What Philosophy Can Tell You™ about Your Lover

What Philosophy Can Tell You™ . . .

What Philosophy Can Tell You about Your Cat
   edited by Steven D. Hales

What Philosophy Can Tell You about Your Dog
   edited by Steven D. Hales

What Philosophy Can Tell You about Your Lover
   edited by Sharon M. Kaye

What Philosophy Can Tell You™ about Your Lover

Edited by
SHARON M. KAYE

OPEN COURT
Chicago and LaSalle, Illinois

To order books from Open Court, call 1-800-815-2280, or visit our website at www.opencourtbooks.com.

Open Court Publishing Company is a division of Carus Publishing Company

First printing 2012

Printed and bound in the United States of America.

Library of Congress Cataloging-in-Publication Data

What philosophy can tell you about your lover / edited by Sharon M. Kaye. . . . .
p. cm. — (What philosophy can tell you about—)
    Includes bibliographical references and index.
    ISBN 978-0-8126-9763-6 (trade paper : alk. paper)
    1. Sex. 2. Sex (Psychology) 3. Love. 4. Interpersonal relations. 5. Philosophy.
I. Kaye, Sharon M.
    HQ21.W68 2012
    306.7—dc23

                                                                    2011050289

Contents

Come-On   vii

I | Foreplay   1

1. The Secret of Lust
   SHARON M. KAYE   3

2. Riding the Magic Carpet with *Twilight*
   UMMNI KHAN   13

3. Kant and Kinky Sex
   JORDAN PASCOE   25

4. Pussy and Other Important Ps
   ROBERT ARP   37

II | Role Playing   47

5. Hips Don't Lie
   PAUL LOADER   49

6. Porn Lovers
   JACOB M. HELD   55

7. Machiavelli at the Bar
   STEPHANIE ST. MARTIN   67

8. Platonic Lovers
   CHARLES TALIAFERRO AND M. PONTOPPIDAN   81

III | Positions   93

9. Wilde Expectations
   MIKE PIERO   95

10. How to Find Yourself a DIRTBAG
    CAROL V.A. QUINN   105

11. The Unexamined Love
    EMILY BARRANCO   115

12. Love in the Time of Self-Gratification
    SCOTT F. PARKER   125

13. It's All about Me
    JAMES BONEY   133

IV | Intercourse   143

14. The Single Life
    WEAVER SANTANIELLO   145

15. Who Do You Love, Simone de Beauvoir?
    MARGARET BETZ   155

16. The I Who Says "We"
    STACEY E. AKE   165

17. Friendly Lovers
    RONDA LEE ROBERTS   179

V | Afterglow   187

18. Up all Night with Socrates
    BENJAMIN STEVENS   189

19. Socrates the Seducer
    CHELSEA C. HARRY   199

20. The Gift
    KATARINA MAJERHOLD   207

21. Winnie the Pooh in Love
    ADAM BARKMAN   215

22. A Single Soul in Two Bodies
    SHAI BIDERMAN AND WILLIAM J. DEVLIN   225

Under the Boardwalk   233

Blueberry Hill   239

Come-On

It's a stormy night. You're out of town at a boring conference. With no place to go and nothing to do, you duck into a restaurant.

To your surprise, there, sitting at the bar, are some of your favorite professors from college. They beckon you to join them.

You chat for awhile about your travels and your lives. Soon the conversation turns to relationships. Your interest peaks. On the one hand, these professors have experienced all the familiar ups and downs of love. On the other hand, they have also studied what all the great sages of history make of these ups and downs.

Tonight, you have them all to yourself. They are in the mood to talk. Teacher and student facades have fallen away.

The conversation pauses for a moment. They turn to you. You raise your glass and propose a toast to lovers everywhere. Then, smiling mischievously, you add, "No one leaves tonight before you tell me what you really think."

I

Foreplay

1
The Secret of Lust

SHARON M. KAYE

> At the moment of orgasm it makes absolutely no difference whom, if
> anyone, you are with.
>
> — JOHN MOULTON

This chapter is for the ladies. (Ladies first, you know.)

What I have to say is of no concern to you, men. And besides, I'm liable to say a few things that might insult your manhood. So just run along and leave us girls to ourselves.

Now then.

Ladies, when I say this chapter is for you, I do so with the caveat that your time may in fact be better spent doing something else. After all, it will take you at least ten minutes to plow through the following pages—a valuable chunk of time for busy people, as are most women in this day and age. You could be doing something more important.

No, really. I'm not just being modest. I actually know there is something better, much better, you could be doing—because, well, because you could be getting yourself off.

Before you sprain your eyeballs rolling them in their sockets at my suggestion, let me just remind you of what you might be missing.

Petting the Pussy Cat

Hopefully, you know the process well: first there's the playful tickle, then the build-up, and the rush, and finally an extraordinary release.

The reason you feel release when you orgasm is because a multitude of wondersubstances are literally being released into your body.

First there are the endorphins, which relax the parts of the brain that cause fear and anxiety. Then there's phenetylamine, a chemical that curbs appetite, and hence aids in weight control. Next we have seratonin, which has a calming effect and generates a satisfied feeling. And don't forget DHEA (dehydroepiandrosterone), which reverses aging, improves brain function, increases fat metabolism, revitalizes the cardiovascular system, promotes healthy skin, and strengthens the immune system. Those who have regular orgasms have much higher levels of immunoglobin A, an antibody that fights infection such as colds and the flu.

Most importantly, at the big moment, the hypothalamus releases extra oxytocin into your system. Called the "cuddle hormone," oxytocin creates the urge to bond, be affectionate, and protect. New mothers are drunk on the stuff. It's like a natural form of ecstasy.

Considering all of these benefits, and more, you may just want to put this book down right now and get busy. . . .

On the other hand, perhaps you rolled your eyes (and I'm not saying you did, I'm just saying I wouldn't be *surprised* if you did). Perhaps you rolled your eyes because you thought it rather inappropriate for me to bring up the subject of paddling the ol' canoe at all.

Now why would I think you might think that?

The Problem

Well, even in our enlightened day and age, many women are apparently scandalized by this topic. Oprah recently devoted an hour to it and received a boatload of ridicule for her trouble.

People often ridicule things that make them uncomfortable.

According to a study Joyce McFadden published in the *Huffington Post*, seventy percent of women feel guilty about trolling the triangle and eighty percent of them were never taught about it as a normal aspect of female sexuality.

Despite being generally skeptical about such studies, I am inclined to believe this one because I myself have had plenty of bad experiences with the topic.

Just one story to illustrate.

I used to get myself off manually and several years ago I sort of sprained my hand doing it. Actually, I was diagnosed with a condition known as "trigger finger," which is similar to carpel tunnel. And so, I finally bought a good vibrator and wore a wrist brace for awhile. Naturally, when friends and colleagues saw me wearing the brace, they would ask what happened.

In a few cases, I told the truth. I was none too pleased with the reactions I got.

Why should I have to lie about such an important health issue? Why are so many of us so uptight about this topic? Well, that's actually what this chapter is about. It's a problem of the utmost importance to your love life.

Who's to Blame?

I'm here to tell you that we have philosophers to blame for the notion that checking for squirrels is anathema. And we ought to be plenty pissed off about it.

As the makers of the HBO series *Rome* bravely revealed, the ancient progenitors of Western Civilization were a bawdy bunch, male and female alike. Sex was a festive part of Roman society and women, or at least women of privilege, got what they needed.

Witness ancient Roman mythology, which, as just one small part of an outrageously sexy panoply, portrays a woman named Leda getting off with a swan. Of course, some will insist that Leda was being raped by Zeus *disguised* as a swan, but it amounts to the same thing. At any rate, ancient mythology, which I studied in high school English class, was the best sex education I ever had, fodder for many, many, many fantasies to come.

You might call today's Budweiser party culture "bawdy", but it sure isn't because those crazy "Girls Gone Wild" are riding the unicycle.

What happened? What did the philosophers do?

To make a long story short, they vilified *lust*, the sine qua non of auto-eroticism.

What's Lust?

No woman in the history of womankind has ever gotten herself off by thinking about the amazing health benefits of getting herself off. You can (sometimes) get yourself to eat health food by thinking about its health benefits and you can (sometimes) get yourself to exercise by thinking about its health benefits, but polishing the peanut, despite being just as important as these other things, requires a special state of mind.

In his interesting little book devoted to the subject, the contemporary British philosopher Simon Blackburn defines lust as "the enthusiastic desire, the desire that infuses the body, for sexual activity and its pleasures for their own sake" (*Lust*, Oxford University Press, 2004, p. 19).

This definition demonstrates how lust differs from the not-so-closely related concept of romantic passion, with which women often confuse lust. Whatever else it concerns, romantic passion concerns another person; lust does not. It is not a desire for someone. It is a desire to *do* something.

Lust is a bit like an itch that needs to be scratched. Think of a figurative itch—like the craving for a long, hot shower after a day of skiing.

This is what baffles a lot of women about lust and makes them think that it's a male thing—kind of like belching or farting loudly and uncontrollably. A lot of women just don't feel the itch, and therefore just don't see any point in scratching.

But notice that you wouldn't crave a long, hot shower unless you had spent the day skiing! There are things you have to do to get yourself to feel the itch. And here's where there is a real biological difference between men and women: most men, especially young men, don't have to do much, if anything at all, to feel that itch. The reason is that they have gargantuan genitals and mega-octane hormones to go with them. The slightest suggestion of sex can put them in the zone. Most women, on the other hand, with our sweet petites, need a little more imagination.

What Lust Requires

In Blackburn's view, people are circumspect about lust because it is inherently private. But this, I think, is a cop out. We're circumspect about peeing and pooping and picking our noses. These activities are private. People are more than circumspect about lust.

And there is a reason.

The state of mind that gives one the itch is a little bit crazy. I, for one, do not care to discuss my sexual fantasies with other people or even think about them except when I am actually using them to reach the big O.

I would be quite embarrassed about the thoughts that buff my muffin if it weren't for my understanding of evolution. The limbic system is responsible for sexual arousal and it is the oldest, most primitively "animal" part of the brain.

For sexual fantasies to work, they have to yank your limbic system out from under the tight control of your cerebral cortex. The thoughts capable of accomplishing this (by triggering adrenalin and other chemical messages) are uncivilized, violent, absurd—in a word, irrational.

And that's okay. They don't mean anything. They're just a vehicle: the necessarily rather distasteful means to a very valuable end.

As you may have noticed, philosophers are big into rationality, which instantly discredits lust in their eyes. But the story is more sinister than that. We can trace a very specific line of philosophical thought that has for a very long time supported a grand conspiracy against lust.

Philosophy's Betrayal

The story begins, of course, with Christianity swallowing up the Roman Empire.

The fourth-century Roman philosopher Augustine sealed an ugly fate for Western thought when he converted from paganism to Christianity and proceeded to co-opt ancient wisdom into institutionalized religion. A very central part of his program was his attack on lust.

According to Augustine, there are two kinds of people: the "City of God" and the "City of Man." If you indulge in lust, well, then, you know who you are. Truly holy people do not even experience lust, much less pursue it. Augustine goes so far as to assert that Adam and Eve reproduced without lust in the Garden of Eden before their fall from grace.

But perhaps Augustine's agenda never would have made much impact if subsequent medieval philosophers had not sold out to the Church. The Church was the only edifice that survived the collapse of the empire. It was the only place you could go to learn to read or even get your hands on a book.

Did the Church keep the weak flame of learning alive, or did it monopolize intellectual resources? To each his own conclusion. Either way, the upshot was that, rather than standing up to intellectual tyranny, as their great predecessor Socrates had, medieval thinkers used the Church to get their education and then became ensnared in its grip. Augustine was the most popular reading, second only to the Bible, for hundreds (yes, hundreds) of years.

Ahh, the Dark Ages.

Augustine's popular influence was later rivaled by the thirteenth-century philosopher Thomas Aquinas. He condemns lust as one of the seven deadly sins. If you die without divine forgiveness for lust, according to Aquinas, you have an irreparable defect in your soul and therefore cannot be admitted at the gates of heaven.

Even after philosophy finally pulled itself out of its medieval funk, lust continued to languish. The arguments against it are so bad they don't bear repeating. For example, the eighteenth-century philosopher Immanuel Kant, reaching a breathtaking height in philosophical lameness, writes that, though he can't think of an argument against masturbation, everyone simply knows it is wrong.

Why?

In the end, the classic Western philosophers, upon whom we were supposed to rely for liberating, free-thinking, authority-challenging arguments, instead propagated a damaging religious doctrine.

One lone voice, however, boldly rang out against the insanity.

In a little known and neglected work he wrote toward the end of his life, the early nineteenth-century philosopher Jeremy Bentham attacks religion for systematically undermining human happiness.

People don't need religion unless they're unhappy. So, in order to stay in business, religion has to keep people unhappy. What better way to do this than to forbid physical pleasures?

Bentham writes that the temptation to perform any act is proportional to the magnitude of the pleasurable, and the smallness of the painful, consequences by which it is attended. Those deeds, therefore, which are the most delightful, and the most innocuous, will meet with the severest prohibitions in the religious code, and be represented as the most offensive to the "divine majesty." Because such deeds will be most frequently repeated, they will accordingly create the amplest demand for the "expiatory formula," which, of course, only the Church can provide.

So, religion is a racket: by propagating guilt, it creates the need for forgiveness, and then offers to supply that forgiveness, for a price. While the price is often literally monetary, the intellectual loyalty that religion demands is by far the more tragic.

There is a twist to the problem, however, that not even Bentham explored. While lust is an unavoidably frequent temptation for most men, most women, due to the charming demureness of our genitals and hormones, can quite easily ignore lust completely, to the point where it simply disappears. The condition is popularly known as "frigidity." (Perhaps this is why women as a whole have always been more devoted to Christianity than have men as a whole—they feel they have a chance of living up to at least one of its expectations.)

The Solution

What can be done about the dysfunctional attitude toward lust we have inherited? The only solution is to restore it to the respectable and celebrated position it enjoyed in the ancient world. My proposal is to think of lust as a type of love that should be actively cultivated and admired.

We can seek guidance from the twentieth-century novelist C.S. Lewis, who distinguishes and defends four different kinds of love. *Storgé* is the affection you feel toward people and things you find present in your life by chance. *Philia* is the friendship you deliberately develop with people who share a common interest with you. *Eros* is the romantic passion you share with a lover. *Charity* is the unconditional love you might devote to God.

If you are thinking that Lewis has already given sufficient recognition to lust because "lust" is really just another word for *Eros*, then you are falling victim to a dangerous confusion, which I mentioned earlier. Romantic passion and lust are not the same species. The difference is evident in this: romance might put you in the mood to be physically close to someone, to touch them, embrace them, even roll around naked with them. *But it will never get you off.* It is too cerebral and beautiful. It cannot awaken your reptile brain.

Although every man knows this in his bones, very few will admit it. (And most men are not consciously aware that they know it, so don't bother trying to discuss it with them.) You see, their anatomy is so *gross* (in the sense of big, I mean) that, once they are in sufficient proximity with a potential sexual partner, they slide seamlessly and effortlessly from romance to lust without even noticing.

To his credit, Lewis recognizes and mentions this confusion. Romantic passion and lust can and often do go together, but you can have a romantic passion for someone without ever getting sexual with them and you can get sexual with someone without ever having a romantic passion for them.

Reinforcing our theme of returning to ancient Roman values, Lewis calls lust *"Venus."* Though working in the same prissy Christian intellectual tradition launched by Augustine, entrenched by Aquinas, and championed by Kant, he finds himself at the slightly more enlightened, modern end of it. He shyly grants that *Venus* is natural and has its place.

It is not, however, to be elevated to the status of a love.

Shame on you, Mr. Lewis, for taking Venus *for granted. Without* Venus, *you men would never be able to come. How would you like that, huh? Obviously,* Venus *is the fifth love. So, put that in your pipe and smoke it!*

The Fifth Love

You may think I'm proposing to elevate lust to the status of a love on the grounds that it constitutes self-love. After all, we call masturbation "auto-eroticism."

But I actually don't experience lust as self-love at all. In fact, I'm a connoisseur of lust without being especially fond of myself. Mainly, I just annoy myself a lot, and I honestly don't think I would be able to make soup at all if it were about me.

What kind of love, then, is lust?

Lewis makes room for the love of objects under his notion of *storge.* For example, many people love the house they grew up in simply because it's so familiar. But what about love of an *activity*? As mentioned earlier, lust is not a desire for someone or something; it's the desire to *do* something. I therefore think lust should be cast as an activity love.

The best way to understand this is by analogy with skiing.

Skiing, like getting off, requires a considerable degree of concentration and athletic ability. When you are skiing, you need to be thinking about skiing, or rather, not thinking at all but rather, engaging in a kind of trance.

While instantaneously taking in all the physical variables she encounters, the skier experiences a free flow of deeply motivating images and volitions. As her coach will tell her, it doesn't matter what the thoughts are, so long as they put her in the zone. She nurtures this trance during training and then lets it loose when tackling a personal challenge, such as a race or a new mountain.

At bottom, my view is that all sex, if it is to climax, is essentially lust-driven, and at the final countdown, it is essentially the same as getting yourself off.

Airing the Orchid

By all means, find yourself a lover, if you want, and cultivate *Eros*. Having a lover is especially nice in those tantalizing moments before, and glowing moments after, a mutually satisfying sexual experience. This doesn't change the fact that, when it comes to the process of climaxing, *Eros* has nothing to do with it.

Now in my old age, I realize that I learned this great wisdom when I was a tender freshman at the University of Wisconsin, Madison. I took the last aesthetics course the philosopher John Moulton taught before he died. We were discussing various controversies surrounding nude paintings when we suddenly swerved into the topic of sex. The class sat blushing as Moulton boldly, yet almost off-handedly, made the astonishing claim that, at the moment of orgasm, it makes absolutely no difference whom, if anyone, you are with.

These words shook me to my very core and probably had a more profound influence on my life than any other single phrase I learned in school.

Because I was in love. I had already met the man that I married upon graduating. Like so many romantic young women, I was completely convinced I had found my soul mate.

Though the union was not to last, I have never to this day doubted that I really was in love and that I really did experience *Eros* in pure form. And I came plenty with him.

But Moulton was right: the coming itself had nothing to do with him.

Though this sounds like a terrible thing to say, it actually makes perfect sense if we go back to the analogy with skiing. At the moment you go flying down the slope, it makes absolutely no difference who, if anyone, you're with.

Granted, a ski trip can be much more fun, and can even be a genuinely meaningful experience, if you go with someone you care about. You get to ride up the chair lift together, take in the scenery, perhaps even enjoy a nice meal or a cuddle by the fire in the chalet. But if you're thinking about this person while flying down the slope *then you are doing it wrong and you will never be good at it.*

Auditioning the Finger Puppets

I stake my claim that lust is a true form of love against the dictate of the twentieth-century philosopher Mortimer J. Adler, who once said that sexual love can truly be love only if it is not selfishly sexual or lustful. I think he and the entire Western philosophical tradition he stands for are self-deceived and dead wrong.

My position is this. If you want to have a lover, then you'll want to have sex. If you want to have sex, then you really should be climaxing. Simply letting someone else have sex with you while you fake it is an extraordinary waste of opportunity. So, you'll want to climax with your lover. And if you want to climax with your lover, then you should keep yourself primed by squeezing the peach on a regular basis. This way, whether or not *Eros* works out, you'll always still have *Venus*.

Find the category of porn that triggers your reptile brain and you'll be tossing the salad in four minutes flat. If you have objections to the adult video industry, you can use hard-core animation or even literature to the same effect. With practice, you'll accumulate a store of motivational images in your own head, ready for use at your convenience. . . . Hey, how about now?

2
Riding the Magic Carpet with *Twilight*

UMMNI KHAN

When I was a young teen, just learning how to masturbate (yes, I really did teach this to myself—from a book), I realized that fantasizing intensified my arousal. Before this important realization, I could not—for the (sex) life of me—figure out what the problem was.

My self-love manual explained that you had to stick with it for one hour every day, and that eventually you would discover which rubs, tugs, strokes, or circles would weave that magic carpet and fly you over the mysterious edge. Orgasm. But no matter what combination of moves I tried, I would find myself stalled, the carpet unraveled. And me lying there, a heap of hormones with no place to go.

My manual suggested that I "imagine a sexual encounter" while getting down to the task, but the only sex I had ever seen was in a porn flick that my pals and I surreptitiously watched, gasping and giggling until the money shot. While this was definitely a moment of girl bonding, the scene itself was gross and boring. The detailed close-up of genitals, where you could see every fold, every ridge, every vein, was too much information. Wayyyyyy too much. And somehow the sex itself, with Buddy jack-hammering away, could not launch my libido. Replaying the scene in my head during my nightly practice sessions not only failed to rev up my magic carpet, I think it actually put it in reverse.

But funnily enough, in the daytime, when I was not working on my masturbatory techniques, I sometimes found myself a little jumpy. A little tingly. This was particularly true in the school yard. I had a mixed group of friends and we liked to play freeze tag, which involved someone who was "It" trying to catch the rest of us (I was never It; I was too slow for this role). Once caught, I would "freeze" until one of my faster teammates would crawl between my legs, which—according to our juvenile law—would unfreeze me. And the chase would continue. I began to notice that this left me breathless, and not just because of exertion. It was exciting. Being hunted like that. It was especially hot when the cute new guy was the one who unfroze me.

And that's how I discovered fantasy foreplay.

Instead of thinking about the mustached macho man and his mechanical moves from the porno movie, I thought about being pursued by the baddest boy in our class (well, he was bad in math anyway). And sometimes, I would think about the new kid unfreezing me. In my dream I was not wearing jeans, but a grown-up pencil skirt that had to be hiked up so that my open legs could create a wide enough passage to crawl through. Combining such thoughts with my figure-eight finger technique, I finally learned how to fly.

As my self-love life took off, I created a whole roster of jack-off scenarios that never involved intercourse, but always involved the thrill of the chase, or a moment of frozen anticipation, half-exposed but never naked, never penetrated. I would climax while my pursuer panted after me and I remained just out of reach, suggesting a sequel that I never actually needed to watch.

Twilight: Everlasting Love and Lust

So, what does this obscene anecdote have to do with *Twilight*? Stephenie Meyer's hit saga dramatizes the very same kind of erotic tension that accelerated my pubescent sex drive, as a bit of thought about its premise will show.

The star-crossed, cross-species love story between Bella, the teenage human, and Edward, the tantalizing vampire, concerns the rapturous delight of restrained desire. While Bella is constantly attempting to seduce the stoic Edward, he represses his sexual lust in order to control his bloodlust, lest he accidentally devour the one he loves. To further complicate things, another captivating creature enters the picture. Jacob, a part-time werewolf and Bella's BFF, comes down with a serious case of puppy-love for the vamp's girl. Bella, believing at first that both men are ordinary humans, slowly comes to discover just how dangerous they are.

Like many runaway success stories, *Twilight* has received its fair share of criticism. Intellectuals read it as faux literature and bemoan its absurd plot, its clichéd writing, and its conservative sexual moralism. Feminists further contend that the main love story between Bella, the awkward adolescent, and Edward, the broody blood-sucker, romanticizes domestic abuse. From this perspective, if you scratch the surface of Edward's pale skin, you find a cold, controlling stalker with violent tendencies.

But such interpretations take the series too literally, when in fact, it should be interpreted more pornographically. In other words, *Twilight* is not a prescription for behavior; rather, it is a stimulus for arousal. If I'd had a copy of the book when I was a teen, I would have gotten that magic carpet up and running a lot sooner.

Furthermore, *Twilight* does something few simplistic love stories dare: it provides us with a rival who, depending on your philosophy on love, might be more attractive than the romantic hero. In the second and third books, Jacob, with his canine charisma, becomes a serious contender for Bella's affections. And *Twilight* does not predispose the audience to pick one suitor over the other in the way the literary classic *Pride and Prejudice* does. In that love story, it's clear by the end of the book that the deceitful and greedy Wickham is no match for the honorable and generous Mr. Darcy. *Twilight*, on the other hand, allows its audience to feast upon two mouth-watering monsters, both of whom—feminist critiques notwithstanding—are champions. Both love Bella and both slay villains.

In response to the rivalry between these supernatural studs, fan culture has organized itself into two fiercely opposed camps: Team Edward versus Team Jacob. The enthusiastic members of these teams battle it out on the Internet and at conferences, sacrificing time, money, and their very reputations for their cause.

How can we explain the wild popularity of this fantasy?

Masochism

Leopold von Sacher-Masoch was a nineteenth-century Austrian who wrote some very naughty fiction about a cruel dominant woman and a devoted male subordinate. Sexologists coined the term masochism from his name. Today, the term is usually used pejoratively to convey mental illness or self-destructive behavior. But if we turn to Sacher-Masoch's writings, we see a recipe for some delicious fantasy foreplay that includes worshipful devotion, submission, pleasure in pain, and most importantly, the intensification of desire through sexual frustration and the postponement of gratification.

When Bella falls for Edward, it's no ordinary crush. She practically deifies him—which makes sense, because compared to her fragile, klutzy, aging self, he is a god. Edward enjoys superlative strength, speed and grace, and is basically immortal. Throughout the saga, Bella obsesses over his stunning physique, which she continually likens to that of an angel.

The way Bella idolizes her boyfriend is not unlike how some infatuated lovers behave at the beginning of a relationship. We see our sweeties through rose colored glasses and from this viewpoint become intoxicated by their divine perfection. Of course, we eventually sober up and notice their plebeian way of, say, leaving dirty socks at the bottom of the bed.

Masochism is about suspending our disbelief and consciously continuing that worshipful gaze, using a kind of romantic alchemy to turn the dirty socks from an annoyance into a sacred gift from a glorified master or mistress. In the world of *Twilight*, Bella is able to maintain this worshipful role with ease, since her perception of Edward's excellence is a fairly accurate assessment of his exceptional vampiric attributes.

Although we can accept Edward's flawless exterior, what many of us find harder to swallow politically is his dominant personality and Bella's submissiveness. As their relationship develops, Edward becomes more and more of an authority figure: he controls Bella's movements, cajoles her into marriage, decides who she will spend time with, and even has her monitored and kidnapped, supposedly for her own good. He further infantilizes her by singing her lullabies to soothe her into sleep. If this were a real-life relationship, I might have some doubts about its healthiness. But we have to remember that Bella is a fictional character within an extremely artificial world of vampires and werewolves. It's a fantasy or, as masochists would call it, a scene.

I was discussing *Twilight* with a friend who is a faithful member of "Team Edward." Initially, her choice seriously puzzled me. She self-identifies as a control freak, and her partner is sweet, boyish, and much more like the cheerful Jacob than the overbearing Edward.

I now realize why her choice makes perfect sense. Fantasy is not about what we have or want in real life, but about experimenting with exotic and even opposite experiences. After all, one of the remarkable things that professional dominants have recounted is that their clientèle are often men who exercise a lot of authority in their day-to-day life: business tycoons, judges, cops. The fantasy of submission is a temporary antidote to the daily responsibility of power.

Twilight readers get off vicariously on Bella's submissiveness, not because they necessarily want such a domineering boyfriend for themselves, but because it's exciting to lose control within the controlled setting of a novel. And while the dominant player may appear to hold the power, we all know that Bella, the "submissive," subtly instigates scenarios to further her own agenda, sexual and otherwise.

The ultimate example of this is when Bella finally gets laid before turning vampire. Edward had been resisting her sexual demands, fearing that his monstrous passion would damage her feeble human body. But after hovering at first base for three books, Edward and Bella finally hit a homerun on the first night of their honeymoon in *Breaking Dawn*, the last of the four novels in the *Twilight* series.

Of course, masochistic Meyer, who always wants the sexual consummation to remain out of narrative reach, does not allow the reader to witness this long anticipated moment of union. Instead, what we read is the foreplay and the aftermath. In the morning, Bella is stiff and sore, with the odd sensation that her bones have become unhinged at the joints. Later, when she looks at her post-virgin body, she finds her lips swollen, and her skin discolored with large purple bruises. To top it all off, she is covered in feathers because, in his attempt to resist biting his bride, Edward's fangs ripped apart the down-filled pillows. Edward is consumed by guilt, but Bella does not recall the force ever being unwanted. She enjoyed his violent passion and is anxious to have more of it.

The second time they do it, again through Bella's instigation, her lingerie is torn to shreds and the bed frame is broken. To put it mildly, they have rough sex. To put it more accurately, they have sadomasochistic sex. And Bella loves it. This is the physical dimension of masochism: pleasure wrought from pain. Again, this does not necessarily mean that a reader who finds this hot is a hardcore pain-slut (not that there's anything wrong with that!). Rather, it points to ways that sexuality demands intensity, loss of control, a desire to obliterate all boundaries. It's also a fact that when we're aroused, what might otherwise feel uncomfortable or unpleasantly painful can feel intensely good; ergo, the popularity of the hickey.

So far, we've been considering how Bella demonstrates masochistic tendencies. But Edward too is implicated in this erotic dynamic. In order to understand his masochistic tendencies, we have to return to the first book.

When Edward finally falls in love after a century of bachelorhood, Cupid plays a mean trick on him: Edward's romantic desire for Bella intermingles with his thirst for her blood. As a human, she is his basic and most preferred food group. But his family, a coven of vampires, lives an ethical "vegetarian" diet: instead of feeding on humans—their natural prey—they hunt wild animals. Not as tasty, or as satisfying, but nourishing enough to keep them going.

When Edward meets Bella, it's love at first whiff. He wants her in multiple ways: romantic, sexual, and edible. However, because he loves her, he must protect her—not just from her hapless and accident-prone existence, or from other bloodthirsty fiends, but from his own desire to literally suck the life out of her. Bella does not make it easy for him, as she continually tries to get him in the sack. Edward fears that if he ceases to repress his sexual instincts, he will be unable to suppress his predatory impulses—which would be bad, because then he'd kill her. The agony of this situation, the withholding of gratification, is at the crux of masochistic eroticism. Climactic release must be postponed as long as possible in order to heighten the bittersweet anguish of intense longing. This is fantasy foreplay at its most sublime.

Masochism haunts not just our self-denying vampire, but also his rival. While sexual fulfillment remains out of reach for Edward because he might accidentally kill Bella in his passion, Jacob the werewolf is also obliged to tame his intense desire, this time because Bella's heart belongs elsewhere.

Jealousy

If Jacob's burning desire and virile presence get you to cheer for the underdog, you relish the helpless devotion and selflessness that can only come from unrequited love. The appeal of Jacob can be illuminated through the philosophical poetry of Sappho, whose birthplace, Lesbos, gave us the term "lesbian." Through Jacob and Bella's flirtatious friendship, we see that Sapphic verse is actually a universal expression of the dialectic between jealousy and erotic desire that can occur across genders (and species!).

An excerpt from Sappho's work that scholars have named, "Fragment 31," conveys not only a passionate love, but the piercing pleasure of Jacob's situation: the intensification of passion through jealousy.

The first four lines begin:

> He seems to me equal to the gods that man
> Whoever he is who opposite you
> Who sits and listens close
> To your sweet speaking
> And lovely laughing

In the opening verse, the narrator assesses the man lucky enough to have captured the heart of the beloved. The rival is likened to a "god," which, as discussed above, is a remarkably accurate description of Edward. But for Jacob, Edward has godly status, not because of his extraordinary strength or beauty, but because he is allowed to be with Bella.

Later the poem reads:

> When I look at you, even for a moment
> No speaking is left in me, none
> My tongue breaks and thin fire races under my skin.

Again, this is an uncanny description of Jacob's phenomeno-
logical experience. The unspeakable agony of unrequited love
suggested in these lines explains Jacob's decision to shapeshift
into a wolf when he is overcome with jealousy. He wants to
escape the world of language because the pain of losing Bella
to Edward leaves him literally speechless.

Furthermore, since he acquired werewolf capabilities, his
temperature blazes ten degrees higher than a normal human.
On a symbolic level, the fire racing under his skin signals the
constant state of frustrated desire that Sappho outlines. The
fervent intensity of this desire, Sappho suggests, is generated
precisely because someone stands between the admirer and the
object of affection.

Thus Jacob and Edward are both implicated in the exquis-
ite torment of unfulfilled desire. However, unlike Edward—
who never wavers in his sexual self-control—Jacob, at least
sometimes, breaks the rules and succumbs to carnal temptation. Ironically then, even though Jacob is the werewolf, it is
Edward who is more bark than bite. Edward's ability to resist
nibbling on his girlfriend, and Jacob's transgression of propri-
ety, now brings us to the ancient Greek philosopher Plato and
his understanding of the struggle between transcendent and
embodied love.

Control

Though written in 370 B.C., Plato's dialogue, *Phaedrus*, nar-
rates an archetypal lesson that we can see repeated in
Twilight's love triangle. Plato explains that when the lover
looks upon his darling, a struggle commences. Plato compares
the situation to a chariot driver with two horses: one obedient,
chaste, and controlled; the other defiant, lascivious, and uncon-
trolled. The lover must tame the defiant horse so that bodily
impulses can be channeled towards higher pursuits. If not, the
wicked horse will drive the chariot, its driver, and the beloved
to indecent destruction.

In Edward's case, Plato is vindicated. Edward manages to
steer the naughty horse all the way to the honeymoon bed,
never allowing his moral commitments to be trumped by carnal urges until passion can be legitimated by holy matrimony.
In Jacob's case, Plato is disregarded. Jacob blithely follows the

shameless horse. He ignores Bella's non-single status and her rejection of his advances, and instead fights for her love, using sex as his weapon.

In two key seduction moments, Jacob dissolves Bella's resolve. He kisses her twice; the first time she protests, the second time her protests transform into passionate response.

I must admit that at first this really, *really*, bothered me—I mean, besides getting me hot and bothered, it also troubled my feminist sensibilities. If we read this as a prescription of what is acceptable in life, then *Twilight* is legitimating sexual assault between friends as an avenue of courtship. But I slowly came to the conclusion that we need to read *Twilight* as fantasy and philosophy. Within the safe confines of a fantastical novel, these are erotic scenes that allow the reader to relish being stalked and hunted while that ill-bred horse pulls her into the quagmire of forbidden pleasure.

In the first kissing scene, Bella does not sexually respond, and indeed, is infuriated by the smooching onslaught. In a fit of anger, she punches him—which results in her breaking her own hand. While not explicitly sexual, this subtly evokes masochism for Team Jacob members by linking the pain in her hand with the pleasure of his kiss. When Jacob kisses her for the second time, she has agreed to the intimacy, ostensibly for the sole reason that he has made suicidal threats.

When his lips claim hers, Bella at first remains passive and detached. But Jacob urges her to stop "overthinking it," and then later says, "For once, just let yourself feel what you feel." Bella soon follows this advice and finds herself hungrily responding. What is particularly exciting for Bella is that she does not need to be careful with Jacob, the way she must be with her volatile vampire. And even more thrilling, Jacob is not, like Edward, urging them both to follow the good horse on the righteous path. Instead, he lets his libertine steed liberate Bella from the burden of rationality, restraint, and morality, pulling them both towards beastly bodily love.

The contrasting approaches of our wanton wolf and our virtuous vampire thus exemplify Plato's comments on the two directions a lover can take. Those who root for Jacob enjoy the fantasy of transgression and loss of control, allowing carnality to trump conscience. The card-carrying members of Team Edward—the majority of fans—prefer their fantasy beau to be more in control of that chariot, where the suspended tension between rapacious longing and modest restraint feeds the eroticism.

So how does Meyer resolve this love triangle so that everyone can live happily ever after? With ingenuity (and a little perversity)! In *Breaking Dawn*, Meyer conceives of a utopian solution that combines the sexual pleasure of masochism with the moral guidance of Plato.

As mentioned above, Edward and Bella finally consummate their marriage in a violent night of passion. As a result, Bella becomes pregnant and the pregnancy precipitates her vampiric conversion. When Bella and Edward are equals, their sex life is no longer masochistic.

But mental masochism is still at play. After Bella engages in vampire-on-vampire sex for the first time, she asks Edward whether this "craving" ever stops. We learn that vampires never tire of sex, never need a break, and are never satiated. Thus, the dilemma of desire—namely, that it is eradicated by gratification—is conveniently sidestepped. This is magical masochism: having your sex and desiring it too. In other words, vampires get to enjoy a never-ending appetite for sex and sexual consummation.

Of course, once Edward is able to engage in unrestrained sexual passion with Bella, Jacob becomes a third wheel wolf. But Meyer does not leave him in frustrated heat forever. Instead, she devises an ironic solution where Bella's union with Edward results in Jacob finally getting a piece of Bella all to himself.

This solution is foreshadowed when Bella, herself heartbroken from breaking Jacob's heart, wishes that she could split herself in two so that a part of her could stay with Jacob while the rest runs off with Edward. In *Breaking Dawn*, Bella basically gets her wish. The birth of her daughter Renesmee, conceived on that fateful honeymoon night, allows the part of Bella that loves and desires Jacob to live on in the next generation. When Jacob lays eyes on this human-vampire hybrid, he realizes he's been barking up the wrong tree the whole time. His devotion to Bella is irrevocably transferred to her progeny. We learn later that from her own infantile perspective, Renesmee is equally smitten with Jacob's wolfish ways.

Putting aside the weirdness of Jacob falling in love with the baby of his rival and unrequited love object, it is noteworthy that the readers will not get to witness Jacob's romantic and sexual fulfillment. When werewolves imprint on a child, their affections are familial, and do not become sexual until the beloved reaches an appropriate age for romance. In other words, Jacob's love of Renesmee is platonic, not pedophilic.

The concept of "platonic love" is premised on the writings of Plato, which privileged spiritual and cerebral connections over embodied and carnal relations. With the lover-as-chariot-driver allegory, Plato was not simply laying out two equally valid paths from which to choose. The allegory is instead supposed to inspire us to tame the salacious steed, channeling our desire to more elevated aims. And this is what Jacob finally learns to do when he falls for Renesmee. All of his sexual desire is temporarily frozen while protective brotherly love is activated.

So, the conclusion of the *Twilight* series celebrates eroticism driven by the unattainability of sexual satiation. Edward and Bella enjoy unabated sexual stamina no matter how many times they bang their fangs. Jacob postpones the pleasures of the flesh as he plays nanny for his baby beloved.

And They Lived Happily and Hornily Ever After

And so, this is why I think the *Twilight* series is a form of literary freeze tag that functions as fantastical foreplay. Bella gets to be hunted by two hunky heroes. As was the case when I was a kid being chased by my schoolmates, she wants to be caught. Within Edward's icy embrace, she is frozen in a continual state of sexual longing.

When Jacob comes to unfreeze her with his fiery touch, she experiences the thrill of sexual surrender to promiscuous passion. Yet this state is only temporary, as Edward comes to finally claim her affections for eternity with the gift of climactic triumph paradoxically combined with constant craving.

But every dog has his day. When Jacob finally finds true reciprocated love with Bella's daughter, Renesmee, he too learns the importance of delayed gratification. And as for the reader, she has learned that the philosophic lessons of Masoch, Sappho, and Plato not only endure, but are an excellent source of inspiration for anyone who wants to fly their magic carpet to new destinations of desire.

3
Kant and Kinky Sex

JORDAN PASCOE

My lover is not a vampire. Which is a shame, because vampires are sexy. More than that, vampires are synonymous with sex—sex as hunger, appetite, an act of devouring.

Think about the way sex is presented in the vampire narrative of your choice (be it *Buffy the Vampire Slayer*, *Twilight*, *True Blood*, or any number of other examples): sex is dangerous, because it involves twin desires. For the vampire, sexual desire is always also bloodlust; for humans, sexual desire is intertwined with the desire to be consumed. In these stories, sex involves both release and restraint, and it requires a radical form of trust. After all, humans can survive sex with vampires only if the vampire stops short of treating them as an object to be devoured, only if they resist the impulse to suck them dry.

Why do we find these stories so compelling? Well, *aside* from vampires being sexy, it's because stories about sex as hunger, consumption, surrender, and restraint are compelling. Many of us have never taken a vampire as a lover (though not for lack of trying), but we may have encountered sex with our human lovers that took on a decidedly vampiric flavor. We may have craved a lover, or wanted to be consumed by a lover in a way that seemed dangerously dehumanizing. We may have crossed that invisible line between desiring someone and downright devouring them, using them for our own pleasure even if that meant sucking them dry. Sex is a tricky thing, and (if we're doing it right) it has the potential to unleash the monster in all of us.

Immanuel Kant, the eighteenth-century German philosopher, put it another way: the trouble with sex is that it's cannibalistic. (Cannibalism being, when you think about it, rather like egalitarian vampirism, only with less sex and more ick.) In the *Appendix* to the *Metaphysics of Morals* (1798), Kant argues that "carnal enjoyment is *cannibalistic* in principle (even if not always in its effect)." He goes on to say that sex is like consumption "by mouth and teeth" and to compare it to the way a woman "is consumed by pregnancy" and a man "by the exhaustion of his sexual capacity from the woman's frequent demands upon it." (Apparently, Kant thought women's sex drives have a decidedly vampiric quality.) Kant worries that sex leads us to treat one another as "consumable things" and that sexual desire is inconsistent with respect for another person—a claim that poses rather serious problems for your relationship with your lover.

Kantian Cannibalism

We have good reason to be skeptical about Kant's account of sexuality. First, he most likely died a virgin, so we might want to take his views on sex with a grain of salt. Beyond that, his arguments are out-dated, highly conservative, and shaped by his personal tastes and general feelings about women (which, as we've already noted, weren't particularly warm or respectful). And finally, Kant's arguments about sex are mostly kind of *bad* as philosophical arguments go: they rest on questionable premises, are conceptually confusing, and lack the consistency that is central to his otherwise painstakingly consistent moral system. So why take heed of something an eighteenth-century misogynist virgin said about sex?

There are two things about Kant's moral philosophy that may encourage us to think about his views on sex, no matter how skewed they might be. First, Kant's moral philosophy is centrally concerned with the relationship between our reason and our desires. Second, Kant is concerned about our tendency to use other people. Morality, he says, is the obligation to treat others as ends in themselves, and never merely as a means. And we act morally when we're guided by our reason, not our desires.

This isn't to say that our desires are *bad*—they're just morally irrelevant. Sometimes our desires lead us to do good things: we're nice to people we love, and we occasionally save adorable puppies. But Kant thought that, to be moral, an action had to be motivated by reason and respect for persons as ends, not just a desire to be nice.

Think about it this way: if we choose good deeds for no reason other than that we enjoy them, we can't be counted on to choose good deeds when we don't feel like it. So, if my only reason for caring about you is the pleasure it brings me, what's to stop me from using or abandoning you when the mood suits me? Kant's moral philosophy, in other words, is concerned with constancy and reliability, which are important questions in sexual relationships.

Given this brief account of Kant's moral philosophy, it's easy to see what Kant might have to say about your relationship with your lover. He might say that this relationship presents a conflict between reason and desire, and that our natural sexual desires conflict with our moral obligations to respect each other as persons and ends in ourselves. Sex may lead us to care deeply for our lover, to desire to bring them great pleasure, and to do nice things for them because doing so adds to our pleasure. But if sexual desire is only about pleasure, then it won't make me a reliable or trustworthy lover: I can't be relied on to care for my lover when doing so won't bring me pleasure, and I can't be relied on to treat my lover as an end in himself.

In other words, sex is like other desires: it's not bad, just morally irrelevant. And all this seems like a reasonable account of the problems sex poses: if sex poses the same sorts of challenges to relationships as other desires, then sex is vulnerable to the same kinds of moral solutions. As long as we temper our desires with reason, and make sure that we're not using others in unacceptable ways, there's no reason sex couldn't be compatible with a healthy moral relationship.

But that's not the end of the story. No, Kant thought sex was much worse than other desires, and that it posed a uniquely dangerous moral problem. Kant, remember, called sex "cannibalistic": sex, he said, is the *only* case where I use another person directly as an object to satisfy my desires, and it's the only case where my desire is so graphically appetitive. My sexual desire for my lover, says Kant, is likely to be at odds with my moral concern for my lover, and even the best moral intentions are likely to be corrupted by the appetitive nature of sexuality.

Before we accuse Kant of overstating the case, let's note that the language of appetite, hunger, and consumption comes up a lot in talk about sex, whether or not vampires happen to be involved. We say that we hunger for someone, that we crave someone, that we want to be consumed or devoured by someone. And a fair number of sexual euphemisms (we bite, we nibble, we eat someone out) use the language of appetite. So, okay, sex has a cannibalistic flavor.

Kant thinks sex deserves special attention because it leads us to objectify both others and ourselves. This seems hyperbolic, of course: we don't commonly think that our sexual relationships are necessarily morally corrupted. But I don't think we should dismiss Kant that easily. Kant is concerned that, when we move through the world as sexual objects, motivated by sexual appetite, we treat ourselves and others differently.

When we're "on the prowl," we present ourselves differently and we engage with others differently, and too often we think and behave in ways that are contrary to our moral obligation to treat others—and ourselves—as persons possessing dignity and deserving respect. Sexual impulse is a particular kind of orientation towards the world, and if unrestrained, it threatens to undermine our duties to ourselves and others. The trick, then, is to find a way of restraining sexual impulse so that we are not tempted to objectify ourselves and others.

Kant's proposed solution to the moral dangers of sex is, at first glance, predictable: we must only engage in sex within a legally sanctioned marriage. Which, sure, sounds like exactly the sort of thing an eighteenth-century moral philosopher *would* say. But, we might ask: if sex is such a thorny moral problem, can even marriage redeem sex? Why does Kant think that marriage can radically transform the cannibalistic nature of sexuality?

How Not to Cannibalize Your Lover

Kant thinks marriage is the only way to make sex morally permissible because marriage involves a mutual surrender that is both bigger and broader than the surrender involved in sexuality: through marriage, my lover and I give one another our *whole person*, of which our sexuality is a part. Only this total, unified surrender can make sexual use and objectification acceptable.

Kant's account of marriage is a tricky thing. Here's what he *does* say about marriage: it's a monogamous, equal, legal agreement that produces an exchange of equal and reciprocal rights that gives partners shared ownership of all their stuff, and it must occur through public law rather than private contract. Here's what he *doesn't* say about marriage: he says nothing about love, or about how partners ought to treat each other, beyond the basic, universal requirement that they are bound to respect each other as persons. He says a lot about what makes marriage a useful legal institution, but almost nothing about what makes a marriage "good."

The puzzle, then, is this: how, exactly, does marriage as a carefully defined legal institution transform impermissible, cannibalistic sex into principled, morally permissible sex? What kind of transformation is marriage supposed to create? One argument is that marriage "blocks" sexual objectification: if sex is just one part of a relationship in which partners are legally required to respect each other as persons, and to take each others' ends and goals as their own, I am less likely to objectify or dehumanize my partner. Or, to put it differently, marriage creates a kind of "psychological transformation" where sex becomes a respectful encounter with my lover, rather than a dehumanizing one.

But if what we need is a "psychological transformation" of our relationship with our lovers, why is marriage necessary? Wouldn't a loving, committed relationship be enough to block the urge to cannibalize? There are two criticisms to make here: first, if respect brings about this transformation, and respect characterizes any loving, committed, monogamous relationship, why is sex only permissible within marriage? And second, if Kant defines marriage as a legal relationship and tells us nothing about what makes a marriage good, why assume that marriage *per se* will be loving, committed, and respectful enough to bring about this transformation?

To answer these criticisms, philosophers have argued that we need something more than marriage to bring about the transformation of sex that Kant describes: we need an account of a morally robust, committed relationship. This relationship doesn't need to be marriage, but it might benefit from some of the qualities that Kant ascribes to marriage: it should be equal and committed, and require partners to respect each other and take one another's ends as their own.

Within such a relationship, we can easily imagine that sex, like other parts of the relationship, would be concerned with equality and respect. Cannibalistic sex is humanized: my vampiric desire to consume my partner becomes a moral desire to love, respect, and enjoy my partner. The idea is that sexual desires themselves are transformed so that my tendency to objectify my partner is checked by the deep respect that our loving, committed relationship has instilled in me.

Kant discusses just this kind of relationship in his *Metaphysics of Morals*, where he describes moral friendship. Moral friendship, he says, has the following characteristics: it is a friendship between equals with a genuine concern for one another as persons (rather than a friendship of "mutual advantage"). It's a relationship characterized by respect.

Kant says that moral friendship is based on "mutual respect" rather than on feelings (since feelings have a pesky tendency to change) and that true friendship involves limited intimacy, since too much intimacy tends to undermine respect. Respect, in this way, counteracts love: while love draws two people closer, Kant argues, respect urges them to maintain a reasonable distance from each other.

Friends, Not Lovers

Curiously, though, Kant didn't think moral friendship was compatible with a sexual relationship. He thought this for a number of reasons, not all of which are good—for example, he didn't think this kind of friendship was possible with women, who lacked equality and tended to be emotional rather than reasonable. But more basically, I suspect, Kant thought sex was incompatible with the respect moral friendship requires. And this is not simply because sex involves objectification and debasement, but because it involves too much intimacy. The intimacy of a sexual relationship threatens to undermine the respect required to maintain a moral friendship.

The respect that characterizes a moral friendship requires distance, and so Kant tells us that friends shouldn't become too familiar with each other. Friends don't need or depend on each other: they can't care for one another when they're sick, for example, because doing so might create a troubling intimacy. And, by the same token, friends can't have sex with friends, since this kind of basic, consuming need would conflict with the distance that friendship requires.

This lets us see Kant's argument about marriage in a different light. Sex involves an unacceptable kind of intimacy, and intimacy necessarily undermines respect. Marriage doesn't make sex any less cannibalistic, but it creates a legal space in which we are allowed to indulge in sexual cannibalism. It's not that sex itself is morally transformed. Instead, it's quarantined: I'm no longer "on the prowl" with my rampant desire to cannibalize others. I'm now legally required to cannibalize only one other person, who has agreed to a lifetime of reciprocal cannibalization (which is exactly how wedding vows ought to put it), and we engage in this thorny sexual behavior behind closed doors.

The "behind closed doors" bit is critical to Kant's argument. If we take Kant's concerns about objectification and dehumanization seriously, sex undermines respect in a bunch of ways. When I present myself as a sexual creature, Kant suggests, I present myself as an object of desire, and in doing so I make myself unworthy of respect.

This argument is deeply troubling, and we have excellent reasons to reject claims that our sexuality makes us unworthy of respect (which spurred, most recently, the rise of the SlutWalk protest marches, originally prompted by the advice of a Toronto police officer that, for their own safety, women had better not dress like sluts).

But the idea of sexual quarantine is still resonant: I want my lover to see me as a sexual creature and an object of desire, but I would rather my students and colleagues not think of me that way. I want to be free to explore my sexuality in one part of my life without it spilling into all the other parts.

Marriage, as Kant defines it, performs precisely this kind of quarantining function by legally allowing one person to objectify me, and simultaneously demanding that everyone else stop objectifying me (coveting your neighbor's wife and all that) and respect my relationship with my spouse (cannibalism and all). Only a legal institution, he thinks, can publicly compartmentalize my life so that I'm free to be sexual and intimate in one part of it, and deserving of dignity and respect in all the other parts.

This doesn't mean that there aren't better or worse marriages, or that moral friendship doesn't have a place within marriage. Certainly, good marriages, like all good relationships, involve a balancing act between intimacy and respect. And it doesn't really tell us that legal marriage is necessary to managing this balance. We could surely imagine a committed, morally robust relationship that could both morally transform sex and create a space in which intimacy is possible without compromising respect. A number of philosophers have done just this by borrowing from Kant's concerns about sex and his account of moral friendship. But Kant himself didn't—and we ought to ask why.

Kant focused on marriage as a legal institution that quarantines sex rather than as a form of moral friendship. Kant didn't think sex could be morally transformed in the straightforward way that we might think it can. In other words, Kant thinks that sex is *always* cannibalistic. There's no such thing as morally unproblematic sex. And given this, his solution is simply to contain it, and to allow just one relationship in a person's life to be contaminated by it, which in turn allows that person to engage in all kinds of other relationships without fear of cannibalizing or being cannibalized.

Kant and Kink

If marriage can't transform sex, but only contain it, then sex is really never morally permissible—and this seems like a ridiculous conclusion. So we might return to our opening gambit: Kant was conservative, reactionary, and (most likely) a virgin. So why should we take his thoughts on sex seriously?

Here's a reason: there's one way in which Kant was rather radical about sex. Unlike many other philosophers and religious figures of his day, he rejected the idea that sex was about procreation and that sex was permissible only if it was procreative. Kant understood that sex was about pleasure and pleasure alone. This still totally freaked him out, as we've seen. Kant thought that sex was about the heedless pursuit of pleasure at the expense of one's own humanity and the humanity of one's lover. He thought it was the desire to objectify and be objectified, to debase and be debased, and an appetite so consuming as to be cannibalistic.

Kant thought sex was unimaginably kinky. And, given that he knew very little about sex, this is not surprising. He's wrong to think that sex is inherently kinky, cannibalistic, and debasing in this way. Lots of sex is loving and respectful and even (imagine!) motivated by an appreciation for the humanity of yourself and your lover. Lots of sex is totally consistent with dignity and respect and moral friendships as Kant understands them, and in this sense, Kant's concerns about sexuality seem like hyperbolic relics of another age.

But we can think about this in another way: some sex *is* unimaginably kinky. Some sex is about hunger and devouring and debasement and objectification. So Kant is right, in a sense: sex is about pleasure, and some pleasure is kinky. And the trouble with kinky sex is that (much like vampire sex) it's awesome and consuming and highly pleasurable— and totally morally dangerous. Often, it means seeking out scenarios in which we are debased and dehumanized just because this is pleasurable. Sometimes, what we want is precisely to be used, to be dominated and devoured, and to take a break from all that respect and dignity. So I suggest that we *can* take Kant's thoughts on sex seriously, as long as we understand that he's taking on the moral perils of unimaginably kinky sex.

And if we read Kant's concerns about sex is this way, his claim that kinky sex can't be *transformed*, but only *quarantined*, seems more reasonable. After all, we don't want to transform kinky sex and make it all moral and respectful and stuff. That would completely defeat the point of kinky sex. And, by the same token, we may not want the dehumanizing elements of our kinky sex lives to spill into other parts of our lives.

A relationship that's consistent with kinky sex isn't one that transforms our kinky urges, but one that creates a space in which we can explore them. A kinky sex life requires us to design relationships with the capacity to compartmentalize sexual cannibalism on the one hand, and moral respect for our lovers and ourselves on the other.

I'm not suggesting, as Kant does, that marriage is the solution to the untransformable kink that sex entails. But I think he may be on to something when he emphasizes the quarantining function of successful relationships, which allow us intimate spaces in which to explore our most cannibalistic urges within a broader relationship characterized by mutual trust and respect.

Moreover, by emphasizing the moral dangers of kinky sex, Kant suggests that we need to think carefully about the kinds of structures that would allow us to explore the rampant, morally troubling pleasures of uninhibited sex lives while maintaining loving, moral, and respectful relationships. The very presence of the moral dangers of sex require us to think more carefully about our relationships with our lovers—which is a good thing, because it's likely to make us better lovers. I have to be *more* careful to respect my lover than the other people in my life, precisely because we often also objectify each other, devour each other, and allow ourselves to be consumed by each other. Sex poses a useful challenge to our relationship by forcing us to construct a relationship that can maintain respect in the face of intimacy, desire, and even kink.

The risky moral presence of sex may in fact teach us to engage more directly in questions about responsibilities and obligations, and to develop more careful moral relationship with our lovers. And the kinkier the sex (be it with vampires or not), the greater the challenge to developing a sustainable moral relationship.

We see this challenge play out in vampire stories, where the dangerous and devouring nature of desire requires vampire lovers to engage with questions about respect and restraint (for several thousand largely uninterrupted pages, in the case of the *Twilight* series). But it's this tension that makes vampire heroes like Edward (*Twilight*), Bill (*True Blood*), and Spike (*Buffy*) so sexy: these vampires have a dark and dangerous desire to devour their lovers, and can restrain themselves only out of a deep, awe-like respect for the object of their desire.

Vampire sex, in this sense, shares some characteristics with Kant's idea of moral friendship. Both involve a delicate balance of need and restraint. One force (love or desire) draws us towards each other into a perilously dangerous intimacy where one's very humanity (or, you know, life) is threatened; another force (respect or restraint) urges us to tread carefully, to maintain a safe distance, so that we can enjoy each other safely. And this constant balancing act, this continuous resistance to our deepest impulses, is exactly what keeps vampire sex sexy (and moral friendship respect-y).

So Kant, perhaps surprisingly, gives us some tools to engage safely in kinky sex. He reminds us that kinky sex can't, and shouldn't, be morally transformed. Even radically objectifying your lover is okay—as long as you build a relationship that balances that objectification with respect. A successful relationship is one that can make room for kink while safely quarantining it.

Within my relationship with my lover, reciprocal cannibalism is totally permissible—provided we're still talking about sexy cannibalism, and not actual cannibalism. Because that's still not okay, even with vampires.

4
Pussy and Other Important Ps

ROBERT ARP

What is true love? Is it a cosmic force that unites us all? Is it a general concern for the welfare of all human beings? Is it reserved only for our most intimate friendships? Is it the erotic passion one finds in sexual relationships? Or, is it something more than that? Can there be anything more than that?

Throughout the journey of my life, I've discovered six kinds of love. What I really want to talk about is the one I like to call "Pussy Love." However, in my saner moments, I've come to believe that everyone needs to experience a little of each kind of love. And I've further come to admit—very, very reluctantly admit—that Pussy Love may not be the end all and be all, the true love we are all searching for.

Partridge Family Love

Let's start off with the kind of love I experienced first in life. I'll call this kind of love *Partridge Family Love*, in honor of the 1970s sitcom that featured a family who "love each other, no matter what," to quote Shirley Partridge, the mom of the family.

Partridge Family Love is unconditional and unending. I'm forty, and my mom still tells me: "You'll always be my baby, and I'll love you no matter what." In a similar vein, my older sister still introduces me to people as "her baby brother." She has often also added this little tidbit: ". . . and I used to change his diapers, so I've seen his winky . . . ha, ha, ha" (in a cackling way). I have kids now and regard them in much the same way that my mom and sister do me—though I will never talk about their private parts in public.

The kind of love we're talking about here is underscored by the Christian concept of *agapé*, as discussed by the philosopher Thomas Aquinas (1225–1274). Christians see their god as an all-good, all-merciful, all-loving father who created all of reality, and who loves his creation with a profound bond that nothing can *ever* break. Even when the Christian god's children reject him and sin by doing something absolutely horrible, like murder, he will always be there to forgive and forget.

Though I've never killed anyone, I have borrowed lots of money from my parents, only *some* of which I have paid back through the years. As a parent now, I know what it's like to be on the other side of that kind of deal. But somehow it just doesn't matter. Blood ties are the ties that bind.

Another aspect of *agapé* Aquinas discusses is self-sacrifice. The Christian god was embodied in the person of Jesus Christ, who not only said "There is no greater love than to lay down one's life for another" (John 15:13), but also claimed to be giving his life to save all of humanity from death and damnation.

Self-sacrifice is a familiar idea to most parents. I would give up my life in a second to spare one or both of my girls. I would trade places with them if they had cancer, or were being tortured, or had to endure any kind of suffering whatsoever. (Wow! I just realized that I *would* do "what Jesus would do" . . . I need one of those shirts, or at least a cool bracelet.)

It shouldn't be too controversial for me to assert that all people need to experience Partridge Family Love. In fact, gobs of data indicate that it's required for psychological stability. Without it, we become sociopaths, unable to care about other human beings.

Nevertheless, Partridge Family Love isn't enough. Ultimately, the problem with it is that it is just a little on the dull side. I mean, except in apocalyptic times, who wants to spend Saturday night with their parents? As I grew up, I began to search for something more exciting.

Prevalent Love

In my first philosophy class as a gangly teen-ager, I learned about the ancient Greek philosopher Empedocles. He envisioned Strife and Love as polar principles at work in the universe. Strife is the source of all that is destructive, separate, chaotic, and evil, while Love is the source of all that is generative, unified, harmonious, and good. The universe balances in tension between the two, with either one dominant at various times. Here, love is not just something that affects human relationships, it literally "makes the world go around" as a prevalent force.

Many people think of love and hate as awesome and inescapable powers that lead people either to peace, harmony, and respect, or to war, chaos, and violence. This is a very Sixties notion that recurs with even greater frequency than bell bottoms and sideburns. Although, as a child of the Seventies, I could never be a true hippie, I was inspired.

In the end, however, Empedoclean love suffers from the same pimply vagueness found in adolescent poetry. Slogans like "All you need is love" are so general that they become meaningless. A grown adult needs true love to be something *more specific* than an underlying source of harmony—something that lives and breathes and walks and talks. Hence, while retaining a healthy dose of cosmic consciousness, I plodded on.

People Love

Deciding to enter the seminary, I studied more philosophy and became increasing drawn to the Greek Stoics, whose founder was Zeno of Citium (334–262 B.C.E.). The Stoic conception of love is a deep respect for all of humankind that I'll call *People Love*.

People Love requires that you should be detached enough from this world and its pleasures to appreciate the beauty and goodness of all of humanity. Such a detachment would bring about universal harmony and peace, which is the ultimate goal of a happy life. Stoic love treats all people equally as "Citizens of the World," as opposed to being concerned only with one's own family or friends.

People Love is also supported by the philosophy of Immanuel Kant (1724–1804). Kant calls for each person to uphold their duty to humankind, and the moral law underlying this duty goes something like this: "Always treat yourself and others as an end and never as a means." This can easily be interpreted as a form of love, echoed in Biblical passages such as "Love your neighbor as yourself" (Leviticus 19:18; also Matthew 22:37); and "love your enemies" (Matthew 5: 44–45). For the Stoics, Kant, and Christians, love very specifically requires daily kindness toward our fellow human beings.

Now I'm no Desmond Tutu (and certainly not Mother Teresa!), but while in the seminary, I worked in my share of homeless shelters and soup kitchens ministering to poor people, as well as to people with mental disabilities and mental illnesses. And I want to make the case that everyone needs to experience a bit of People Love through some such experience. Once you allow yourself the emotional vulnerability of engaging with disadvantaged individuals, you begin to count your own blessings and become more empathetic toward people in general, whether they are disadvantaged or not.

So, People Love, unlike Prevalent Love, is very satisfyingly down to earth. And yet it leaves a certain hunger. . . .

Pussy Love

Well, I put this topic off as long as I could. There is no stopping me now.

Boy do I *loooooooooooooooooooove* pussy! And I always have. Of course, at this point in my life, it's my wife's and only my wife's. Nevertheless . . . I *do* love pussy.

Throughout my youth, I enjoyed many carnal pleasures, from masturbating to magazines and videos, to kissing and fingering, to oral sex, to sexual intercourse. I did all these things and more with different chicks in the appropriate chronological sequence and then I went back and did them again, and again, and again, and again, and again. Then I tried different combinations of these things with different chicks again, and again, and again, and again, and again, and again, and again. Then I switched it up a bit by doing it with different chicks wearing various different outfits again, and again, and again. You get the picture.

Actually, despite my interest in different chicks, I usually stayed with one chick at a time. Though I was a one-pussy man, for the most part, I never went without it for long, even throughout my time spent in the seminary. (Please don't tell my old priest professors, and don't show this chapter to my wife, my kids, my mom, my sister, her husband, or anyone I work with, or anyone who has the power to damage my professional career).

Now, I mention all of this not only to tantalize (or possibly offend) you, but also because a lot of people associate love with an emotion involving passionate desire. This association has a long history in Western philosophy that begins with the ancient Greeks, who developed a conception of love known as *Eros*.

In Greek mythology, *Eros* was a god who had great power over mortals, causing them to do crazy things like lie, steal, cheat, and murder—mostly for some kind of sexual payoff. The epic poet Hesiod characterizes Eros as the enemy of reason. This characterization was influential in the Golden Age of Greek philosophers, who envisioned human beings as having a rational, controlled, prudent part of their personality that must keep the irrational part of their personality in check.

The irrational part of one's personality is shared with animals—and often has to do with sex. In Greek mythology, when mortals and gods weren't trying to screw each other over, they were trying to screw each other! So, *Eros* came to be associated with sexual desire, and that's why, today, erotic desire is so closely linked with sex and sexual relationships.

As with Prevalent Love, Partridge Family Love, and People Love, I think that all people need to experience Pussy Love (or Penis Love) at some point in their life. Now, I want to be crystal clear that I am not advocating any kind of dangerous, promiscuous, Don Juan-like sexual behavior here. It's just that we're animals deep down, and those urges will be met, one way or the other.

I eventually came to terms with the fact that I am not cut out for the priesthood. Fortunately, I escaped the Church without ever being molested. Through my experiences there, however, I learned that a lot of priests are homosexual. What these homosexual priests do, despite the fact that they have taken vows of celibacy (where they are not supposed to even masturbate, let alone have any kind of sexual contact), is "act out" on the weekends or on vacations by engaging in sexual activities at all kinds of places like bathhouses, bars, and bike trails! The other percentage of priests who are not gay end up acting out too, often with prostitutes.

I always admired the older guys who went into the seminary as a second or third career. They lived, lied, *and loved* a bit before consciously making the decision to be celibate. Nevertheless, their choice always mystified me.

As mentioned, I enjoyed erotic love throughout my life. And I still do with my wife. We have hot, horny, sweaty, super-satisfying, monkey sex—just like other animals. And so, knowing that there are those who voluntarily give sex up, I've had to ask myself, why?

Upon leaving the seminary I embarked on a career in philosophy. This required intensive study of great thinkers, who gave me new perspective on pussy. While I myself would never go so far as to give it up, I have come to appreciate that purely physical love leaves the mind wanting. We must now examine two other kinds of love that fill that void, though I will have occasion to return to the topic of pussy (if only because it so amuses me to see the word in print).

Platonic Love

The ancient Greek philosopher Plato was one of the most brilliant writers who ever lived. He so ardently defended another conception of love that it has been given his name.

In contrast to the irrational and animalistic *Eros*, the Greeks had another conception of love called *philia*, which can be understood as the appreciation of another's beauty or goodness. Plato developed an elaborate metaphysical foundation for this philial notion of love, casting it as an intellectual "Form" of Beauty Itself in which all beautiful things have a share.

According to Plato's metaphysics, reality is divided into two basic realms: 1. the imperfect, corruptible, changeable, "visible" world of our sense experiences; and 2. the perfect, incorruptible, unchanging, "intelligible" world of ideas or "Forms." Each kind of object, event, thing, or action that one experiences in the visible world corresponds to a Form that one can come to know in the intelligible world.

A Form is like the ideal essence, core, or fundamental "nature" of something. So, for example, all of the different chairs we see around us are chairs in virtue of the Form of Chairness, which can only be "accessed" through our minds. We need only use reason and serious logical thinking to "see" these Forms.

For Plato, the Forms are what humans should be striving to know, as these ideal universals fulfill the twofold purpose of: a. making the things in the visible realm *known as* what they are; as well as b. making the things in the visible realm actually *be* what they are. Plato expressed this by saying that things in the visible world "participate" in the Forms. So, if you want to be able to recognize and understand objects and events around you—as well as be able to explain how it is that these objects and events have come to be—then Plato suggests that you get to know the Forms. To know and understand the essence or fundamental nature of something is good, as it will help you avoid bad reasoning or making decisions based upon too little information that could lead to unwanted consequences in your life.

Plato argues that *philia* can lead a person from the changeable and imperfectly beautiful things of this world to the unchanging and perfect universal Form of Beauty. This is Platonic Love. Unlike any erotic experience, it will be satisfying to the *mind*, rather than the body.

In erotic encounters, our bodies make contact with beautiful objects in the visible realm, and physical pleasure is produced (Mmmm, pussy). In philial encounters, our minds make contact with the Form of Beauty in the intelligible realm, and mental pleasure is produced.

True love, for Plato, is knowing and understanding the ideal Form of Beauty in which beautiful things in the visible world participate. This kind of satisfaction is most readily found in philosophy, where one studies the nature of beauty and other universal concepts. (The English word *philosophy* comes from the two Greek words *philos* and *sophia,* meaning *love of wisdom.*)

As contrasted with erotic love, in which sexual or bodily desires are met (pussy, pussy, pussy . . .), philial love is concerned with a desire for the Beauty that underlies persons, places, and things *for Beauty's sake.* Hence, the term *Platonic relationship* refers to a situation in which two people enjoy lofty, intellectual pursuits together without having sex.

Like the Prevalent Love of Empedocles, all people need to be at least *aware* of Platonic Love. After all, Plato is one of the most important thinkers in the history of Western civilization, and his conviction that we should try to know the essences of things is central to any rational investigation. Plato wrote philosophy in the form of dialogues, and they are timeless classics precisely because the discussion he started continues to this day and beyond.

One cannot, however, have a dialogue alone in one's ivory tower. Without explicitly claiming that one could, Plato devoted remarkably little attention to the Platonic relationships that foster intellectual pursuits. His philosophical program is frigidly abstract without others to share it with.

Pal Love

And so we turn to Plato's illustrious student, Aristotle (384–322 B.C.E.), who advanced an extremely influential analysis of friendship.

For Aristotle, love entails an appreciation of the beautiful qualities of another person standing before you right here and right now, not in some abstract world. This is someone you really know and can really talk to, whether or not you are also having sex with them. According to Aristotle, love is best understood as a relationship of friendship between two people who strive to promote each other's good.

More or less everyone "has friends," but not everyone pays attention to the quality of these relationships. Aristotle argues that there are three types of friendship.

Friendships of utility are those relationships where mutual benefit is to be gained from each other's services. For example, I bring my car to a mechanic on a regular basis. We are friendly toward one another, no doubt, and I "love" him insofar as he serves the purpose of fixing my car. We chat about our interests, our vacations, and even our families. He is a utility friend. I feel the same way toward: my dentist, because he is useful for keeping my teeth clean; my doctor, because he gets paid to keep me healthy; and my gutter-cleaner guy, because he keeps my gutters clean.

Friendships of pleasure are those relationships where pleasure is to be gained from engaging in mutually enjoyable experiences. For example, I was on a softball team just after I got out of college. You can't really socialize while playing softball, not if you're a serious player, but we'd all go out together after a game and socialize while playing pool.

So too, throughout my life there were people I'd simply go to a movie with, or play in a band with, or enjoy sushi with, or bone (pussy, pussy, pussy . . .), and that was about it. (I recall at least one of my relationships with a woman that kind of degenerated into my coming over for sex, then "coming," then coming to my senses and immediately leaving.) Sure, we'd shoot the bull and get to know each other a bit, but our friendships centered on the pleasurable experiences.

While friendships of utility and friendships of pleasure are legitimate and even desirable relationships, the best and most noble, in Aristotle's view, are *friendships of virtue*. These are also the most difficult to achieve because they require the friends to be wise and good. In this kind of friendship, as Aristotle so poetically puts it, "two bodies share one soul," in that they develop a deep desire for one another's highest good—a good that is concerned with the most true and virtuous kind of life.

I think Aristotle's friendship of virtue, which I more modestly call Pal love, is the most mature, most self-actualized, and most valuable form of loving one can engage in. Commitment, loyalty, honesty, integrity, trust—these are all qualities crucial to this kind of love. When you are reunited after time apart from a true pal, you feel as if no time has passed, and a little part inside of you is always excited to see them.

I would say there is really only one woman with whom I share Pal Love, and that's my wife (even though I like her pussy, too!). You know how people say that they have found their soul mate? Well, I understand what that means in this Aristotelian way. Similarly, there is one man I regard as a true pal, and that's an ex-priest friend of mine. He's my male soul mate, but in a non-gay way, since, in case you haven't heard—I like pussy.

Everyone should have at least one Pal Lover in life. There are gobs of data indicating that not only the most successful people but also the happiest people have intimate friends who they can "come home to." A real pal helps us get through good times and bad, inspires us to become more than we are, and loves us with all of our strengths and flaws.

Life's Love Journey

So, that's what I've learned—at least so far—in my search for true love. It's really not the case that any one kind of love is true love. It's rather that love is a multifaceted reality, including what I've called the six P's: Partridge Family Love, Prevalent Love, People Love, Pussy Love, Platonic Love, and Pal Love. Granted, I may be a little bit obsessed with Pussy Love (Mmmmmmm, pussy . . .), but that's only to be expected, given the passionate sort of desire that Pussy Love is. What philosophy has taught me is that you can have many different lovers of many different kinds.

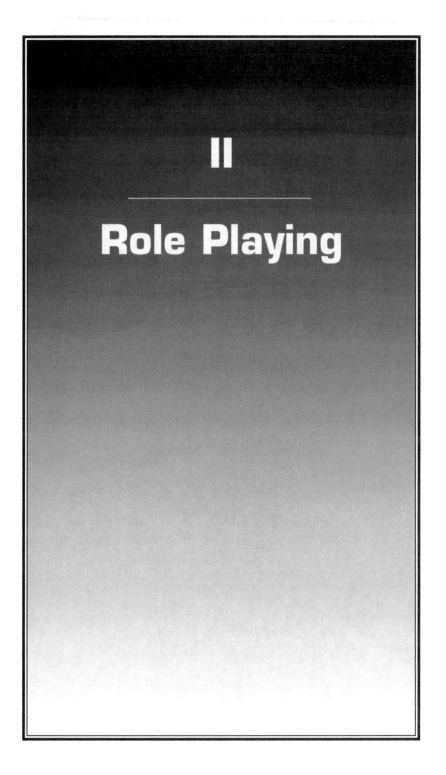

II

Role Playing

5
Hips Don't Lie

PAUL LOADER

Philosophy and the study of the actual world have the same relationship to one another as masturbation and sexual love.

— KARL MARX AND FRIEDRICH ENGELS

My hips don't lie.

— SHAKIRA

1

Ex-Professor John Cohen was in a bit of a quandary. With his hand on her knee he was willing to say almost anything to keep the situation moving. What were words anyway? Just a means to an end. And those legs meant more to him than a thousand pages of Marx. They were a critique of philosophy in themselves, an immediate, sensuous critique that demanded his urgent and sustained attention.

But then she had to mention Richard Dawkins. Dawkins the Bore. Smugface Fuckhead Dawkins. She might as well have spat in his face. Actually no—not that. He realized his sexual tastes were so degenerate nowadays that he might enjoy her spitting on him. . . .

"Are you going to Dawkins's talk on Friday?" she had asked, all innocence.

"I don't think so" he said, conveying with a wrinkling of his nose just how unlikely this was.

"Why? Don't you like him?"

He tried to sound casual, "Oh, I just think he's a bit unimaginative, that's all."

And then, blindly, with no sense of the possible impact of her words, she had said, "I don't agree. I think he's really clever and imaginative."

He should try to stay calm. It shouldn't matter. If he rode things out Dawkins would fade from their conversation as quickly as he had appeared and all would be well again. Maybe later, once they had slept together, he could explain things to her carefully, show her the error of her ways.

But could he sleep with her at all knowing that the figure of Dawkins loomed large in her consciousness, suffused with a halo? That she valued Dawkins's opinion above his? That, in some sense, she'd rather be fucking Dawkins than him? Not that she had ever explicitly entertained such a proposition, he supposed—or probably not.

God, what if she had? Maybe she imagined Dawkins sitting at his desk explaining some passage from the *Selfish Gene* to her. He'd be all authoritative and distinguished. And she'd imagine him putting one of his authoritative distinguished hands into her panties whilst he talked about sexual reproduction. . . .

He took a large gulp from his beer. He needed to get a grip. She was a grad student. She liked Richard Dawkins. So what? All grad students liked Richard Dawkins.

Perhaps when they got back he could just fuck the Dawkins out of her. He'd take her savagely from behind. Make her renounce Dawkins as he thrust into her. What should she say? Maybe she should say "Fuck Dawkins!" in rhythm with their lovemaking, getting louder and louder until she screamed "Fuck, fucking Dawkins, the fucking bastard!" when she came.

But would this be enough?

He felt that more needed to happen to exorcise Dawkins completely. His work would have to be defiled somehow. Pages from one of his books would have to be incorporated into the sex act in a way that expressed complete contempt for their content. Bodily fluids would certainly have to be involved.

As various unfeasible acts of defilement passed through Ex-Professor Cohen's mind the student placed her hand on his:

"Anyway, shall we get going?"

2

Blundering around in the dark, he ended up tripping over a pile of shoes.

"Wait" she said, "Let me get the light!"

The lamp was Barbie-like. Not Klaus Barbie, which would have been rather disconcerting, but some kind of kitschy pink and purple creation involving a ballerina in a tutu. Its suggestion of innocence cast a pleasantly disreputable light over the whole proceedings. He was pleased with the effect. This was a world he felt at home in. This was why they had forced him to become an *ex*-professor, a title which over time he had come to regard as an honor. Where was there to go after 'professor' anyway? Genuine progress meant realizing that all the abstractions of academia were empty, useless nothings. It meant rediscovering the world of physical desire and embracing it wholeheartedly. Or something like that. . . .

He had the idea that he might try to use a phrase like "help with your homework" or "been a naughty girl"—not that she was really that much younger than him, but he had found such talk to be effective in the past. In this instance, however, it proved unnecessary, for before he could formulate a single suggestive sentence she was already lying back on the bed, legs dangling over the edge. He leant over her, kissed her on her lips and began moving his hand up between her thighs. She laughed a bit at first then closed her eyes, relaxing into his rhythmic hand movements.

This would show Dawkins, he thought. *His* distinguished hands were nowhere to be seen. It was his own hands—Cohen's hands—that were here, now, living in the moment. He was exploring a truth that Dawkins would never know—the truth at the apex of a grad student's thighs! Dawkins—the fool was probably sitting in a room by himself, peering over his bifocals at some lesser known work of Darwin's, making assiduous footnotes. Or banging on about God to an audience of earnest young men.

That was the problem with Dawkins—he didn't know what life was about! Which was ironic given that he was a biologist. What was the point of perpetually rallying against religion if one had nothing worthwhile or imaginative—nothing passionate—to replace it with? Just a sterile 'scientific' world view. A cold barren landscape of biological processes. What was that charming phrase of his? We were "survival machines" for genes. "Survival machines"—two miserable ideas contained in one phrase. Well he wasn't a machine, and neither was he interested in mere survival—he wanted to live!

Cohen paused to scratch his nose. Anyway—what did it even mean to say that we were survival machines for genes? How could Dawkins justify turning things on their head in this way? He was simultaneously stripping us of our own humanity and anthropomorphizing genes. It was absurd. It was like saying—it was like saying we were just 'walking machines for shoes' . . .

"Everything okay?" she said, propping herself up on her elbows.

Cohen realized he'd been staring into space.

"Yes—I'm fine. Sorry!"

"What were you thinking about?"

"Oh nothing. . . . I was . . . I don't know really."

"It's just that it *is* kind of off-putting when someone fazes out like that, right in the middle of sex."

There was an uneasy silence. He felt awkward. Part of him was still thinking about the 'shoes' metaphor. 'Walking machines for shoes' . . . he could write a paper called 'Walking Machines for Shoes'. That was the best way to get at Dawkins—ridicule him. Most people probably wouldn't read the paper in its entirety but the title—the central idea—would stick. . . . But where could he get it published? Maybe in the *Journal of Biology and Philosophy*—or if not, then the *Journal of Philosophy and Biology* . . .

"I'll make some coffee." she said, getting up.

"No! I mean—let's not have coffee yet. I didn't mean to get distracted. I was just . . ."

"No—let's leave it" she said. "I'm a little tired now anyway."

3

Saturday afternoon. There was a pleasant spring breeze and Cohen was feeling chirpy as he walked up the hill towards her flat. He'd been a fool to let his obsession with Dawkins get the better of him. Well there'd be no more of that now. He would go round there. Ask her if she wanted to go out for a walk—a ramble in the country. They could make love in the woods.

As her house came into vision he could see that her door was already open. He hadn't considered this. She may have planned something already. A picnic with friends maybe. Well he could still say hello. Arrange to meet up another time.

A man appeared at the door, a rather old man dressed in a tweed suit. He walked out into the street then turned around to wave goodbye to the girl who was now standing in the doorway.

How sweet. Must be her father come down for a weekend visit. Probably with a carload of provisions. Cohen imagined the boxes of items the father had brought—half of which she would never use. Things to keep her warm. Healthy foodstuffs. Maybe a magazine with an article he thought she would be interested in because it mentioned the word 'philosophy' in some irrelevant way.

Cohen stopped by a mailbox. He would wait a while. Better to avoid any lengthy and potentially embarrassing introductions.

The girl stepped out into the street to hug her visitor. Then something odd happened. As the hug progressed the man appeared to run his hand down her back and on to her behind. An affectionate fatherly bottom patting perhaps? Was there such a thing? But now the hand was squeezing her behind rather vigorously, and moving up inside her skirt. . . . The girl jumped back laughing. Her face was flushed. She leant forward to give the man a final peck on the cheek, then waved good bye and returned to the house.

When the door closed the visitor turned back to the street and began walking in Cohen's direction—allowing Cohen his first clear view of that distinctive face. Suddenly Cohen found himself rooted to the spot, a cocktail of emotions invading his system—shock, anger, jealousy, bewilderment, disgust—inducing in him a kind of paralysis.

As the man drew close he noticed Cohen staring at him. He smiled back. The face was unusually relaxed, conveying a sense of inner satisfaction, smugness almost.

"Lovely day!" he said to Cohen, with a wave of one of his distinguished hands.

Ex-Professor Cohen said nothing.

6
Porn Lovers

Jacob M. Held

Two students, Jan and Cal, have just left their Gender Studies class.

JAN: Where ya headed, Cal? You wanna grab some lunch?

CAL: Nah, I thought I'd go back to my room, watch some porn, and rub one out.

JAN: Oh my God! I can't believe you just said that. You are so disgusting!

CAL: Whatever, Jan! Didn't you hear our prof say that masturbation is a normal and healthy part of male and female sexuality?

JAN: Sure, I heard that, but I didn't hear him recommending porn. In fact, didn't you do the reading by Catharine MacKinnon? She argues that porn isn't just disgusting, it's harmful.

CAL: Yeah, I read that. But I also read the one by Nadine Strossen, who shows that MacKinnon's full of it. Tell you what: I'll go to lunch with you—hell, I'll even buy you lunch—if you let me show you why your reaction just now was so wrong.

Cal and Jan begin walking toward a restaurant.

CAL: So, it seems to me that you and MacKinnon have a personal distaste for porn, and you're trying to force your preferences on everyone else.

JAN: We don't just dislike porn, Cal. We're saying that it harms us—that it harms all women. And beyond that, it distorts our understanding of sexuality, and that affects everyone.

CAL: Oh, come on. How has porn harmed you or anyone you know?

JAN: Well, it's like sexual harassment. In a workplace you can't go around telling bawdy jokes or making lewd comments to whomever you chose.

CAL: No, you can't. Some overly sensitive woman is bound to complain.

JAN: Be reasonable, Cal. In addition to being illegal, sexual harassment is morally wrong because it creates a hostile environment for women, making it difficult for us to function as well as we might otherwise. Suppose my boss ogles me and calls me a cock-tease. This is not only a direct assault on my self-esteem, it affects my ability to deal with him professionally and thus diminishes my opportunity to succeed at that job. It creates a discriminatory atmosphere, one premised on gender inequity.

CAL: Fine. Your boss is a pig and should be reprimanded. But what does this have to do with porn?

JAN: Porn does exactly the same thing on a societal scale. It's the dirty joke men tell and women are forced to hear. We live in a society that accepts that joke and thus implicitly accepts the premise that women are sexual objects, built for male pleasure.

CAL: You've got it all wrong, Jan. Porn is nothing but a fantasy, and responsible users know that. It's not like we expect real women to be into gangbangs, anal sex, or threesomes, just because that's what we want to see the professionals doing. The fantasy turns us on, we take care of business, and then we move on with our lives. No harm, no foul.

JAN: But through continued porn use, men start to view the world through a pornographic lens. They judge women according to whether they meet the pornographic ideal. They start to see women in general as objects for their pleasure, things to be used and thrown away just like the Kleenex after a late night Internet session.

CAL: You're talking about your asshole of a boss again. He would treat you like shit whether or not there was such a thing as pornography. But decent guys like me don't do that. My personal beliefs would never allow me to treat a woman like a spooed Kleenex. The porn industry is not some organized society aiming to brainwash men. It couldn't if it tried.

JAN: It doesn't need to be deliberate, Cal, and it doesn't need to work on all men. Think about how sexual harassment works. The sexist boss creates a sexist climate. Not all the male employees go along with it and not all the female employees are targeted—maybe none are directly targeted. But everyone's experience is tainted.

CAL: Okay, so think porn is like sexual harassment. But even the law about sexual harassment is vague—there is a strong and a weak interpretation of it. Everyone will agree that direct targeting—such as touching or sexual remarks—is wrong. But it's very controversial whether things like joking about sex or pinning up a poster of a nude in your office constitutes harassment. In fact, I can just as easily argue that prohibiting such things creates an unpleasantly chilly climate that kills employee camaraderie.

JAN: You could make that case, although not very convincingly.

CAL: Really? What's your favorite TV show?

JAN: Well, I like *True Blood.* . . .

CAL: You and I wouldn't be able to talk about the latest episode of that show in the lunchroom at work under the strong interpretation of sexual harassment. The bottom line is that porn does not directly target any woman—it cannot physically touch you, and it cannot make sexual remarks to you. And so any "targeting" it did would have to be indirect—the kind that, in the case of sexual harassment is controversial.

Cal and Jan sit down at the restaurant and order lunch.

JAN: All right then, let's pick up a related thread. Part of the problem with sexual harassment—even the indirect kind—is that it proliferates a negative attitude toward women. For instance, if someone at work jokes that women are whores, and the comment goes unchecked or receives the seal of approval by those in authority, then the idea "women are whores" and all it entails, their degradation and humiliation, becomes an acceptable and supported attitude in that workplace.

CAL: Believe me, Jan, no one with any backbone is going to be influenced by a stupid comment like that.

JAN: But with pornography it's not just one comment in one environment. It's everywhere and it's over and over again. Consider advertising. It inundates us, influencing our view of the world. We know ads set unreasonable body-image ideals, and some people may be able to disregard them. But most people can't, as is evident from the epidemic of body-image disorders in our society. And it's not all about our conscious responses, a great deal of media operates at the non-conscious level setting expectations and forming attitudes we're unaware of.

CAL: Well, advertising is everywhere. Porn isn't.

JAN: Man, you're dense. Porn is everywhere. It's on the best seller shelves in bookstores, in music videos, all over the Internet, and even trickles in women's and young girl's fashions. Hell, pole dancing is being pimped as an aerobic exercise. What does that say about how we view women, their place in society, and what we think they are good for? We live in a pornified nation. Jesus Christ, the average age of exposure to hardcore porn is eleven fucking years old! And on the Internet, any category of porn you can think of is just a click away: amateur, public, lesbian, interracial, bukkake, golden shower, enema, fisting, she-male, double penetration, bondage. . . . I could find you midget-clown-rodeo-gang-fucking if you wanted. Or how about pterodactyl?

CAL: I'll do pterodactyl porn with you any time you want, Jan. And don't worry: I won't accuse you of sexually harassing pteranodons.

JAN: Seriously, Cal. Do you think these genres ever just occurred to someone? Do you think a normal, healthy little boy ever grew up and just spontaneously said, "Hey, you know what I think would turn me on?—Seven ripped, enormous black dudes pounding a blonde school girl and gagging her with their pricks until she vomits."

CAL: Wow—for someone who doesn't like porn, you sure have been watching quite a bit. . . .

JAN: Don't dismiss this, Cal. A young man might begin with something simple, like wanting to see a blow job while jerking off, but soon he needs more—he looks for something more intense. Facials. Then maybe threesomes or orgies. Pretty soon he's viewing things he never imagined would turn him on. And there's no going back. Once you're desensitized your sexual appetite is calibrated to a pornographic ideal of sex. Porn shapes your view of sexuality through sheer repetition. Continually consuming women as sex objects turns them into a consumable commodity, at least in the consumer's mind. This mentality distorts our view of sexuality and each other.

CAL: So, you think porn causes people to have certain sexual desires. But you've got it backwards: the sexual desires people have cause the porn industry to produce what it produces. You say porn is like advertising. Well, think about how advertising works. It says—"You want food? You want to be popular? You want to have fun? Then buy our product!" It doesn't convince people that they want food or popularity or fun. Humans naturally want these things.

JAN: Really, Cal? Advertising doesn't affect our desires or expectations? All it does is provide info so we can make informed decisions about desires we already have? That'd be news to advertisers. They know they can create artificial desires and then feed them with whatever product they're selling. Human beings may naturally crave food, but that doesn't mean we crave Twinkies. Twinkies are a completely synthetic exploitation of our innate cravings. Advertising works by exploiting our innate needs with false palliatives. Consider cosmetics companies. Everyone wants to be liked and accepted, that's natural. But cosmetics companies set up artificial standards of beauty—unachievable ideals—in order to perpetuate a culture where women are always uncomfortable in their own body. This guarantees that they will always have a market for their newest product. Porn's the same way. People may crave sex and want release, and porn may provide that, but it promotes a culture. Watching women get slapped and called "cunt" while being ravished by abusive men is a cultural phenomenon—and a fairly new one. And constantly consuming this will affect the consumer. The hyper sexualized, unattainable ideals of femininity found in advertising have been linked to eating and body image disorders, so what do you think a culture of porn is going to lead to?

CAL: Okay, so your second argument is that porn is like advertising. I'm content to accept your analogy without drawing the conclusion that porn is morally wrong. There is a whole host of food on the market—from bread, to chips, to Twinkies. It is up to the individual to make responsible choices. I'm glad the variety is there and I'm not ashamed to engage in some harmless indulgence from time to time.

Cal and Jan leave the restaurant and begin walking back to campus.

JAN: Let's look at the issue on a more personal level, then. Turn the tables for a minute and imagine your girlfriend is into porn. She loves to watch porn stars like Lex Steele and Shane Diesel—ripped, muscular men, with ten-inch cocks as round as Coke cans. You know she's janing-off to their videos and fantasizing about them. How does that make you feel about your body? Do you think it might make you a little uncomfortable or insecure to know that you don't and can't possibly ever measure up to what's getting her off? Do you think her porn consumption might affect her expectations of how your sex life as a couple should be?

CAL: Perhaps. . . .

JAN: I think you'd find it troubling. Men's use of porn indicates that they're bored and dissatisfied with their lovers. They may as well just cheat for what it does to their emotional bonds and commitments.

CAL: Okay, but if you say porn is wrong because it's like cheating, then you have to say why cheating is wrong.

JAN: Well, I think it's about desertion. It's a betrayal to be sure, but what it really does via the betrayal is create a distance between the man and the woman. He's giving his time and energy to another person.

CAL: I'll agree with your assessment of cheating—while denying that it applies to porn. Guys don't run away with porn stars. On the contrary, they might be more likely to stick around if they can get their rocks off at the computer screen. Porn doesn't take any more time or money than other hobbies—like bird watching or listening to music.

JAN: But it creates an emotional distance. If he can get his rocks off without her, then he doesn't need her. And if she knows about his porn use, then she feels unwanted. And if she doesn't know about it, then he's keeping a secret from her. Either way, their intimacy is destroyed. In fact, counselors and therapists, as well as lawyers, point to frequent porn use and porn addiction as a leading cause or contributing factor in a great number of divorces. Porn destroys relationships. It destroys the man's ability to form meaningful relationships by reinforcing a distorted sense of sexuality that is caustic to a reciprocal and loving bond.

CAL: I wouldn't be at all surprised if there was a correlation between excessive porn use and relationship trouble. But there again, you've got the cart before the horse. There's no reason why reasonable porn use would cause relationship trouble, though I could see why relationship trouble could cause excessive porn use. People often point at surface symptoms as the cause of a problem when really there are deeper issues.

JAN: What exactly do you mean by "reasonable porn use"?

CAL: I mean, first, that she knows about it. You're right about secrets being a problem in a romantic relationship. Second, they should talk about it. He should be clear about why he's using it. Maybe it's because he just needs more sex than she does. It would be selfish of her to keep him from meeting a genuine physical need. Or maybe it's because he just wants fresh excitement. But in that case, he should invite her to participate.

JAN: Yeah, and how often do you suppose that happens?

CAL: Not very often, I suppose. But I think it's too bad. It would be a lot of fun.

JAN: Maybe for the guy!

CAL: I have to remind you not to assume that women don't like porn. Even supposing that some might like different types of porn, there's no reason why the couple can't find something that pleases them both. You ask me to imagine a world that is porn-free. I'll ask you to imagine a world where women and men are equal porn users. Everybody's getting off and everybody's happy as clams.

JAN: When porn is produced primarily by men, according to a male narrative of power and orgasm, women can't be equal users, they're merely used. You're asking them to buy into the image of women in porn, which is produced by men for men. Equality requires reciprocity and all I hear from you is, "My porn use is perfectly fine, and women should deal with it." That's not equality.

CAL: But there's nothing wrong with the porn I consume, or the sex it presents. Women are sexual slackers. They could learn a few things from porn. I don't need to quote the statistics to you about how many women have trouble reaching orgasm and how many women feel sexually unfulfilled. You just need to get after it a bit, you know? Porn is just the ticket.

JAN: There is a better way. Men could stop "learning" from porn and try to be responsive to actual women's needs.

CAL: Jan, your problem is you think the two have to be mutually exclusive. Actual women can enjoy porn. Your own conservative view of sexuality is not the only way to exist as a sexual being.

Cal and Jan arrive at the gate to the campus residence halls.

CAL: So let's recap. You've made three arguments to convince me that porn is morally problematic. First, that porn is like sexual harassment; second, that it's like advertising; and third, that it's like cheating. While I think you made some good points, I'm not convinced. If porn is like sexual harassment, then it's only like the indirect type that isn't really harassment at all. If it is like advertising, then it's a matter of the consumer's personal responsibility and media literacy. If it's like cheating, then it reveals deeper problems in the relationship, which I maintain could be solved by more porn, not less.

JAN: But honestly, Cal. How can you stand what porn has done to our society? Jenna Jameson is mainstream. Little girls are wearing risqué costumes and clothing. Pop stars like Miley Cyrus sell themselves as sexualized teens. Porn stars are on reality TV shows, and some people only become famous because of their porn-star-style antics. Hello, Kim Kardashian and Paris Hilton. And don't even get me started on *Girls Gone Wild*.

CAL: Look, Jan. You're preaching to the choir when it comes to pop culture. I don't listen to pop music and I don't even have a TV. The fact that mainstream culture is cashing in on porn is no argument against porn itself.

JAN: But if you recognize the problem with over-sexualizing girls and you see porn as part of that problem then, yes, it is an argument against porn as an element of a raunchy and destructive cultural trend. Add to that concerns about harassment, discrimination, and relationship stress and we have myriad reasons to be concerned about the impact porn has on our lives.

CAL: But attacking porn is overkill. Suppose soft-drink companies started marketing a drink for children that has a small amount of alcohol in it. The ads for these drinks are aimed at kids. They glorify bar culture and glamorize alcoholism—you get the picture. This would be really bad, right? But would the solution be to ban alcohol for everyone? Of course not. The solution would be to crack down on the leak into the wrong demographic. You can crack down on Miley Cyrus and her ilk all you want. Good riddance, I say. But keep your paws off my porn. Like alcohol, it's for adults to use responsibly.

JAN: But I see a difference between alcohol and porn. Alcohol is a concrete, containable substance. Porn is more diffuse. It comes across in words, and images, and even gestures.

CAL: That's true. But anti-porn words, images, and gestures are just as strong in our culture as are pro-porn messages. In particular, religion has been making people feel guilty about exploring their sexuality for hundreds of years. The fact that I can't even tell you that I'm going to go watch porn and rub one out without you yelling at me is proof that our society suppresses it.

JAN: The fact that I can't turn on the TV without seeing pornified images or raise concerns about them without being attacked as an anti-sex shrew shows exactly how prevalent and acceptable porn is. Porn isn't suppressed; it's so abundant that it has become the background noise of our lives. We don't even see it anymore, and so we are blind to how it affects our culture and us. I'd be happy at this point if you'd just pull your head out of your ass and acknowledge that porn exists and has an impact, one that merits consideration.

CAL: And I'd be content if you'd stop demonizing porn and admit that there can be beneficial uses to erotic material. In the end, the problem with you women is that you're too ashamed to explore your sexuality. I bet you don't even know what turns you on, much less how to get yourself off.

JAN: Don't be so sure about that! Just because it takes women longer doesn't mean we don't know how to do it.

CAL: It would take me a lot longer too if I had an old bag like Catharine MacKinnon watching over my shoulder and tsk tsking every time I started thinking dirty.

JAN: Thanks to porn, you men just don't know the difference between sleazy and sexy. That's the bottom line.

CAL: Fair enough. I really don't see much of a difference there. I would actually be very interested in hearing all about what you think is sexy. . . .

JAN: Whatever, Cal. You'll have to go to the Internet for your fantasies. Have fun rubbing one out. Alone.

7
Machiavelli at the Bar

STEPHANIE ST. MARTIN

How the hell is it already 7:00 p.m.? I thought to myself as I glanced down at my watch. I had been sitting at the corner of a local bar for more than two hours in the hopes of getting a jump start on correcting midterms. My jump start, however, had turned into complete and utter disdain for every one of the students in my class.

"What can I get for ya?" The bartender was standing in front of me.

I lifted my head up from the papers now dripping with red ink. Exhausted, I nodded over to the bottles of liquor, brilliantly lined up, row by row, column by column. "You see all that liquor on the top shelf? Put everything in a big glass, add a cherry, and bring it to me."

He empathized with me, "One of those days, huh?"

"I didn't realize the letter 'u' has become a word in the English language. I don't know why on Earth I expected my students to write out the word "you" in their essays. Next time I'll just have them text their papers to me."

The drink was placed in front of me as he chuckled. "If you need anything else, let me know. My name's Greg."

"Well, Greg, if this thing you made here doesn't kill me, let me know when the next train comes by . . ." I continued to correct, circling every contraction, misspelling, and lowercase 'i' I could find. I finally took a sip of the concoction, making a face as if I had just sucked down an entire lemon. "On the other hand," I mumbled to myself, "they don't *deserve* to kill me," and I slid my drink back towards the bartender.

"I can't believe you're grading papers at a bar!" I had apparently caught the attention of some guy about six barstools away from me. He wore a faded Red Sox cap, so I decided to humor him and respond.

"Well, I once had a professor who said that all the bourbon in the world could not get him through teaching, but I was hoping it could work for me."

"Yeah, teaching high school must suck. The kids are assholes and they're just trying to get through the four most awkward, sex-crazed years of their lives."

"Oh, what a *wonderful* opinion of our youth!" My voice reeked with sarcasm. "I hate to disappoint you, but I'm not talking about high school, I'm talking about college students . . . who apparently have not yet mastered the English language!" I began furiously engraving a red circle onto a student's paper, "Since when is 'kinda' a word!"

"Whoa, whoa, . . . wait. You teach college?!?!" He seemed surprised, but this reaction was something I was slowly getting more and more used to. At twenty-six, I was regularly asked to leave the Faculty Room on my campus because the staff there *still* seemed to assume I was a student. I nodded to him as I tried again to take another sip of my hemlock. Again, I choked and again, pushed the glass away. "What do you teach?" he asked.

"Philosophy," I responded. "I teach Ethics and Intro to Philosophy."

"No shit? Philosophy? That seems . . . well . . . kinda useless." He chuckled and elbowed the man in the suit on the stool next to him. "I mean, you don't seem like the philosophy-type."

"That's because I'm not an old man in glasses with patches on the sleeves of my tweed jacket saying things like: 'Interesting, but highly overrated.'"

He laughed.

"And no," I continued, "it's not useless."

The businessman seemed slightly annoyed by my response. Pulling the olives off the toothpick in his martini, he rolled his eyes and glanced over in my direction. "Sweetie, philosophy *is* overrated. It's all bullshit, and you'll never be successful."

"Thank you, Mr. Enron. And I suppose you don't need ethics to close a business deal?"

"Business deal, love deal, whatever the hell you want to argue—I know how to win."

As much as I wanted to stop this conversation, order another drink, and get back to the stack of papers I had waiting for me, the douchebag vibe that this guy was displaying just had to be dealt with. I mean I could easily ignore him and continue correcting, but the uncharted conversation seemed far more interesting. Besides, what kind of philosopher would I be if I didn't argue my case? I slid the stack of papers back towards the drink and began to mentally prepare for battle.

The Game of Love

"Hey Enron—what's your name?" I asked as I now turned toward him.

"Nick," he responded.

"And I'm Sully," the Red Sox cap guy chimed in, not wanting to be left out. He slid from his stool to one closer to me. Nick followed, sitting beside Sully. Even Greg the bartender followed the duo down towards the corner of the bar, seeing where this conversation was headed.

"Stephanie." I pointed to myself and then proceeded to shake hands with both of them. "Alright, Nick, can I ask you a question?" He nodded and took a sip from his martini. "You married? You got a girlfriend at home?"

"Sweetie, when I make time for women, I have them at my beck and call."

"Your beck and call? Who the hell do you think you are, Richard Gere in *Pretty Woman*?" I teased. Sully laughed, nodding his head in approval. I'm glad someone thought I was amusing. Nick on the other hand was not impressed.

"Look, Sweetie—"

"First of all, I'm not your Sweetie so you can stop with that bullshit. I read enough bullshit in these papers my students have written for me," I said, holding them up. "I don't need any more."

Sully leaned in and whispered to me, "That's because all philosophy is bullshit, Stephanie."

I ignored him and tried to focus on my opponent. "Do you call all your girls "sweetie," or is it the select few?"

"Look," Nick replied, "I treat ladies well. I am not looking for a girlfriend, but I can get just about any girl I want into bed."

I nodded sagely. "And how do you accomplish this?"

"It's just like closing any business deal. You do what it takes." Nick took another sip of his martini, smirking.

"So, Nick, you will lie, cheat, and steal to get a girl home with you?" I asked.

"The girl is the prize, right? And I'm a winner. All is fair in love and war."

"Alright, then, how about an experiment," I said to Nick, hoping he'd humor me. "Let's play the game of love. You play your way and I'll play the 'philosophy' way. Loser pays for the other's tab and Sully here will be the impartial judge. You up to that challenge?"

Nick nodded and called to Greg. "Get me another martini—if I'm going to play, I'm making sure the victory is sweet."

"So what's the game?" Sully asked.

"You and Nick are going to attempt to pick up the same woman."

Nick barely got his sip of martini down. He grinned at Sully—"No offense kid, but the professor here needs to give me a bit of a challenge." His eyes then began to comb the bar. "Can I pick the girl?"

"You mean the lucky girl who gets to come home with me?" Sully teased.

"That's your first mistake, Sully—Luck's got nothing to do with it."

And that's when it hit me. Nick was a modern-day version of Niccolò Machiavelli, the philosopher who is famous for 'lowering the bar' when it comes to morality.

Machiavelli believed that you do whatever it takes to gain and keep power. Being virtuous wasn't important; in fact, virtue was nothing but the skill used in gaining power. Machiavelli wasn't like other philosophers who believe in pursuing the good life—that's just 'pie in the sky' stuff. Instead, you learn when to caress and when to crush.

Just then, Nick spotted his poor victim and proceeded to entice her to walk over to our corner of the bar. I cringed, hoping he would be more 'caressing' than 'crushing' with this challenge.

Nick stuck out his hand to her. "Hi...oh," he paused and pointed to the corner of her eye, "it seems you have something in your eye there." He then cupped her face in his hand, "My mistake—it's just a sparkle."

"Oh geez!" Sully apparently had the same sentiments I did. He stuck out his hand to her as well. "My name is Sully. How are you doing tonight?"

"Hi, I'm Jane. I'm good, thank you."

"Jane. I'm Stephanie. Can I ask you a question?" She looked puzzled but nodded. "Which guy's approach was better? Who were you more comfortable talking to?"

Jane smiled and seemed to understand what was now going on over in this corner of the bar. "By looks or by approach?"

That's definitely a fair question. I may be a philosophy pro-fessor, but I'm not immune to the goods of the body Nick had going for him. If only it didn't come with a douchebag vibe.

"Like there's a difference!" smiled Nick. He was trying to sweet talk his way to into her heart.

"Pick the guy in the Sox hat!" Apparently our little experi-ment had received some attention from a group of women down at the other end of the bar. Team Sully had just been formed.

"I think I'd go with Sully," Jane replied. "He just had a more natural approach. No offense—" Jane said as she looked back at Nick, "but you didn't even introduce yourself to me. And that line—I mean, I guess some girls might be impressed—it's far too cheesy for me though." She started to giggle, "Do girls really like that? I mean—seriously—has any girl ever given you their number?"

"Only the desperate ones!" The women on the other side of the bar were again chiming in.

"Ladies, if you want to be a part of this class discussion, please raise your hand!" I called over to them and I gestured for them to join us. "Just come on down here so we aren't giving Greg a headache by screaming across the bar!"

"It's worse on karaoke night when the girls are all singing 'I Will Survive'—trust me on this one," Greg said as he started to prepare a drink for another patron. Meanwhile, Team Sully made their way towards our corner of the bar.

That's What Friends Are For

I glanced over at Nick, who looked . . . well . . . flabbergasted. I'm sure he had been turned down before, but I don't know if it had ever been on such a public scale. Perhaps if he and Jane were just talking one on one, he would have had a good comeback in place or pretended as if he didn't care. The problem was that all eyes were on him and he couldn't hide his failure. But just like Machiavelli, he quickly concealed his emotions before everyone else noticed.

"The line works 99.9 percent of the time, Sweetie. It's not my fault you weren't impressed, because in all honesty, I wasn't trying to impress you," Nick said.

Wait . . . what? Umm . . . did I not explain the rules? Now I was the one who was flabbergasted!

"I'm sorry?" Jane asked. She seemed, and looked, even more puzzled.

"Let me explain something to you," Nick began.

I guess I have now been relieved of my teaching duties.

"Women—you all have friends. You talk to them . . . every day . . . about everything. I don't know if there is a single decision you actually make on your own. The women in your inner circle help you make decisions and as much as I need to impress you, I need to impress your friends even more. Because even if you're unsure, they can tell you how wonderful I am and how cute they thought the line was when you all go to have that little pow-wow in the bathroom."

An eruption of applause sounded. Men throughout the bar were applauding for Nick's soapbox speech. Smiles were spread ear to ear and one by one, guys were coming up to shake his hand and pat Nick on the back.

"Oh, give me a fucking break!" I couldn't contain my outburst.

I glared belligerently into the eyes of every guy who had just erupted in applause. The look on their faces was as if I just told them girls don't pillow fight naked at sleepovers.

"I know you all think Nick just gave the best locker room speech ever, but are we not forgetting one, *tiny* detail?" Again, the eyebrows were raised. "Nick's single! I'll admit a girl's friends are one key to his success, but do you really think that all the bullshit is going to get passed them?"

"It worked for *NSYNC," Sully remarked.

"Fair enough . . ." I smiled at Sully, but I still wanted to make my point. "It's true that a girl's friends are important to her, but remember, a girl's friends are also her protectors. Why do you think one of us is always designated to drive? Because there has to be one set of sober eyes on all our friends. We aren't going to let you get a free pass at any of our girls! When we have that pow-wow in the bathroom, we may like you, but that doesn't mean we grant you the power to take her home. It takes a lot more than a *lame ass* pick-up line for you to get our approval!"

Boom . . . now the girls were applauding. It was definitely me versus Nick now, and I felt it was time I schooled him on real love.

Jane, however, had been waiting her turn to rebut Nick for some time. She watched me eagerly, waiting for me to call on her. I had to get my teaching authority back from Nick.

"Umm . . . Jane, is there something you would like to say?" I asked.

"Yes, thank you," she said as she readjusted herself on the barstool. "Of the two, Sully was the more natural approach, but I would have given Nick props for trying. I mean . . ." she glanced over at Team Sully who seemed to be huddled-up discussing their decision, "what do you girls think?"

A bleach-blond with orange fingernails piped up. "Well, personally, I don't think it matters how a guy picks me up. But it does matter how he treats me. And Nick has a point—I tell those three everything. We are like the *Sex and the City* girls," she said, sounding pleased with her statement.

"Well, which one of you is Samantha?" Greg quipped. I felt the need to applaud for that one. *Very well played.*

"No we *totally* are!" chimed in another one of the women. "We even have epic conversations. The other day we were all out and there were two guys. Chelsea asked if we should hit on the blond or the brunette and then Robin asked if you can even call boys 'brunettes.' So we began discussing how to differentiate between guys who are blonds and guys who aren't. So Meg said we should call brown-haired guys 'brunos.' It was really funny."

"I'm sure," I said. Suddenly my students' papers were looking far more appealing. Somewhere the judge from *Billy Madison* was telling Team Sully 'I award you no points and may God have mercy on your souls.'

The captain of Team Sully continued with her point. "Nick's right because, if a guy does something nice for me, I really will tell my friends. Brianna's totally got us pegged—we do have epic conversations but I will always turn to my girlfriends for help. And if he wants to stay with me, he has to get their approval," she said.

Nick started to smile thinking he was swaying the jury in his favor. "All I have to do is take the time to send a girl flowers, and chocolates,—and promises I don't intend to keep—and I will always have girls wrapped around my finger."

"No, no, . . . no." Sully was shaking his head in mock sympathy. "Dude—they are obviously going to be able to tell if you aren't keeping your promises. They have follow-up meetings. I mean no human being, unless they are eight beers deep, has to pee that much. You girls are always in the bathroom, analyzing information, decoding every word out of our mouths—and the tone we used . . ." Sully looked around, apparently surprised he was holding everyone's attention. "Even over texting. Honestly, if I don't include a smiley or a kissy-face on my texts, all hell breaks loose. This whole 'love' thing sucks when you are a guy because you don't have a jury of your *peers* judging you—you got a jury of twelve *fucking jaded* women who want to make your life a living hell!"

Love the Way You Lie

Are relationships only about symbols? I thought to myself. Are we really just consumed by kissy-faces on texts and hearts and 'xoxos' in cards? Sully had given me an open door to make my next point.

"So, hang on," I interjected, addressing Nick. "Would you include a smiley face on a text if say, you are up to no good, so your girl wouldn't suspect you are up to something?"

"Well," said Jane answering for him. "People don't always talk on the phone now so if a guy is sending me a text or an email that seems 'off', it's going to make me suspicious."

"But, Jane—let's take it a step further, shall we?" The professor in me was clearly coming out now, "what if a guy does text you and includes those symbols, but he doesn't call you his girlfriend? Are you worried if you aren't called the 'girlfriend' in front of his friends?"

"Look, I've made that slip," Nick answered. "—you just have to appear to be innocent."

I stared at Nick, dumbfounded. It was as though he'd been studying Machiavelli's handbook. In *The Prince*, Machiavelli always said you just have to know when to appear virtuous but secretly act vicious. As long as you maintain a good image, you can keep your power. *The Prince* could basically be the blueprint for every cheater in America.

I looked Nick over. *Come to think of it, thank God no one reads philosophy.*

Nick continued, "Tell her you think she's great and she should know she's your girlfriend without having to put a label out there. Send a random text so she 'knows you are thinking about her' and, definitely, without a shadow of a doubt, you *have* to make sure she'll post how awesome you are on Facebook."

Again, applause erupted. For the next ten minutes, Nick went into a long tangent about how weirdly sensitive girls are about Facebook. Girls need to show their friends how wonderful their lives are because every girl is in competition with every other girl. In order to be the envy of their friends, girls will post cute pictures of their boyfriend, tell him to post sweet-nothings on their wall, and even announce amazing dates and his sweet gestures themselves through their statuses. Nick said that every girl wants to be number one and prove that their love life is better than that girl in high school who made them feel wretched. This is how they claw their way to the top of the social ladder. And they will do anything to keep that power.

At last I broke in. "So, what you are saying is that women are just as appearance-conscious as men?"

"They're worse," Nick said. "Girls will manipulate men to get what they want. Kanye West tells us about gold diggers—they will flirt with you just to get a Louis Vuitton purse."

"But you guys are manipulating us to get what you want . . ." Jane said, ". . . sex. Men rummage around the bar to find the girl who will just drop her pants. . . ."

"They are looking for margarine," I added. "They want the girl who will just spread." Laughter ensued.

"But let me continue on what Nick said about Facebook," I began again. "Women use Facebook to appear to be 'innocent' too. I have a friend who was dating this guy for about a year, and he just didn't want to commit to her, or put a label on things. He broke up with her and she was devastated, but rather than pine over him in her apartment, she got her closest girlfriends together. Every night, the girls went out to the bars, having a blast. One of her friends invited a good-looking guy to come out and party with them. He knew the situation with her ex and offered to help her 'trick' him into coming back to her. Her friends would take pictures of her and the guy in 'suggestive poses'. I'm not talking about sexual poses, but poses that kept you guessing: 'Are they together or aren't they?' Her friends posted the photos on Facebook . . . but she didn't post any or even tag herself. After one month of this her ex suddenly changed his tune. And she appeared innocent through it all! Guys may have an agenda to sleep with any girl they can find, but girls have their own agenda too. Anyone can all appear innocent even when they aren't."

On the Hunt

It took a while for the 'class' to digest my story. Finally, I heard someone murmur, 'That's a brilliant idea!' I sighed. Apparently, my goal to sway them to the side of excellence had failed. . . . I had just given out ammo against another commitment-phobia-prone guy.

"But Jane has a point," someone said, trying to restart the conversation. "Guys literally hunt for prey at bars. It's like you're a pride of lions and you are sniffing out the weak, desperate ones in the general area. Women don't have that kind of radar."

This point seemed to sit uncomfortably with the guys. It's like they all knew that 'man-code' had been broken and an important secret had been revealed.

"We don't have a strategy," Sully objected. "I mean if a girl is drunk and we take her home, that could come back to bite us in the face. Not all of us are going to prey on the weak ones who have no clue what's going on."

"But there's a big difference between preying on a drunk girl and preying on a girl who has no self-esteem. You guys can smell desperation like we can smell Old Spice," said Brianna. Another solid comeback from Team Sully. *I really hope someone is keeping score.*

Suddenly Jane seemed concerned. "You guys seemed to get all uptight when Meg mentioned the strategy on how to pick up women at bars. What's wrong?"

Nick immediately took the question and ran with it, "Well, would you rather us be up front about it or sneaky?"

"There's a difference? I mean it's the same end result that you are looking for—to get us in bed," Meg said.

Now this was a good question. It was a philosophical question. I dove in.

"Let me ask you guys a question." Hearing the conviction in my tone, everyone turned their attention to me. "Do you think it's better to be loved or feared?"

The group was silent. I knew where I wanted the discussion to end—I just had to be the pied-piper and lead them there. I could almost see the wheels in their heads turning, so I continued.

"The reason I ask is because if a guy is upfront about it, you might fear him. Think about what Meg said about guys hunting like lions. Lions are powerful and strong. Most people are afraid of lions—they're dangerous. And once you know you are dealing with a lion, a guy who is in-your-face powerful, you may be scared. You could run away, or not trust him as much, but the bottom line is that a smart woman *will* walk away. He's too dangerous.

Think about this animal though: a fox. A fox may not be as big and powerful as a lion, but it's sneaky. Foxes are known to be sly and clever and, although they may not be able to get their prey with the direct approach, they will sneak up on it and attack when the prey least expects it. Guys who are foxes may be sneakier about their desires and not as direct, but does the sneaky approach work?"

Sully, who was following my words closely, was ready to answer. "Well it depends on what the goal is."

And there it was.

"What do you mean by that, Sully?" He had totally become my favorite 'student' at the bar tonight.

"Well, why does a guy pick up a girl? If he wants her for a one-night-stand and 'beck and call' purposes *like some people we know*, then the sneaky approach works. But it won't work if you are trying for a higher goal . . . if you are looking for an actual relationship and love. . ."

Go Team Sully!

Don't Stop Believing

"That's a great point, Sully," I said, trying not to show too much favoritism. Depending on what your goal is when you meet a girl, the end could justify the means. If you don't care about how you get her into bed, the end could be . . . unfortunately for our society . . . justified.

"Can I tell you guys an example that I use in my class about this topic?" I asked. Some members of the group were drifting away in a boozy haze. My core competitors, however, huddled up around me in hopes of hearing some kind of wisdom.

"There are people in the United States whose job it is to create tornados so that we can build stronger defenses against them. They literally set up warehouses and use technology to create these storms, supplying the winds, the rain, and even the debris. The amount of energy is measured perfectly and the time and effort that goes into creating these storms is ridiculous. They literally have to plan out each storm: when the wind gusts, the direction the funnel will be spinning, how big the hail is going to be—all of it. The insights they gain from the results will ultimately save lives. But there's a problem: even with all the technology, none of these artificial storms will even come close to that perfect tornado that Mother Nature creates herself. When that F-5 twister comes along, no research will be able to hundred-percent protect the people. Houses reinforced using information from the test results will still be destroyed. It's when that perfect storm hits that you finally understand the true power of nature."

My remaining listeners seemed to be wondering if I even had a point.

"You are probably wondering why I told you this story. Well, I agree with Sully. If you are manipulating love—buying gifts, saying sweet nothings and promises you don't intend to keep, real love can't exist. Just like the tornado-makers who are measuring the amount of wind, you can't measure the amount of time it should take for someone to 'fall in love with you.' You can't plan love—that's why I hate those classes that have become popular lately—you know, the ones where guys learn how to pick-up women. They go into a bar with 'a plan' and use this knowledge to time when they will say this and do that. You are building up a lie or you are attempting to create something that prevents a natural connection from occurring. You are creating the storm, not letting it happen. But, maybe if you do what Sully did, and just introduce yourself, a real connection can exist: an *authentic* connection. One that doesn't have all these internal gadgets and plans. Because the authentic power of love can bring down any defenses that we have built up. When love hits you, you fall; your defenses fail. Real love can't be man-made. It's a cosmic force stronger than all of us."

There were some vague murmurs of approval. Greg chose this moment to take more orders. I waited, musing to myself. Only Sully and Nick returned to class.

Sully looked at me hard. "So does that mean I win?"

"Well, remember, it's up to Jane," I said.

Hearing her name, Jane turned from another conversation and smiled seductively at Sully. "I would like to buy a vowel," she teased and dropped into a chair next to him.

"And I would like to buy your drink," Sully said, smiling at her.

Nick rolled his eyes and turned toward Meg.

I gathered my things and began to stuff them in my brief-case. The song "Don't Stop Believing" started playing on the juke box. *How apropos.* Even knowing that there could be sucky guys out there, do we ever stop believing in the power of love?

Sully and Jane seemed to be getting better acquainted, making small talk on the barstools beside me. I paid Greg and thanked him for putting up with my nonsense, but as I turned to leave, Sully stopped me.

"So is that what you learn in philosophy class? You learn about love and the 'life of excellence'?"

I had to smile. I placed one hand on Sully's shoulder as the other hand clutched my heavy briefcase. "Sully—what do I know about love?" I began. "I'm twenty-six and single. Clearly I'm the fucking expert," and with that I ventured outside and into the night.

8
Platonic Lovers

CHARLES TALIAFERRO AND M. PONTOPPIDAN

The following is an enhancement of a real conversation between three philosophers who met at a conference in Denmark. Most of the talk was between the pleasantly present-day Platonist Charles Talliaferro and a spirited young Ficinian (Renaissance Platonist) called Jenny Inn.

But a weird medievalist in a green—sort of Arthurian-looking—tight leather suit, M. Pontoppidan, was listening to most of it and made a few interruptions at the end, which we include to show you one type of reaction Platonists risk meeting with today when defending the beauty of their vision.

Although they were in fact wearing soft shirts of good quality and black pressed pants, the two Platonists should be imagined in togas and wreaths for dramatic effect. All present were drinking wine from chalices, of course.

In the Elevator

CHARLES: Hello again, Jenny. I wanted to tell you that I really enjoyed your presentation yesterday!

JENNY: Thank you.

CHARLES: As it happens, I'm writing a chapter for a book on the same topic.

JENNY: A book about love?

CHARLES: Yes. The volume is called *What Philosophy Can Tell You about Your Lover*.

JENNY: How interesting! And what do you think philosophy can reveal about lovers?

CHARLES: Well, I think it tells us that the best lovers are Platonic lovers.

JENNY: That sounds odd, considering that a Platonic relationship is supposed to be sexless. Are you saying that the best lovers don't have sex?

CHARLES: No. I think Plato never meant for his notion of love to be sexless.

JENNY: Hmmm. Perhaps Plato himself was a bit ambiguous on that point, but I think his great Renaissance interpreter, Marsilio Ficino, makes it clear that sex is a no-go.

CHARLES: Perhaps we could meet later and talk about this. . . .

Over Coffee at the Hotel Cafe

JENNY: So, what makes you reject the idea that Platonic lovers had better renounce sex?

CHARLES: Plato's central claim, on my reading, is that when the lover and the beloved unite, they are fruitful. So, Plato was not centrally concerned about whether there was or was not sex; the important point is that in a Platonic relationship each person desires the good of the beloved, there is a desire for unity with the beloved, and there is fecundity or, to use an odd term, there is *fruit*.

JENNY: Right. Plato was referring to the great thoughts that he and his fellow philosophers produced together.

CHARLES: No doubt. But I'm also wondering whether Plato would include something more concrete, like children, in which case Platonic lovers would definitely have sexual relations.

JENNY: He might count artwork, but he is not likely to recognize marriage as a model of love.

CHARLES: You are right, and I wouldn't say that Platonic love could ever be typical. But if philosophers can cultivate true love in producing books, and artists can cultivate true love in producing art, then why couldn't parents cultivate true love in producing children?

JENNY: I think Plato would insist that a life catering to the body in one way or the other will distract from love's higher purpose.

CHARLES: It would tend to, yes. But not necessarily. I'm not saying that every set of parents automatically share Platonic love any more than any set of philosophers or artists do. I'm just saying, the fact that parents *could* share Platonic love, and the fact that their product *requires* sex, proves that Platonic love needn't be sexless.

JENNY: But Marsilio Ficino, who invented the expression "Platonic love," thought of this relationship as a way of seeking an immaterial, purely rational God. The attraction between the two humans involved was not the real purpose, just the means to get high enough to touch God.

CHARLES: I am not so sure Ficino was right to suppose Platonic love *has* to come about within a religious framework.

JENNY: His reason for thinking Platonic love is purely spiritual is that Platonists see union with the divine as the highest thing a human being can strive for. In seeking union with the divine, Platonic lovers experience love as the unifying power of the universe. This is an idea as old as the Presocratic philosopher Empedocles, who thought that love keeps every living thing together—that without it, we would quite literally fall apart.

CHARLES: I am very drawn to such a philosophy. It is very beautiful and I know that without the love of my life—Jil— I would fall apart. But aside from the philosophical thesis that love needs to be all around, I now seem to be arguing for two positions that may be in tension with each other. On the one hand, I think that a Platonic, loving relationship can be sexual, but I also concede that, if we stick with Plato and Ficino, the love is going to seek out the good of the soul of the beloved. And for Plato and Ficino, the soul is more than the body. So, in a sense, I concede that Platonic love has to at least transcend bodily love. Can I get away with claiming that in Platonic love, both lovers seek to cultivate and be united with a virtuous soul—whether or not sex is involved?

JENNY: Ficino would be very happy with the connection between loving and developing the virtues of the soul. But I think that both Ficino and Plato himself might respond to you with the question: "Just why do you insist sex is so important? Aren't you mistaking the real nature of your desire?" I think that what Plato wanted to show was that sexual desire is really a spiritual longing, and that once you understand its true nature you will no longer need to feed the body with sex. Of course, it was very provocative in his day to make such a claim. And it still is today!

CHARLES: You are making sense, but why exactly should Platonic love have to *exclude* sex?

JENNY: Because Plato insists that body and soul are separate entities and, in a way, even opposites. So that the body by its nature tends to pull the soul in the wrong direction. Ficino frequently returns to this point, claiming that true love prohibits touch. He argues that a Platonic relationship is based on sight, hearing and thought, and that touching the beloved indicates a "falling down," from love to lust.

CHARLES: Ficino seems to be presupposing that all sex is based on lust. I think lust is a shadow or inversion of true love. When you truly love your partner in a romantic, Platonic fashion –desiring her or his good and seeking unity with the beloved—there can be quite the opposite of falling down.

JENNY: To be continued?

CHARLES: To be sure.

Walking in the University Park in Copenhagen

JENNY: You seem bent on redefining the term Platonic love. Why?

CHARLES: It's true that I would rather people not use Plato's name as a synonym for sexlessness. But it's not so much the word I care about. I'm really concerned to show that lovers today—including those in a sexual relationship!—can gain something by inspiration from the special strengths of Platonic love.

JENNY: That sounds interesting. Please define those strengths.

CHARLES: A friendship that renounces certain sensual plea-sures can display a beautiful, even ecstatic restraint. A Platonic friendship ensures that benevolent love will always trump lust and egoism. It ensures that the point of love is delighting in the good of the beloved rather than selfish sat-isfaction. This could be a first step toward virtue. So, while I started out defending the idea that Platonic love can involve sexuality, I also suggest that Platonic love is first and foremost about goodness. And because sexual fulfilment on a Platonic model must involve the good of both parties, in a way I agree that Platonic love will always subordinate sex to some idea of virtue and the soul. But the first strength I see in Platonic love is that it makes room for the other person and her or his good. As a Platonic lover, one thinks about the other person in a substantial fashion, and not only about oneself.

JENNY: Yes, I can see that if one cannot make room for the other person, then there is no space for lovers to meet. In that sense, restraint is the first lesson anyone who would aspire to be a lover must learn.

CHARLES: Excellent. While I began defending the idea that Platonic relations can include sexuality and my own view that the best of lovers are Platonists, I will come round to offer a modest defence of Ficino.

JENNY: Thank you.

CHARLES: I think that a strictly sexless friendship can strongly highlight some features that are good to have in *any* intimate relationship. It is reassuring that friendship between two persons of any gender combination can blos-som without sex. Harry Potter and Hermione do not have to have sex to have a treasured, even passionate, transforming friendship, and thank heavens Luke Skywalker and Princess Leia did not sleep together!

JENNY: Er, yes. . . . But in what way do Harry and Hermione reassure us?

CHARLES: By showing us how rich two persons can be in each other's eyes, how much two persons have to build upon. Sex is great, but it isn't everything. And remember, Plato was right about the physical—it always passes away. Perhaps there are some lucky couples who will never stop doing it, even at 122 years old and beyond, but many passionate romantic relationships may have to resort to what might be called Ficinian love.

JENNY: Speaking of Ficinian love—did you know that Ficino, like many Platonists, mainly describes love as an intimate attachment between two males? The love of his own life, Giovanni Cavalcanti, was a young man famous for his beauty. I have the impression that women are not seen as relevant for this kind of love—are not included in it, perhaps?

CHARLES: I don't think Plato ever meant for true love to be for men only. After all, in his *Symposium,* it is a wise woman, Diotima, who reveals to Socrates the real nature of love. And Plato did have female students—something that was certainly not the norm in his culture and age. Furthermore, it's hardly a coincidence that the majority of female philosophers from Ancient Greece known to us today by name were either Platonists or else Pythagoreans (who were the nearest thing to Platonism before Plato!). Finally, Plato explicitly argues in his *Republic* that it is possible for women to become philosopher kings. So I don't see why Plato wouldn't recognize true love between two women or between a woman and a man.

JENNY: Okay. . . . So you're saying that we all, men and women alike, need to train our self-restraint in order to be good lovers? I think that's good advice. Without restraint, our ability to give also becomes limited. If we couldn't postpone or set aside our own needs, human life would be a fight of all against all. And if we could not restrain ourselves *willingly,* then the best relation we could hope to establish with others would be a contract of the form "I'll-scratch-your-back-if-you-scratch-mine." In such an arrangement, each participant remains alone with his or her own needs. There's no shared experience. So in these models, there is little room for love.

CHARLES: Right. So I propose that Ficino has something to teach us about the non-romantic aspect of love and friendship. But when it comes to romance, I think the thirteenth-century philosophical-mystic and poet Jalal ad-Din Rumi is the better guide. He may be thought of as a sexy Platonic lover!

JENNY: Good heavens! The conference is nearly over but let's try to talk at the closing dinner.

At the Closing Dinner

JENNY: I see you brought your copy of Rumi with you tonight.

CHARLES: I realized he can make the case for Platonic sex much better than I can.

JENNY: Let's hear him, then.

CHARLES: Rumi was married and wrote many poems to honor his wife and relish their shared sensual pleasure. Unlike Ficino, Rumi fathered children with his wife. When she died, he remarried.

Let me read you one of his poems, "The Love of Women" (translated by Michel LeGall just for this volume):

If you dominate your wife in outward things, but you are dominated
by your heart's desire—this is the mark of being a man. Love is
lacking in other animals,
and they are thereby not as great as man.
The Prophet said that woman prevails over those who are wise,
while thoughtless men rule over her.
Truly, in those kinds of men, their animal inferiority is evident. Love
and gentleness are the marks of being human,
whereas animals are given to anger and lust.
Woman is a ray of God: she is not the earthly beloved.
She is creative: in fact, it may be said that she is not created.

JENNY: Rumi has a rare talent as a poet. I wish I could read his works in the original Persian.

CHARLES: Note that he condemns domination in a loving relationship. He also advances a very Platonic idea: lust, because it is physical, is base and animalistic, while love is properly human. For Rumi, to love a woman fully involves a kind of divine devotion.

JENNY: I agree with him that when we love someone, we see them as infinitely valuable. It is a great burden, however, for a human being to be idealized as a divinity. . . .

CHARLES: It's *as if* the person were divine.

PONTOPPIDAN: Excuse me, may I interject?

CHARLES AND JENNY: Eh? Certainly.

PONTOPPIDAN: It's just that the last thing you said—"as if divine"—reminded me of a beautiful saying of the early medieval church father St. Augustine. He was a Platonist too, and when recalling in his autobiography how once he had lost a close friend to a fatal illness, he simply wrote: *He whom I loved as if he should never die, was dead.* It is a favourite quote of mine, because I think it describes so clearly how love is experienced. The description holds good whether we are in fact immortal or not: we love as if we are.

CHARLES: Yes, so one of the ways Platonism can help the lovers of today is to give them a language strong enough to describe what they are really going through. Nothing short of eternity can express love.

JENNY: Hey, Charles, it now sounds as if you're the mystic. Earlier you seemed reserved about Empedocles?

CHARLES: Reserved, but not a non-believer. I think that when you truly love a person, you do love their soul, and this means that you would love them even if they were in a plane crash and became physically disfigured.

JENNY: Yes, Plato says, too, that the real reason why bodily beauty attracts us is that it resonates with something in the soul—reminds it of an idea. Bodily beauty is only a signpost signalling a deeper, ideal affinity between the lovers. Ficino says the same thing: Love is a form of recognition—of your "soul mate". And once the beloved is recognised as the one you were longing for—the reality behind the image you carried in your soul—then you no longer need the visible beauty as a sign post and can stop focusing on it.

In the Bar at the Airport

JENNY: Thank you, Charles, for a most enlightening discussion. It's great fun to have the rare opportunity to openly discuss sexlessness as a serious option. In this age where carnality is sort of presented as the new spirituality it *is* a sort of taboo we've been breaking, isn't it?

CHARLES: Yes, and I should say that our talk would convince people who heard it that Platonic love is worth learning from even today! Do you think it might help readers of *What Philosophy Can Tell You about Your Lover?* In fact, I would like to scrap the idea of writing up the chapter for that collection myself. How about we reconstruct our dialogue and submit that to Sharon Kaye?

JENNY: Oh great! And why don't we, for a start, right now ask that medievalist who chipped in with the Augustine quote what our exchange has done for her? I noticed she was listening quite absorbedly nearly every time we talked—and smiling as if it interested her a lot.

CHARLES: Sure. Hey, Squire (if I may call you that)—have we made a convert to Platonism out of you yet?

PONTOPPIDAN: Not exactly a convert, no, but I consider myself greatly entertained, so thank you. And the point you both made about restraint as a condition of giving and receiving more fully seems important. Also, I think it's healthy to challenge one's own faith every now and then! Prevents you becoming a fundamentalist of the boring kind. About sex, though—I must confess I'm worried that the Platonic way of splitting apart body and soul, and calling them opposites, is a troublemaker. . . .

CHARLES: But if we couldn't see the difference between thought and action, mind and body, we would not be capable of any restraint, or respect for the other person.

PONTOPPIDAN: There's a point in restraint before reaching the point of sex itself, sure—but in the act, the joy will depend on the ability to fuse body and soul, won't it? Then, the idea of the split, and of bodily desire as inferior to the spiritual, may inhibit the lovers. . . . So I must admit that I personally prefer an erotic encounter to be modeled rather on the wild Christian doctrine of incarnation ("entering the flesh"). I mean—Jenny said that in Ficino's Platonic love, human lovers reach for a purely spiritual God by renouncing the body and refraining from touch. Whereas in the incarnation, love is shown as having such a nature that it makes spirit and flesh *merge* . . . and turns even God human! I find the idea of spirit actually becoming flesh attractive—and erotic—because it hallows the whole human being, not just the soul.

CHARLES: I want to agree with you fully on this, but I confess that maybe I am still in sympathy with Plato and Ficino about a certain primacy of soul over body. Though perhaps, rather than what you might call a hyper-dualism (meaning that the soul sort of inhabits the body), I think the Platonic lover can think of his beloved as an integrated unity of soul and body. In fact, the Platonic lover might desire above all for the unity of soul and body, so that the soul and body act as one—as opposed to the soul wanting to dance while the body is confined to a bed.

JENNY: I really like that image; it's beautiful. But I don't know if any of the old Platonists would accept it. Wouldn't they protest that an attempt to unite soul and body is as futile as trying to unite a body with its shadow, or to embrace your mirror image? They wanted us to see and desire in the beloved only that which is free of change, that which cannot be lost. . . . So the body, to them, was beside the point. . . . Or do you think that I read them too uncharitably?

CHARLES: Alas, you may be quite accurate historically, but contemporary Platonists like myself try to make a case for the goodness of the ensouled body or the embodied soul.

JENNY: Well, I think it is lovely that we are being so true to Plato as to, like many of his dialogues, end up with an *aporia*—meaning "no way out," no final answer. That's just as it should be: choosing a guide in love is, like religion, the most deeply personal thing there is. Some have one need, others another. Just like some humans are vegetarians, and others carnivores, so not everyone has a taste for flesh and blood in love. That, too, is as it should be.

CHARLES: Funny you should say that; since some famous followers of Plato were actually vegetarians. Probably inspired by the Pythagorean faith that Plato more or less belonged to himself. Pythagoreans believed in the transmigration of souls, from humans to animals or the other way around, so the eating of any creature thought to possess a soul was forbidden. They would find a cannibalistic ritual such as the Eucharist revolting!

PONTOPPIDAN: Yes, well, whatever else one may say about Platonism, it is undoubtedly more civilized at the table.

CHARLES: I'll drink to that.

JENNY: I too! Cheers.

In the great tradition of the Platonic dialogue, it's customary to blend fact and fiction artfully. So of course you're not surprised to learn that Jenny Inn is a purely ideal Platonist in the straightforward sense that she doesn't have a body. (Rumi would have called her Jinn instead of Jenny!) We invited her for this occasion because it can be a little difficult today to find someone who'll break a lance for the sexless interpretation of Platonism. But this voice should be heard too. So we hope you liked befriending Jenny as well as the two more fleshly speakers. Cheers again, in wine and good spirits.

III

Positions

9
Wilde Expectations

MIKE PIERO

I stepped out of the shower. It was a cool Saturday morning. My wife was already up and diligently working to set up her easel and paints out on our deck. As I reached for the towel to dry myself off, I quickly discovered that the towel rack in the bathroom was empty . . . once again. So, dripping water across the floor and carpet, I hunted down a towel in the hallway closet, dried myself off, and prepared myself for a confrontation; for, certainly, the situation needed to change.

That's not entirely accurate, I suppose. I didn't exactly prepare myself; I went more out of irritation. Now, before you think I'm some sort of domineering, controlling monster of a husband, let me briefly clarify how things in our household work.

We each take turns doing most of the chores around the house. There are some, of course, that we don't take turns doing, but only because one of us hates the chore (for me, those damn dirty dishes) and the other doesn't mind it so much. Washing the laundry, however, does not fall into that category, so we take turns. This past week was my wife's turn to do this particular chore, and time and time again, she would wash the towels, but never stock the bathrooms with them, like I did every other week. So, I regularly found myself cold, naked, and in want of a towel; and on that Saturday morning, I thought, "Enough is enough."

"Why are there never any towels in the bathroom?" I demanded, standing at the sliding glass door looking at her.

"Put some in there," she retorted, refusing to be distracted from her work.

"But that's not my responsibility this week! You do it."

I'm sure you can guess what comes next: she gets upset, yells "Fine!" storms inside the house, rifles through the towel closet, and seemingly in one motion chucks a bunch of towels into the bathroom. I resist the temptation to say, "Now see, was that so difficult?" and walk away.

If you've ever been in a committed relationship, I'm sure you've had at least one moment like this one: a stupid fight over the most ridiculous situation! Such moments are as embarrassing as they are painful, I must admit.

Yet, it was only after thinking about the towel incident that I came to see how so many conflicts between me and my lover stem from the unrealistic expectations we project onto one another. On closer examination, it becomes evident that these expectations are rooted in philosophical problems. The nineteenth-century playwright and essayist Oscar Wilde provides witty signposts for three such problems worth exploring in detail.

"It is Difficult Not to Be Unjust to What One Loves"

Our first quotation from Wilde propels us into the philosophical realm of ethics. Ethical theories try to answer the question: How best should I live? A difficult damn question, especially when it comes to interacting with our lovers.

One theory of ethics that has become very popular over the past decade or two is *utilitarianism*. It was first proposed by the early nineteenth-century philosopher Jeremy Bentham and later developed by John Stuart Mill—a contemporary of Oscar Wilde, incidentally. Utilitarianism says we should always act in a way that results in the greatest amount of happiness or pleasure and the least amount of pain.

It's not hard to see that pursuing our own pleasure is often the culprit in our conflicts with lovers. Utilitarianism argues that we must not pursue our own pleasure, but rather strive to maximize the total amount of pleasure for everyone affected by our action. So, when considering whether to confront my wife about the towels, I should have calculated what I could say (or not say) to bring about the best consequences for both of us.

John Stuart Mill goes so far as to assert that one has an obligation to lie if that lie will produce more pleasure and less pain for the parties involved. Such lies—"white lies" as they're usually called—are given much attention in our culture, from television and movies to novels, newspapers, and magazines. How many times have you seen a scene in which a girl asks a guy something like, "How do these pants make me look?" We know how this script goes! The guy, if he is "smart," is obligated to say that her pants look great regardless of whether they do or not.

White lies often meet the cost-benefit requirements of utilitarianism, and they are a popular choice in our day and age. Critics of utilitarianism, however, contend that that happiness should not be given priority over other values, such as truth.

The most prominent alternative to utilitarianism is *deontological* ethics, which requires us to do what is most rational regardless of the consequences. Following the eighteenth-century philosopher Immanuel Kant, a deontologist would argue that it's never acceptable to lie, since lying is a self-contradictory act that violates human dignity.

Although deontology meshes well with many people's religious convictions, critics find it overly strict and unrealistic. In presupposing universal rules that apply to everyone at all times, it ignores legitimate differences in perspective.

A third type of theory, known as "care ethics," sees morality as based on personal relationships. The twentieth-century philosopher Nel Noddings argues that in order to treat others ethically, we must understand them and identify their genuine needs. According to care ethics, it might be best to tell your lover that a particular pair of pants just doesn't look right. Setting aside abstract values such as happiness or truth, this approach emphasizes the importance of maintaining a strong commitment to those we love, even when it's difficult.

Care ethics is especially useful in dealing with lovers. With it, we are not subscribing to unrealistically strict laws, nor are we burdened with the task of computing consequences in a complex and unpredictable world. Care ethics prompts us instead to see the world from another's eyes, to make the other truly significant.

Going back to the towel incident, care ethics implies that I acted both ethically and unethically. My decision to raise the issue of why my wife wasn't stocking the bathroom was right, yet the words I chose and the attitude they reflected were wrong. I was casting her as a minor character in my own life story, as a person who simply relates to me by what she does (or does not do) for me. In order to have the proper expectations for your lovers, you must be willing to treat them as their own "major characters," with her own ideas, thoughts, rationalizations, problems, and life stories.

Lovers must relate and interact towards one another as two major characters inhabiting one another's lives. This means I must recognize and respect my wife's interests in an absolute way, as if they were my own. If I had put myself in her place that fateful Saturday morning, I would not have spoken to her so harshly.

"The Very Essence of Romance Is Uncertainty"

This quotation comes from Wilde's play, *The Importance of Being Earnest*, in which Jack is planning to propose to his love, Gwendolen, but his friend, Algernon, takes issue with this plan. In fact, Algernon says, "I really don't see anything romantic in proposing. It is very romantic to be in love. But there is nothing romantic about a definite proposal." Romance, for Algernon, hinges on the uncertainty of the very relationship, the indefiniteness of it all. With marriage, or even the proposal of marriage, "the excitement is all over," he claims.

This thought, one could argue, is oftentimes (but not always) confirmed not only in cultural scripts on marriage and commitment, but even in our own relationships. We've all been there, right? Fading excitement, seemingly dulling senses. When the infatuation of young love begins to wane, romance seems to flee quickly behind. No more roses and only the occasional romantic, home-cooked dinner!

Algernon, with a great deal of certainty, has placed romantic commitment in a lowly, marginal position. People often act and speak as though they know a great deal about love. But do they really? Philosophical theories known as epistemology explore the basis of our claims to certainty.

The twentieth-century philosopher Ludwig Wittgenstein argues that certainty is fundamentally a matter of context. A person doesn't know (in the sense of being certain of) something in an isolated way. Each belief, every judgment, presupposes other ideas, beliefs, and judgments. Our relation to the world, therefore, is determined by a *system* of knowledge in which each part of that system, every bit of knowledge, is situated by everything else that we know, or at least claim to know.

While some philosophers would argue that certain beliefs can be justified on their own, apart from any other belief, for Wittgenstein, all knowledge exists in some kind of context, which influences the meaning of that knowledge and how we come to accept or reject it. Wittgenstein asks us to remember the expression, "I thought I knew." If you've ever used that expression, you know that your so-called knowledge is not infallible!

Many misunderstandings with our lovers rise from a pigheaded insistence on our own correctness, our own certainty that we're right. We look for easy and quick solutions to complicated problems. Wittgenstein points out that we can be convinced of the correctness of a view simply by its simplicity or symmetry, to which we often react: "*That's* how it must be."

Thinking back to the towel incident, my certainty lay in a series of beliefs about the situation:

1. **My wife was *consciously* not putting the towels in their correct places.**

2. **The *correct* place for the towels is the towel racks in the bathrooms.**

3. **Since I organized the bathroom this way on my laundry weeks, it was her responsibility to do so on her laundry weeks.**

4. **Not having a towel when I emerged from the shower was not my fault.**

And there are probably more assumptions and beliefs that my knowledge rested on, even perhaps the idea that I need a towel in order to dry off.

A colleague of mine once told me that she doesn't use paper towels to dry her hands in the bathroom, but instead, for environmental reasons, she shake, shake, shakes them dry. Perhaps she does the same thing with showers After all, fewer towels used equals less energy to wash and dry them. I guess I'll never know.

At any rate, in any system of beliefs, some things to us are unquestionable and other things are open for revision. It seems to me that a lover who is open to question more of these judgments will have the advantage of being able to resolve conflicts more successfully.

This, of course, doesn't mean that you go around second-guessing yourself on every aspect of life. Should I have ordered a whiskey instead of a cognac? No, this means that you should be open to recognizing that your knowledge is not absolutely fixed, and that rethinking ideas, beliefs, or problems is the mark of a mature, sophisticated person.

People often suppose that changing their views is the mark of hypocrisy. As the Irish novelist and playwright Samuel Beckett once wrote (in the words of a character), "I have many faults, but changing my tune is not one of them." A true philosopher will regard such healthy change with openness, not stubbornness.

If being too certain of your own position is a problem in a relationship, then the obvious solution must be to become more flexible in your thinking and problem solving. So often, this requires time. It takes effort to think through issues to devise the best solutions. To change one's mind or realize an error in thinking is the sign of a person who is committed to his or her relationship, a lover who isn't in it just for the "ride."

"The Proper Basis for Marriage Is Mutual Misunderstanding"

As this quotation indicates, Wilde's skepticism regarding romantic relationships derives from the prevalence of misunderstandings, which often go unnoticed or unattended for weeks, months, or years. Perhaps, for Wilde, the mutual misunderstanding of each partner is a necessary one, lest they see the true chains of their commitment. This pessimistic view of marriage aside, most of us would agree that our relationships are oftentimes fraught with misunderstandings, both large and small, that we would like to learn how to identify and prevent.

As it happens, philosophers are very interested in misunderstandings, particularly those that result from the use of language. We have to recognize that language is fundamentally unreliable. How easy is it not to "get" what someone is trying to tell us? And with the flourishing of digital social networking, where one is further deprived of the opportunity to read nonverbal cues, the words we use become all the more important! We all know that "communication" is the key to any relationship, but how does this actually play out in our day-to-day lives?

If we are serious about reducing misunderstandings with our lover, we must understand something about the nature of language. Ferdinand de Saussure is widely recognized as the founder of modern linguistics and the sub-field of semiology, the linguistic study of *signs*. According to Saussure, a sign requires: a signifier, which would typically be the word we use; a signified, which would be the actual object or idea that the word describes; and the relationship between the two. Sounds simple, right? The difficulty lies in making a positive connection between the signifier and the signified, since there seems to be an endless play in language that refuses to reduce one word to any single meaning.

We all use many of the same words, but do we use them in the same way? Our signifiers have multiple meanings, personal associations, and histories with older meanings. We're inclined to assume that objects in the world come first, and then we simply give them a name. Saussure denies this. Language is not a set list of words and their significations, but a constantly changing, always fluid system of signs. The value of words is determined by how they are different from other words in the system, or even the same words with different meanings.

The towel incident can be understood in terms of linguistic confusion regarding the one sign: "laundry." To me, "doing the laundry" involved not only washing, drying, and folding the clothes, but also putting them away in their respective rooms. To my wife, the signifier ("laundry") involved washing, drying, and folding, but not putting the clothes away. Therefore, in her language system, she *was* "doing the laundry" while, at the same time, I felt she was doing an incomplete job (or half-assing it, as we say) based on my own meaning of the word.

It was this semiotic difference in how we make meaning that caused me to have these unexpressed expectations of my wife. Once we calmed down and discussed the matter, we realized that we both thought of this task in very different ways. When she was growing up, her mom did the laundry, and would oftentimes set the folded clothes on the couch in the living room for each family member to put away. The towels went in the closet, and each person was responsible for getting his or her own towel. At my house, my dad did the wash and always put our clothes in the drawers and our towels in the bathroom on the racks. To complicate the situation, when my parents were divorced, I began doing my own laundry, and continued the tradition of hanging the towels in the bathroom. Once my wife and I had some open discussion about our past experiences, it was very easy to see that we were using the same words in very different ways.

This sort of thing happens all of the time in relationships! So many misunderstandings occur due to the unreliability of language, and without open discussion, there can be no true resolution. This doesn't mean that we want to give up on language and simply draw pictures or communicate with taps on the back or punches in the arm. But it does mean that in our relationships, we have to look out for misunderstandings that might be caused by differences in language, which are often rooted in differences in experiences. Once you've identified the site of the linguistic confusion, you can be open with your lover about what you each "meant" and come to some kind of (re)solution.

"It Is Not the Perfect but the Imperfect Who Have Need of Love"

To resolve conflicts with our lovers is not always easy. This is because such conflicts are actually philosophical problems. Doing philosophy with your lover needn't be too burdensome, however, especially when the prospect of makeup sex is on the horizon! Motivation can be a powerful resource, but so can the realization that our partners, lovers, and spouses, like ourselves, are imperfect. We cannot expect them to know what we want, or even always know what they want for themselves.

The fact is that we are all "damaged goods" in one way or another. To realize this and allow it to inform the ways in which we interact with our lovers is a great achievement in any relationship! Oscar Wilde poses the question, "How can a woman be expected to be happy with a man who insists on treating her as if she were a perfectly normal human being?"

To expect our lover, male or female, to be "normal" is to mistake them for some kind of neutral, uncomplicated, simplistic person. I've never met such a person. Have you?

10

How to Find Yourself a DIRTBAG

Carol V.A. Quinn

The Irish playwright George Bernard Shaw once said that "if marriages were made by putting all the men's names into one sack and the women's names into another, and having them taken out by a blindfolded child like lottery numbers, there would be just as high percentage of happy marriages as we have seen. . . ."

Now here is a frustrated man, and trust me, there is nothing especially bad about England (where Shaw spent most of his life) in this regard. Shaw went on to say, "If you can tell me any trustworthy method of selecting a wife I shall be happy to make use of it."

Is there such a method—or at least a source of good advice? What about philosophy? Philosophy provides some concepts useful to lovers, such as justice and fairness, even friendship and beauty, but can it tell you how to find a really great lover?

I used to think not. I thought love must be the kind of thing where either you get lucky or you don't. But I thought wrong. Digging deeper into philosophy's nether regions, I found some true wisdom about relationships. And I am proud to announce that it enabled me to find myself a real DIRTBAG.

Don't misunderstand—I have met and, alas, even dated many a dirtbag in my day. I am not going to be talking about *them*. The DIRTBAG to whom I refer is named for an acronym comprised of the following characteristics: dignity, integrity, respect, trustworthiness, bodaciousness, affection, and generosity. What philosophy taught me is that, when looking for a lover, you should look for a person possessing these characteristics. Much as it pains my DIRTBAG, I am determined to air our private life for the higher purpose of sharing this wisdom.

D is for Dignity

In his *Oliver Twist*, Charles Dickens wrote "Dignity, and even holiness too, sometimes are more questions of coat and waist-coat than some people imagine." This was the ordinary concep-tion of dignity before the eighteenth-century philosopher Immanuel Kant came along, and it still lingers today. Dignity, that is, was based on a person's social standing and so came in degrees. Kant changed all that, arguing that all people have it equally, just in virtue of being persons (we say in philosophy, just in virtue of being persons *qua* persons, because we are fond of using Latin words). Though I like Kant, I want to hold on to a bit of the Dickensian view of dignity since many people still use it in this way today.

First, dignity requires choosing and following a worthy life plan. Although he earns his paychecks as an electrician, my DIRTBAG's "real" life plan is helping others, and in particular, though not exclusively, children with cancer. He shaves his head once a year in solidarity with the kids losing their hair to chemo. Says my DIRTBAG: "This way I can support children in their recovery by saying 'it's only hair'."

Dignity also requires acting morally responsibly. This is my DIRTBAG's "life's doing," which I can demonstrate by way of a story. One evening my DIRTBAG was driving home from work during rush hour when he noticed a boy walking alongside the very busy freeway. My DIRTBAG pulled over in front of the boy and asked him if he needed any help. The boy, whose name turned out to be Nick, responded that he was going home. He explained that ordinarily he would take a bus after school to go downtown to his family's restaurant where he would wait for his mom to get off work and take him home. But when he arrived at the restaurant, he forgot that it was closed for the day, and because he always rode home with his mom, he started walking home the way that she would drive home— that is, on the freeway.

My DIRTBAG offered to take Nick home but he refused since my DIRTBAG was a stranger. So my DIRTBAG, having left his cell phone behind (which he often does), offered Nick a soda and sat with him for over an hour trying to flag down a driver who might have a cell phone to call for help. Car after car drove by. Finally somebody stopped and called the police, who arrived and took Nick home.

This was my DIRTBAG acting morally responsibly.

On my conception of dignity, people variously possess it according to what extent they act in dignified ways. Since these actions are within our control, dignity might be considered a virtue and something to be earned rather than something a person simply possesses in virtue of being a "rational, autonomous agent" (to use Kant's sterile language). Moreover, dignity is earned, not through *social* standing, but through *moral* standing. It is something about which we *might* be proud, though it is not in the nature of my DIRTBAG to feel that way. He is just doing what he does—a man exemplifying dignity.

I is for Integrity

Being a philosopher, and in particular an ethicist, I often feel driven to redefine moral terms. Just as dignity acquires new meaning in DIRTBAG, so also does integrity. The word "integrity" comes from the Latin word "integer" meaning "intact," "whole," and "complete." My definition connects with the notion of a whole person, a flourishing person, but it also connects with the view of the twentieth century philosopher Charles Taylor, who held that the self is oriented in a moral space—a space in which important questions arise.

According to my view, having integrity is a process. It requires pondering life's most important questions—questions about 1. what is good or bad; 2. what is worth doing and what is not; and 3. what has meaning and importance and what is trivial and secondary. The person with integrity knows what's good, worth doing, meaningful, and important—and does such to the best of his ability.

In an obvious way, my DIRTBAG accomplishes this by raising a lot of money each year in his fight against kids' cancer, where people donate on his soon-to-be-shaven head. My DIRTBAG visits the barber only once a year so that over the course of a year he goes from squeaky clean to rock'n'roll mop—which shows that his commitment is not token but whole-hearted and round-the-clock.

He has also demonstrated integrity in less obvious ways. The story I am about to tell concerns Troll dolls—which seem about the furthest thing from integrity as one might well imagine.

Once, my DIRTBAG had a co-worker who was going through a really tough time at home. Her not-at-all-cool husband was on meth, and they were separating. My DIRTBAG decided that she needed a distraction. She liked those little naked Troll dolls with their distended bellies and out-of-control brightly colored hair. She in fact had several on her desk. My DIRTBAG took them one day, leaving behind a photo of them being taken at (squirt) gun point, along with a ransom note. Then he found some Troll dolls at a garage sale. He purchased the dolls and put them on her desk (anonymously, of course). But soon these too disappeared with more ransom notes. He even gave some of the dolls to family and friends who were going to be traveling. Soon his co-worker was getting photos of her Troll dolls from all over the country—and even Canada! Two of her Trolls actually got married at a sleazy chapel in Las Vegas.

Was what my DIRTBAG doing something meaningful and important or something trivial and secondary? The woman, who was the recipient of this light-spirited fun, would give an easy answer. No doubt, we can play with Troll dolls while still having integrity—and in abundance!

R is for Respect

The contemporary philosopher Stephen Darwall wrote a famous essay called "Respect," in which he distinguishes two different kinds of—you guessed it—respect. He calls them 'recognition respect' and 'appraisal respect'.

Recognition respect is the respect which all people deserve just in virtue of being persons and which demands a certain kind of (respectful) treatment. This kind of respect does not admit of degrees—all people deserve it equally.

Appraisal respect, in contrast, admits of degrees in accordance with social standing, talent, and other qualities. So, we should have appraisal respect for a musical genius, but not so much for someone like me, who tried and failed to play the guitar. No one—not even my mother—had appraisal respect for me *qua* guitar player (or better: guitar-playing-attempter).

Now, while my DIRTBAG has appraisal respect for people I just cannot, CANNOT, comprehend (like NASCAR drivers!) he rightly has recognition respect for those whom many of us would shun. One Sunday, mid-morning, my DIRTBAG was driving over to his landlord's home to drop off his rent check. On his way, he saw a middle-aged man staggering—not on the sidewalk, but in the gutter—and bouncing off of street signs. My DIRTBAG thought "there aren't any bars around and it's early Sunday morning, *but even if he is drunk*, this guy needs help!"

How many of us have driven past the drunk guy, the homeless guy, on the street, ashamed to even look his way because we *know, we all know* that looking at him would show us his face, a face that tells a story, and no matter what the story, this guy is deserving of respectful treatment—and some help!

My DIRTBAG stopped and asked the staggering man if he needed help. He got no answer—just a blank stare. My DIRT-BAG helped the man sit down and knocked on the door of a nearby house to get help, for he was without his cell phone (again) to make a call. Someone came to the door and called for an ambulance.

When the paramedics arrived, they immediately suspected diabetic shock. This turned out to be true: the man's blood sugar was so off the charts that he was on the verge of a coma. He had abandoned his car a few miles away and was trying to flag someone down for help. As he continued to walk, he was getting worse. My DIRTBAG was the first person who was willing to help. But what if the person turned out to be some drunken homeless guy in need of sobering up? My DIRTBAG would have helped nonetheless—likely sharing a soda with him as he did with Nick.

T is for Trustworthiness

Most philosophical discussion of trust refers to the term as it relates to the business world. DIRTBAGS certainly exhibit trustworthiness in this realm, but my topic is on my DIRTBAG's relationship with me, and since he is not my lawyer, banker, accountant, or plumber, we will look at other ways in which he is trustworthy.

When we think about the word "trustworthy" we think about "loyalty," "accountability," "faithfulness to commitments or obligations"—and all of this relates to "care." Feminist philosopher Joan C. Tronto discusses the importance of care. If we pay attention to some of what she says, we will understand what it means to be trustworthy.

To be trustworthy is not merely to be counted on not to fuck your best friend. It requires (additional) on-going responsibility and commitment. As Tronto explains, the original meaning of "care" comes from the English word meaning "burden"—so caring implies assuming a burden. Of course, "burden" sounds so "oppressive" and heavy, but it needn't be.

A trustworthy person can be counted on to fulfill his commitments. That person, as Tronto suggests, has a lot of responsibility on his plate. He's willing to work, to sacrifice, to spend money and time, to show emotional concern, and to expend energy toward the person he cares for. Appropriate care, Tronto tells us, requires knowledge. We must know about the other's needs in order to be trusted to meet those commitments.

When I first met my DIRTBAG I was on eleven (!) different medications. I was on medications to address the side effects of other medications. I was taking a medication that slowed my thyroid and so I also had to take a medication to speed it back up. I was taking a medication that caused tremors and so I had to take a medication that stopped tremors. I was taking a medication that lowered my blood pressure and so I also had to take a medication to raise it! I was doped up all the time and felt and looked it. My liver was running daily marathons.

Noting my "health" (or rather, lack thereof) my DIRTBAG expressed his concern and suggested I rethink all of my medications, thus making my liver a much happier organ once again! I trusted that my DIRTBAG had my best interest at heart. He, being in a relationship with me, was committed to caring for me (and I for him)—to helping me be the best person I could be (a healthy person in this case, and good health helps contribute to a flourishing life). With his encouragement, and my physician's direction, I am now down to two medications. I and my liver have my DIRTBAG to thank!

B is for Bodacious

Philosophy, on the surface at least, doesn't say much about this term, but if we look closely at the word, we see that it is exemplified in the life of Socrates. "Bodacious" means remarkable, outstanding, and in another sense of the word it means defiant of convention, lively, unrestrained, and uninhibited.

The ancient Greek philosopher Socrates was bodacious. Arrested and executed for "corrupting the youth" by teaching them how to think for themselves, he launched the entire Western philosophical tradition.

Certainly Socrates was uninhibited, for it is said that he often frequented the streets of Athens naked, talking philosophy with any interlocutor who would spare the time for him. Why naked? Some say it was because his wife Xanthippe would often get fed up with him and kick him out of the house in this state (evidently Socrates enjoyed being in his birthday suit while lounging on the living room sofa!). Others say that Socrates left voluntarily in this state fed up with Xanthippe's nagging.

But the most bodacious thing about Socrates was his remarkable and unconventional life, which consisted of driving his interlocutors crazy (and often to tears) with his incessant questioning about truth, virtue, and other important matters. Known as the horsefly of Athens, he never worried about annoying or even offending someone in his pursuit of truth.

My DIRTBAG is bodacious as well—and when it comes to our relationship, this is both a blessing and a curse. On the one hand, I admire the way he interrupts his life at length and at the drop of a hat to help others—as is evident from the stories I have already told. But on the other hand, what does this kind of behavior do to a shared domestic life? Can a truly bodacious person ever settle down to a stable commitment? Would I have to play Xanthippe to his Socrates? In fact, since he and I are both philosophers of sorts (me officially, and him unofficially), are we destined to take turns roaming the streets naked? These are questions that only time will answer. . . .

A is for Affection

Love is the only thing Socrates professed to know something about. Yet he had his share of trouble with it in his own personal life. Or was it rather that he had trouble with affection? Which, after all, is not the same thing as love.

Socrates bore no affection for his "shrewish" wife Xanthippe. Yet he showed a great deal of affection for the Athenian golden boy Alcibiades, who was famous for his great looks, talent, and ambition. Alcibiades once sent Socrates a beautiful cake, which Xanthippe snatched away and stomped underfoot.

Did Socrates flunk when it comes to affection? To have affection for people is to genuinely like them, but what does this imply? It need not imply that one like everyone.

Here we should revisit Tronto, who makes a distinction between 'caring for' and 'caring about.' According to Tronto, caring *about* is characterized by a more general form of commitment whereas caring *for* implies specificity—caring for a particular person. Tronto makes a bold generalization; namely, that men care about and women care for. So men care about, say, world peace, whereas women care for their elderly parents and their children. And caring for, Tronto tells us, is a moral activity, whereas caring about might or might not be (one might care about the outcome of a baseball game).

Against Tronto, I say that women can care about (including outcomes of baseball games) and men can care for (their elderly parents and their children). And caring for need *not* be a moral activity. A woman can care for her neighbors' houseplant while they are away on vacation, accidentally kill it in virtue of her not-so-green thumb (and not some malicious bent toward, say, African violets), and it need not necessarily be considered a moral matter.

I kill my houseplants all the time. Yet I keep buying them and hoping for their flourishing. Does this make me an immoral person? We leave that question to the great African violet in the sky. May it be merciful.

DIRTBAGS care about moral matters, about say the general welfare of humanity, about its flourishing, about justice—all the while caring about whether the Dodgers beat the Rockies. And DIRTBAGS care for particular others. That is, DIRTBAGS have affection for, a fondness for, both humanity generally (= care about), and specific persons (= care for).

Having affection for people, whether generally or specifically is not, as we say in philosophy, mainly a state of being, but a state of *doing*. Caring for someone is obviously so, but caring

about is as well. If one has affection for people, a genuine lik-
ing of people (*qua* people, and also of particular persons) one
will go out of one's way to help another (even another stranger)
when one is in need, and to help in causes of tremendous
importance, such as my DIRTBAG's commitment to the cause
of curing children's cancer.

My DIRTBAG has so much affection for these children that
he helped organize an early birthday party for a dying child
who was not going to live long enough to see her fourth birthday (and sadly she did not). He did not know this child particularly well, nor any of the children who attended the
party—yet he helped organize clowns, and balloon-animal
makers, and face-painters, and jugglers—even a balloon-animal making, juggling clown on stilts—a feat few of us would
attempt! He brought gifts and food.

It was my DIRTBAG's affection for children with cancer
that motivated his action. He cares about the cause of kids'
cancer, yet he also cares for the particular children and their
families. Like Socrates, he may not like everyone. But contrast
him with the road rager, or the guy who yells at the person with
sixteen items in the fifteen-items-or-fewer line at the grocery
store. These dirtbags have no capacity for affection at all!

G is for Generosity

The nineteenth-century German philosopher Friedrich
Nietzsche once said, "He who cannot give anything away cannot feel anything either." Generosity is a cornerstone of
Nietzsche's conception of the noble person. He contrasts the
noble person against the all too common, all too mediocre herd
animals ("sheeple" we would say today—sheep-people). The
noble person recognizes his natural rank and keeps a distance
from these lowly types (who are the majority). He's well on that
path to self-actualization. His generosity is not a bestowing of
gifts or talents on the herd but more of an "overflowing of
being," which might be shared with other noble types.

This is hardly the generosity of the DIRTBAG. Indeed,
Nietzsche's classism and elitism might be properly understood
as dirtbaggish—of the "to be avoided at all costs" variety. I once
briefly dated one of these "noble" guys—a multimillionaire
with way too much money spent on face lifts, eye lifts, neck

lifts—everything was lifted. We were out at a restaurant once where the wait person said something like "Hi. My name is Micah. May I start you off with some drinks?" to which this dirtbag said in serious tone to my utter shock and embarrassment: "I really do not care what your name is. You are here to serve me." Compare this with my DIRTBAG, who has picked up the restaurant bill for an unknown elderly couple and had groceries delivered anonymously to a friend who was down and out.

The relevant part of Nietzsche's view is the notion of realizing our potential for greatness. If we have the potential to do great things, to do virtuous things (and most DIRTBAGS, being the type of person they are, recognize that we all do), then that's what we should strive to do.

And this does not imply becoming a martyr. The ancient Greek philosopher Aristotle said that the truly generous individual knows the right thing to do with respect to the right time, the right object, and the right people, while having the right motive and doing it in the right way. Likewise, the nineteenth-century French moralist Jean De La Bruyère wrote that "Generosity lies less in giving much than in giving at the right moment."

What Does It Spell?

My DIRTBAG, when I try to tell him how wonderful he is, says "No. I'm just Paul." I would add—an "ordinary" guy who does extraordinary things. So my lesson to you, Dear Reader, is this: Don't settle for dirtbags! There are DIRTBAGS out there—the ones we should genuinely seek out. They may not necessarily become permanent partners, but they will change your life and remain a source of constant inspiration.

Postscript (after the above was all typeset and the book nearly ready to print)

Alas, Paul and I are no longer together. This leaves me questioning my own judgment on the grounds that unabashed worship that ignores all flaws is how love hoodwinks us into making crazy commitments (such as staying in this relationship for roughly the gestation period of an elephant—and a baby elephant too long!)

11
The Unexamined Love

EMILY BARRANCO

Love and philosophy have always gone well together. The English word "philosophy" comes from Greek words meaning "love for wisdom," so love was part of the game from the very start. Still, it never occurred to me how much philosophy could help with my love life (and how much it might help others) until I fell in love with another philosopher! This is the story of that romance.

There are a few places that I could start this story. The first is around six or seven hundred B.C. when the first Greek philosophers began their quest for knowledge. These thinkers had a passion for understanding the world and how the world works, and they began to devise a method for gaining this understanding. Philosophy was (and still is) about sorting through complex and challenging issues using nothing more than our rational faculties. It was about problem solving, investigation, and exploration. It was about looking at all the open possibilities and finding coherent solutions. It was about using your mind to examine your life, the world, and everything.

The great ancient Greek philosopher Socrates said "The unexamined life is not worth living." But what about the unexamined love—is it worth having? While the ancients used the tools and methods of philosophy to understand the structure of the world, we can use them to understand ourselves, our lovers and our relationships. I know, because I do.

This story could also start with my days in undergrad, when I first fell in love with philosophy. could talk about the exhilaration of meeting other people who wanted to dissect every

word or thought that passed through their minds. It could start
with my first quarter in grad school. I could tell you about my
time studying ancient tomes or the hours I spent at the bar
having loud debates with the other philosophy students. I could
tell you about writing papers and taking classes and slowly letting methods of logic sink into my subconscious.

But, it seems like it would be more fun to tell you a true love
story and how philosophy is helping it to end with happily ever
after. So that is where I will begin.

. . . Happily Ever After

I had been in grad school for two years, and, addicted to love, I
had spent a good chunk of my free time on the dating market.
It was easy to find a first date—I was young, cute, smart, and
open to meeting all kinds of people—but I was having a hard
time finding anyone I wanted to keep talking to after the small
talk ran out. No one seemed interested in anything . . . well
. . . interesting.

Sometimes I would playfully ask "What's the most interesting thing about you?" One blind date's eyes lit up excitedly at
the question. "I don't have a liver!" he bragged proudly and
lifted up his shirt to display a scar. An hour of dull conversation
proved him right—he had nothing more interesting to report.

After a few brief relationships and a string of endlessly disappointing first dates, I was exhausted, bored, and disenchanted. I decided to take a break from dating. My mind turned
to work and I spent the winter hibernating with my favorite
people in town, a few philosophers who had become my best
friends. Joshua was one of those friends.

I had met Josh two years earlier, when I first arrived at grad
school. He was a year ahead of me in our department and we
ran in the same social circle. Because we were both in relationships when we met, a romance between the two of us had
never crossed my mind. Our friendship was purely platonic and
in my mind it would always be.

Still, when one summer we were suddenly both single, I
noticed a growing chemistry between us. We were staring at
each other for entirely too long. Our fingers would slip playfully
against each other as he passed me a drink or the remote control. We found occasion for hugs whenever possible. Soon we

were holding hands in the backseat of our friends' car. And then there was that one kiss. . . .

Things were getting out of hand. I wasn't at all happy about the discovery of our chemical attraction. Josh was one of my best friends. I relied on him. We had helped each other through bad relationships, break-ups, academic struggles, and everything in between. I loved him intensely and wanted to know him forever . . . but I was pretty sure a romantic relationship would fail miserably after a few months (or weeks) and then our friendship would be ruined. I had a history of turning friends into awkward exes and for the first time, losing the friendship did not seem worth it.

Determined not to develop feelings for Josh, I started dating someone else immediately. So did Josh. He spent a few months back home with his new girlfriend, but it didn't last. A few months later we were both back at school and single again. I was hibernating, he was determined to live the single life, but somehow we ended up spending most of that winter together, trying unsuccessfully not to flirt with each other.

By springtime the tension was palpable. Despite all our time together I was deeply convinced that we would never last. Josh was loud, comical, and spastic. He spent most of his time having epic battles with other philosophers—and then accidentally spilling something. I was pretty sure he was going to be way too much trouble.

I imagined our future. He would talk my ear off. I would sit in quiet resentment until finally reaching my breaking point. He would make himself the butt of the joke for everyone's entertainment; I would turn red from embarrassment as it suddenly became clear that—as his girlfriend—I too was part of the joke. It wasn't that there was something wrong with him. He was amazing; funny, generous, honest, and insanely smart. It was just that I wasn't sure how our romantic interactions would go. We were similar in so many ways, but the ways that we were different seemed impossible to overcome.

Josh was of a different mind. While I was convinced that a romance could only end in drama and heartbreak, he was convinced that we were perfect for each other. We went back and forth for a few weeks, having heart-wrenching conversations and periods of silence that twisted my stomach into a million tightly-wound knots. Eventually, I realized that we had gone too far. We would never be able to go back to just being friends, and it didn't seem like we could stay away from each other, so we might as well try dating for a while.

To my delight and amazement, it went incredibly well. We ran into all the familiar problems lovers do, no doubt. But we handled them differently. We looked at our situation objectively and worked together to understand each other's needs. We became a well-oiled machine: one unit, working together for our mutual goals. Friends started telling us how happy we seemed and how happy we made them by being such a great couple.

Why have things worked out so well for me and Josh? I'm sure that part of it is the luck of good chemistry. But, something that is not at all a matter of luck has made things much easier for us—philosophy. While my previous relationships floundered for lack of any method of discussion, Josh and I were applying a set of rules and techniques that we were already using in our professional lives.

Five Rules for Philosophy and Love

At this point you may be wondering what any of this has to do with you. Two philosophers fell in love and it turned out that their communication was supercharged by their philosophical background. . . .

But philosophical love is not just for professional philosophers. Anyone can learn the basic methods. Some are unspoken rules of philosophy and some are sage advice passed down from professors. While they can help anyone to examine any issue with more clarity and confidence, when applied to a romantic relationship, they can create something beautiful, lasting, and powerful. With practice they will take your relationship to a whole new level of depth and understanding.

Rule #1. Examine Everything

One of the first things that I loved about philosophy was the attitude that no topic was off limits. In my other classes, teachers and students alike would raise their eyebrows and hurry the discussion away from topics that hit on politically or emotionally sensitive issues. In philosophy, we delved into whatever issue arose, playing the devil's advocate and following the trail of the argument to its logical conclusion. Nothing was taboo. It was liberating.

I can't stress enough how important this attitude is in successful relationships. When a couple agrees to rationally examine any problem, concern, or issue that presents itself, they allow themselves to be open to growth. Discuss your problems, your decisions, your challenges, but also discuss your relationship itself. Talk about your individual psychologies and how they interact with each other. Discuss your day and the things you're excited about. Explore all the conceptual space. Most importantly, don't take anything off the table.

Most of us never achieve such transparency—I know I never had before—but many simply choose not to. Concerns about expressing something cruel, unflattering, or hurtful keep many from choosing the path of transparency. I strongly caution against this kind of reasoning. When you hold things back from your partner, you hold yourself back from the possibility of a "shared mind." If each partner has a different set of facts to work with, then it is unsurprising when they each come to different conclusions about whatever issue is up for discussion. When you hold things back, you are stopping the collaborative problem solving process and saying "I know best." Keep in mind that your partner will be doing the same thing and you can say "goodbye" to teamwork.

So how can we deal with the hurt or confusion that often comes with open declarations of our opinions? I deal with it in two ways. First, I always enforce a strict policy of understanding before reacting. I keep myself calm so that I can receive all the relevant information. I let my partner explain himself fully before I let myself react. Then I explain my concerns and reactions to him. We work through it. Second, I always consider carefully the way that I tell him anything that might cause pain. I am supportive and constructive. I listen to his concerns and talk through the issue until we are both satisfied with the result.

When you make an agreement with your partner to put everything on the table, you leave yourself open to pain. Why do this to yourself? Because it's better to understand the things that cause you pain, deal with them, and then never think about them again! You must be gentle with each other, but honest. That way, any challenges are challenges you face as a team.

Rule #2. Find the Root Premises

Here's a quick lesson that you can find in any critical reasoning class. The backbone of critical reasoning is argumentation. An argument is a collection of statements that might be true or false. Most of these statements are premises, one is the conclusion.

If I say "Love, I think we should stay in tonight instead of going to that party. I'm tired, you're tired, and it's a long drive," I've given an argument with three premises and a conclusion:

Premise 1. I'm tired.

Premise 2. You're tired.

Premise 3. It's a long drive.

Conclusion: We should stay in tonight instead of going to that party.

When someone gives a conclusion without any premises, problems come up quick. Why? Because you don't know what's motivating them! You don't know why they don't want to go to the party, because they haven't given reasons. You also can't tell whether they've taken your premises into consideration.

Suppose my partner really wants to go to the party because he wants to see an old friend who will be there. Now we have more premises that need to be considered. It is no longer clear whether we should go to the party or not.

Premise 1. I'm tired.

Premise 2. You're tired.

Premise 3. It's a long drive.

Premise 4. You really want to see your friend.

Premise 5. Your friend will be at the party.

Conclusion: ?

Although the task of finding all the premises in an argument is not hard, it's often neglected. As an individual you know all of your own premises instinctively. They are your beliefs, feelings, preferences—your reasons for doing the things you do. As a couple, however, you have a shared set of premises, half of which you might not be aware of. Once you know what all of your collective premises are, you can reason to the best conclusion, make compromises, or try to persuade your partner towards your view. But, until those premises are clear, confusion will turn an innocent disagreement into an ugly fight.

Rule #3. Put your Emotions on "Pause"

One thing I always loved about philosophy is the dispassionate view it encourages for problem solving. Emotional sensitivity gets checked at the door when you walk into a philosophical arena. As an undergrad, I quickly learned that real philosophers hold a straight face and keep a grip on their logic when the conversation veers into emotionally charged waters. It isn't about ignoring your emotions; it's about putting them on hold and keeping your mind clear. Emotions can cloud even the smartest mind.

In relationships, it's hard to put emotions on pause. Love seems to be the domain of emotions, the one place where they rule supreme and logic has to take a backseat. It's obvious that modern relationships are predicated on our emotions and without them partnerships would be cold, impractical things. Still, lovers beware—we have all seen emotions get out of hand and lash out with uncontrollable force when left to their own devices.

My strategy? Make space for your emotions. Listen to them. Use them in your list of premises. When you're problem solving, express those feelings as premises. Tell your partner how different plans make you feel. Express how his actions make you feel. Make collective decisions based on how both of you feel! But, if you want to avoid fighting and heart-break, learn to avoid actually feeling your emotions while you are talking it out.

This is easier said than done. Sometimes it takes a little acting to get started. You might be able to start off calm and collected but then half-way through he will say something that twists your heart and demands an emotional backlash. Don't let it. Take a breath. Try to calmly express how the comment sounded to you. Talk it out until you understand exactly what was meant. Most of the time, you'll find that there is some miscommunication.

If you get to the root premises and you find a serious dis-agreement, then you have something real to talk about. Shooting emotional reactions back and forth won't help you make any progress. So, put your emotions on hold. They will be there when the conversation is done.

Rule #4. Take the Time to Spell Things Out, One Thing at a Time

Among philosophers, communication is key. Given the complexity of our arguments and theories, it's not always easy to explain them to others. So, we practice, we edit, we do test runs; we carefully craft our papers and presentations to ensure that those reading or listening will understand our point. It's common for two philosophers to spend hours mulling over a single point until finally both parties have come to a mutual understanding. They may not always agree, but hopefully they've at least uncovered where their root premises differ. We've learned that if we want to make any progress we need to take the time to spell things out.

The same principle can be applied between lovers. Relationships are complex and sensitive creatures. They are challenging to understand and each new issue brings a whole host of mysteries to be uncovered. Be explicit and clear. Express each of your feelings, insecurities, worries, and needs.

Once you have a set of concerns to work through, things can get confused quickly. If you have ever had a fight where you aren't even sure what you're fighting about, you'll know what I mean. In the heat of the moment it's easy to skip from topic to topic, issue to issue, before any one thing is resolved. This can lead to some serious confusion, whether that means running someone's brain in circles as they try to follow your reasoning or leaving your lover asking "Wait—what were we supposed to be talking about?"

In both cases, confusion is minimized by dealing with one issue at a time. This can be frustrating and difficult. Likely one problem will run into another and you will be tempted to momentarily stray from your original topic. Do not give in! Keep working on your first issue before you move on to other things. Discuss only what is relevant to that issue and save the other stuff for later. It might seem like a good idea to skip ahead, for just a second. But, ignoring this rule can leave you at the end of a heated discussion with nothing decided on, and no real progress made. Take one thing at a time!

Rule #5. Make a List and Keep Track of What Has Been Settled

If you find yourself challenged by the last rule, you may have too many things to keep track of, using nothing more than your short-term memory banks. Since this is also the case in philosophical disagreements, we have taken to using simple tools like a pen and paper, or (my favorite) a white board.

Imagine a couple, Leo and Amy. Leo is uncomfortable with Amy's behavior at the bar. He feels she's too flirtatious. She starts conversations with single guys and forgets to mention Leo. She giggles and plays with her hair. Leo says he trusts her but feels disrespected. He tells her that they need to talk and tries to explain how he's been feeling. While the conversation starts to address Amy's flirtation, it quickly disintegrates into a variety of other topics. The couple may spend hours fighting about nothing in particular. They may talk of Amy's need for attention, Leo's lack of trust, or a whole host of related problems. A fight can bring many things bubbling to the surface.

Using a notepad or white board to jot down your points can help immensely in staying on track and in remembering what needs to be discussed later. Write down each topic and draw arrows between them to indicate connections. "Amy's flirting" might have arrows from "needing more attention" or "lack of trust." There may be an arrow from "Amy's flirting" to "Leo's feeling of disrespect." As you map out your discussion, you will see that you are actually mapping out the problem at hand. This helps to avoid the feeling that you just spent three hours going around and around in unproductive, emotionally exhausting circles. And it helps to avoid future problems.

There is nothing more frustrating than feeling like an issue is settled only to have it re-emerge without warning during another conversation. If you deal with one issue at a time and write things down as you go, you will find that it's much easier to keep track of what's already been settled. Be serious about your interactions. When you resolve an issue, come to some kind of decision.

Amy may agree that she needs to be careful with her flirtatious nature and Leo may recognize that he can be overly jealous. Still, they will only make progress if they use those realizations to create a concrete solution. If they decide together to cut down on their trips to the bar and spend more time at home, they should record that decision and stick to it.

This can be added to your list of premises and help you to make progress on other issues as well. Make a commitment to those decisions and don't waste time bringing up old issues. Move on with your life. Move on with your conversation. In philosophy and in love, this will save you time, effort and a lot of stress.

. . . Reclaiming the Examined Love

Wrestling with a philosophical dilemma can be a challenging feat, but not nearly as challenging as keeping a relationship in good form. Everyone always likes to focus on the fun, exciting part of having a love affair. But unless you're prepared for the inevitable conflicts, pleasure will soon be outweighed by pain.

Philosophers argue all the time. It's our business. And over the centuries we have learned how to do it in a civilized and productive manner. What I have learned is that these methods can be used to sort out problems of the romantic variety.

Still, this is just the beginning. Philosophy is a discipline dedicated not only to solving problems but also to figuring out the best way to solve them. If you find these methods helpful, you may find that further research into philosophy will add to your arsenal of problem solving skills. Read up on decision procedures, take a course on critical thinking, or just read philosophy on topics that interest you and let the methods soak in by example. There are so many ways that philosophy can help you to better understand your lover. Talk, be open—and most importantly—keep examining your love!

12

Love in the Time of Self-Gratification

SCOTT F. PARKER

> To fear love is to fear life, and those who fear life are already three parts dead.
>
> — BERTRAND RUSSELL

The writer Alain de Botton, pointing out what an odd couple love and philosophy can be, once said, "the philosopher in the bedroom is as ludicrous a figure as the philosopher in the nightclub."

We tend to think of love as being spontaneous, passionate, and beyond the ken of reason. Philosophy, by contrast, is critical, judgmental, and deeply self-conscious—traits which are often not conducive to love and intimacy. No one ever wished a lover more philosophical. And rightly so—anyone who has ever lost himself in abstract musings *in delicto* knows how disappointing and hurtful it can be. (Conversely, just try to do some philosophy when you're sexually preoccupied.)

While love is not rational in all aspects—not least in the particulars: why one is drawn to dimples and another is not, why a certain idiosyncratic pronunciation of the word "celery" can leave a person too delighted to sleep, and why in a world full of beautiful women it is She who is uniquely capable of making my life meaningful—it's rational insofar as there are some good reasons for opening oneself up to it. And even in its non-rational aspects it is not irrational. We do not decide whom to love, and we know the futility of denying whom we do love.

We humans are not purely instinctual animals. Our approach to love is shaped by our attitude toward it as well as by our biological impulses. Love, then, falls under the purview of philosophy if for no other reason than because it consumes so much of our time as we pursue it and as we reflect on what approach to love and sex might best facilitate our greatest flourishing. Philosophy, after all, is at bottom the quest for the good life. And so, while Botton is right that no one ought to think about philosophy during sex, sex and love are such defining aspects of human life that we stand to benefit from giving them some deliberate consideration in a disinterested moment.

A Range of Positions from Philosophers

Many philosophers have shunned carnal pleasure as a distraction from nobler pursuits. The ancient Greek philosopher Diogenes the Cynic was known to masturbate in public and said, "I wish I could rub my stomach in the same way to get rid of hunger." The sexual urge to Diogenes was an inconvenience that should be satiated as quickly as possible. Taking the idea of sex as distraction to its limit, the Christian philosopher Origen of Alexandria castrated himself so he could teach women without arousing suspicion.

But not all philosophers have felt so averse to sex and love. Plato and other ancient Greeks celebrated pederasty; Crates of Thebes and Hipparchia practiced public sex together; Jean-Paul Sartre and Simone de Beauvoir rejected monogamy; Michel Foucault frequented gay bathhouses and wrote about sex as "a possibility for creative life." The variety of approaches various philosophers have taken toward sex suggests an infinite number of possible avenues of insight.

Sexual Naturalism

If Foucault is right that we are each the author of our own sex lives, then the variety of approaches various philosophers have had to sex (in theory and in practice) suggests an infinite number of possibilities. The potential for human sexual flourishing is like a blank page on which any particular story can be composed (keeping in mind that "can be composed" does not mean "should be composed"—ethical considerations come into play whenever two or more consciousnesses interact).

Because of the sense of power and utter originality that goes into composing a sex life, each of us can be forgiven for thinking that, in discovering sex (again and again) for ourselves, we've discovered something new in human history. That thing we hear about, or read about, or see on the Internet, is a different order of experience from what we do, and so we're tempted to think our sex is as significant to the world as it is personally. We recognize ourselves in another line from Alain de Botton: "We embarked on one of the longer and more beautiful kisses mankind has ever known."

But while we feel like world-class authors of our sex, the language we write in is not our own. Foucault no more chose to be gay than you, reader, chose to be . . . whatever you are. He chose what to do with his gayness, but not the gayness itself. How would one get outside of oneself in order to choose who that self is? Who would be doing the choosing? (I only make this digression for the sake of emphasis, so that when I write that if philosophy is good for anything it's for helping us figure out how to live there is no chance of giving cover to the kind of argument that says that all of who one is is self-generated.)

Whatever the causes of our condition, the experience of it remains, and so the question becomes: given our particular needs and desires, how should we act?

Sex and Love

Woody Allen once said, "Sex without love is an empty experience, but as empty experiences go it's one of the best." We can all imagine, if not recall, sex without love.

It is much harder to leap from loveless sex to envision what the twentieth-century British philosopher Bertrand Russell is talking about when he says, "Those who have never known the deep intimacy and the intense companionship of happy mutual love have missed the best thing that life has to give." The insight expressed here, which many eventually experience first-hand and which may be impossible to appreciate secondhand, is that, as great is sex is, there are whole worlds beyond it. A high-school friend of mine once put it to me this way: "When you have sex with someone you love your soul feels the way your penis feels when you have sex with someone you don't."

Love was of primary importance to Russell, who saw in it nothing less than the possibility of breaking down the hard walls of the ego and producing a new being composed of two in one. In the prologue to his *Autobiography* he wrote:

I have sought love, first, because it brings ecstasy—ecstasy so great that I would often have sacrificed all the rest of life for a few hours of this joy. I have sought it, next, because it relieves loneliness—that terrible loneliness in which one shivering consciousness looks over the rim of the world into the cold unfathomable lifeless abyss. I have sought it finally, because in the union of love I have seen, in a mystic miniature, the prefiguring vision of the heaven that saints and poets have imagined. This is what I sought, and though it might seem too good for human life, this is what—at last—I have found.

The distinction here between sex and love is of utmost importance. For while love, in Russell's terms, is the principal means of escape from loneliness which afflicts us all, and while sex features prominently among heightened moments of freedom from isolation in loving relationships, sex outside of love very often leaves a person lonelier than ever, as we are confronted with the unavoidable fact that the physical intimacy just shared has gone emotionally and spiritually unmatched.

Identifying some of the virtues of love doesn't address, however, some of the obstacles preventing its development. According to Russell, one of the barriers to healthy mutual love—and therefore one of the barriers to happiness—is our cultural prudishness about sex (and the ignorance in which we raise our kids that is the cause and effect of same).

Russell published *Marriage and Morals*, his primary work on the topic, in 1929. Attitudes toward sex are much more open now than they were then, and sex education is much improved, but a shadow of shame lingers. Even today, Russell would shock some parents with his recommendation that children be free to explore their sexual impulses. Many parents are still so embarrassed by sex that they avoid the subject of what's going on between their kids' legs—and thereby make it all the more fascinating. But, as Russell points out, attempting to thwart natural impulses will never produce the balanced development essential to a happy life.

Russell sees our society's prudishness as a consequence of the continued influence of Christianity (or, we might amend, the Abrahamic religions, generally). He argues that treating sex as a base desire tolerable only in marriage has made Christianity "a force tending towards mental disorders and unwholesome views of life." Whether one subscribes to Christianity or not, the cultural conditions of our existence are always exerting their influence on our sex lives, and so Christian morality continues, Russell says, "to poison love, filling it with gloom, fear, mutual misunderstanding, remorse, and nervous strain." We will never realize the kind of lives Russell envisions as long as we feel shame about sex or are unable to harmonize it with love.

Dispensing with shame, though, is desirable only insofar as doing so contributes to the end goal of human flourishing. The aim is not to reject ethics but to find a more sensible approach to sex that helps to foster human happiness.

Neither Lust nor Romance

In order to have the kind of value of which we're speaking, love must feel the ego of the beloved person as important as one's own ego, and must realize the other's feelings and wishes as though they were one's own.

— BERTRAND RUSSELL

Undergoing a sexual liberation, one risks overcompensating for past repression through excessive sexual exploits. The danger lies not in violating a lingering sense of religious "purity" but in sacrificing some of the specialness of an intimate relationship.

Russell insists that when you can have sex with anyone, whenever the impulse arises, sex becomes nothing special. That hard-to-define *thing* that makes sex in a loving relationship a transcendent experience is easily lost when sex becomes commonplace.

These declamations for love run another risk, though, of sounding suspiciously like fairy tales—as though you must wait for the perfect lover to appear on the scene and rescue you from your private unhappiness. Though being in love does give you the opportunity to peer over the walls of isolation, it is the act of love not the beloved person that affords this possibility.

This is not to say that partners are interchangeable, but it is to say that the benefits of love present themselves independently of love's object.

What is it that actually ends your isolation? It's not someone's beauty, or sense of humor, or aptitude in bed; it's putting their well-being up front in your consciousness—it's thinking about yourself less and thinking about someone else more. And since a romantic relationship involves intimacy of all kinds—physical, emotional, spiritual—there is an implied commitment associated with love. Caring about someone, loving someone, means committing to them. It's for this reason primarily that romance and passion are insufficient for love: love takes work. Romance is enough to initiate a relationship, but, as Russell argues, it must give way to "something more intimate, affectionate, and realistic."

Alain de Botton distinguishes between mature and immature love, saying that mature love involves an honest assessment of the beloved in a relationship of friendship and sex. Immature love, though more passionate than mature love, swings between idealization and disappointment. The former is so desirable for Botton that for its sake he encourages the tactical abandonment of philosophy. Lovers, he says, should prefer faith to philosophy and "risk of being *wrong and in love* to being *in doubt and without love.*"

I'll agree but with a caveat. To argue for the utility of faith is to put one foot into philosophy—and if love is a good thing for humans, it might be a good thing *for a reason*. The lover needn't forgo his philosophy for the sake of his love. Whatever your outlook and motivations for seeking love, once love is realized these become obsolete. Even the self-interested person looking for love *in order to* bring about happiness will forget his motivation if he does find love.

You can be too eager for love. A friend of mine, out to dinner on a first date, was recently flummoxed to hear "I love you" delivered in all apparent sincerity mid-meal. Love, this friend assessed in declining a second date, is not to be sought indiscriminately, and nothing so indiscriminate can really be love. Another friend, perhaps too discriminating, tells me in a tone of regret that, despite contrary statements to the involved parties, he's never actually been in love with any of his girlfriends. These friends, though expressing different perspectives, have in common a longing for love and a sense that their happiness, in part, depends on it.

A Final Plea, Wherein Author Shows He Has No Shame and Lets It All Hang Out

If my observations of friends and my readings of Russell and Botton offer a consistent and compelling endorsement of love, my first-hand experience only further corroborates it. (Although appealing to my personal life risks the impression that everything I've said is a kind of argument to make a virtue of circumstance, I'm willing to make such an appeal, believing as I do that the way I came to my positions doesn't detract from their mettle. I turn to my life because it's the life I know best.)

One defining effect of love is to undermine the self-centered approach to life. It comes as little surprise when in retrospect I notice now that the years I pursued selfish pleasures most enthusiastically did not bring me the peace of mind and happiness that love has. In fact, the period of my greatest promiscuity overlapped exactly with my period of my greatest unhappiness. Cause is too strong a word to use here, but between these variables arrows of encouragement pointed in both directions. This is easy enough to appreciate looking back, but it was another thing to reach self-understanding at the time.

So if my editor will allow one final confession, I'll mention the night I decided I'd had enough. After a series of gin martinis I ended up in bed with someone who I, when sober, didn't even really like to be around. That's it. But what makes this more than an unexceptional story of regret is the lesson it finally taught me: fast sex is like fast food; it might satisfy a craving, but it lacks nutrients, and the longer you sustain yourself on it the more you'll see your health deteriorate. While it makes you feel good in the short term, in the long term it wrecks you.

I won't begrudge anyone some sex; there are times when you're hungry and junk food might be all that's available—that's far from the worst thing in the world. But—and please take this in the spirit in which it is intended, as some things I've noticed that have been helpful for my happiness and might be helpful for yours—I will recommend not living off candy and cola in a world that also offers fruits and vegetables.

While this may seem like a profoundly off-putting moralism, it isn't a moral issue, not really. Assuming honest, responsible sex, the issue isn't the suffering you cause someone else but the suffering you cause yourself. It's an issue of discernment. Sex is not wrong, and Woody Allen is right—there is no better empty experience. So, while I won't disparage the joys of sex, I must stand by the caution that they are not finally enough. Sex might bring you an orgasm, but if meaning and satisfaction matter to you, work for love.

13
It's All about Me

JAMES BONEY

> There are of course ugly women, but I prefer the ones who are pretty.
>
> — JEAN-PAUL SARTRE

When I was in elementary school, my teacher told my home-room that, should we choose to give cards on Valentine's Day, we must bring one for each person in the class. Even at that age, I felt this was strange. I may not have known very much about love, but one thing I knew for sure was that I did not love everyone in the class. To the contrary, I just barely *liked* most of them—including the teacher.

Though my teacher's intentions were innocent, her rule reinforced a long-held myth of Western culture: that love is to be applied universally. This idea is at best arbitrary, and at worst unattainable. How do you honor your lover if you love everyone? The answer is simple—you can't.

Christian philosophy has made an enormous impact on our understanding of love. In the Bible, for instance, we are instructed to "Love thy neighbor as thyself" at least once in each of Leviticus 19:18, Matthew 19:19, Mark 12:33, and Luke 10:27 . . . the list can go on to include Romans, Galatians, Ephesians, and James. In this tradition, love is compulsory. We are commanded to love. The idea is not subtly suggested but hammered home.

Popular culture chimes in as well. We celebrate literary characters like Ebenezer Scrooge who, after being visited by a trinity of specters, is overcome by a desire to love *everyone*. Our modern understanding of love is that it is, or at least should be, universal and unconditional.

Well, I disagree. Love is far too precious a thing to be administered indiscriminately. In my view, love is a deliberate exchange for the purpose of mutual benefit. In order to see this, we must turn to philosophy—first and foremost, to the great ancient Greek philosopher Plato.

Love Is Beneficial

In his dialogue the *Symposium* (meaning "Drinking Party"), Plato writes of a group of drunk old Greeks who, after just finishing dinner, decide to slow things down a bit by exchanging ideas on love. (We learn that they had far too much to drink the night before as well.) After first skipping his turn because of hiccups, the playwright Aristophanes eventually presents his view in the form of a story.

According to Aristophanes, long before the beginning of history, humans were a very different kind of being. To start with, they were twice as large. They also had two sets of arms, two sets of legs, and two heads. Moreover, they were perfectly spherical. This allowed them to bounce and roll around the world in a carefree happiness.

However, because they had two heads they were twice as smart—and therefore twice as arrogant. Ultimately, this arrogance came to offend their creator, Zeus. To put them in their place Zeus sent out a shower of thunderbolts that would split each one in half. The result was the modern human—one head, two legs, and two arms.

Aristophanes's story is meant to explain why on our own we feel incomplete. And why romantic passion elates us to such an extent. Love is the most intimate reconnection imaginable—it restores our emotional balance, making us whole.

From classic literature to modern cinema, Aristophanes's notion of finding our perfect match is a familiar one. In the 2005 comedy *Wedding Crashers*, John Beckwith (Owen Wilson) proclaims, "True love is the soul's recognition of its counterpoint in another."

The image of two lovers becoming one is beautiful and romantic. Some might even say profound. Nevertheless, as Plato points out, this does not make it entirely true. In the

Symposium, he portrays his beloved teacher Socrates advocating a different view—that love is, instead, a progression of intellectual stages.

For young people, romantic passion typically translates into a desperate physical craving for another person. After their first fling ends, they eventually seek out another. In each successive relationship, the current object of affection seems like the only person in the world. But with a little time and wisdom, they learn that what they really love in other people is beauty as such. The transcendent and eternal form of beauty reflected in the other is the lover's true aim. True love, for Socrates, is the ability to see through or beyond the exterior of any particular person to the form of beauty within.

The *Symposium* provides the philosophic building blocks for the notion that love is a form of completion. For Aristophanes, we are emotionally incomplete without love; for Socrates, we are intellectually incomplete. The popular line, "You complete me," from the 1996 film *Jerry Maguire,* reflects this romantic ideal. And there is something very right about it. What's right is that it acknowledges that true love is a benefit to the lover. It is not a form of selfless charity, but a concrete way of improving oneself. However, there is also something wrong with the *Symposium* accounts: They take it for granted that love is a romantic passion that happens *to* us. The very word "passion" comes from the same root as "passive." While Aristophanes's passion is emotional and Socrates' passion is intellectual, both imply surrender. Pierced by Cupid's arrow, love is something that happens to you. As poetic as this idea may be, it is misguided.

Love Is Deliberate

Plato's intellectual view of love never gained the widespread following that Aristophanes's emotional view did. And perhaps this is for the best: love is more a matter of the heart than of the head. But this should not force us to concede that it is passive. We talk of an experience making us happy, sad, or angry. Implicit in such statements is the belief that we are slave to, not the master of, of our emotions. In fact, we find comfort in thinking that our actions are the product of whatever emotion is influencing us at that time. Our modern legal system even excuses crimes of passion.

The nineteenth-century American psychologist and philosopher William James helped to entrench this idea. According to James, an emotion is the necessary result of a physical occurrence. For example, you interrupt a burglar in your home; your body tenses, your stomach turns, then you feel scared. Fear, in this case, is the emotion that is caused by a certain set of physical reactions. Fear happens *to* you. Likewise for love—it is a set of sensations that are caused by a set of physiological responses which, in turn, are caused by a set of perceptions.

The twentieth-century French philosopher Jean-Paul Sartre sees it differently. According to Sartre, a person actively participates in emotional experience. Emotions are *choices*. In Sartre's view, James missed two crucial elements. First, emotions have intentionality—they are always *about* something. You don't just love, you love someone or something. You don't just hate, you have to hate someone or something. Emotions can't be mere feelings because feelings aren't about anything. A headache is a feeling. It might be *caused* by something (a visiting mother-in-law, for example). But we don't say the headache *is about* your mother-in-law. By contrast, love is not a feeling because it is about someone. This someone not only causes your love but is also its intentional object.

Second, Sartre points out that emotions are purposive. That is, an emotion is a kind of strategy chosen by a person to accomplish something. He illustrates this point with an example from the ancient Greek writer, Aesop. In the familiar fable "The Fox and the Grapes," Aesop writes of a fox that encounters a vine full of voluptuous and delicious grapes. Unfortunately though, even with all his fox-like cunning, the fox can't reach the grapes. Turning away in disgust, the fox says to himself, "They're probably sour anyway."

Why has the fox's attitude changed? It's certainly not as if the chemistry of the grapes has been modified. So what happened?

What happened is what Sartre describes as a 'magical' transformation of the world. While the grapes remain exactly as they have always been, the fox's way of seeing them is transformed. He has come to see them as sour. By refusing to accept himself as a failure, the fox has magically changed the world. He now sees himself as a wise fox who is unwilling to waste anymore time or energy pursuing worthless grapes.

Sartre's point is that emotions are a mode of escape. They are not caused within us. We generate them within ourselves in order to deal with the world. They provide us a way to see ourselves as better off than we would have been otherwise. We deliberately love and hate in order to create a coherent life for ourselves. Because emotions are strategies, and strategies are always chosen, we must hold ourselves responsible for our emotions. In this way, Sartre liberates us from the excuse. No longer can we dismiss our behavior on account of being angry. Sartre thinks that we're even more accountable because we were angry.

By turning the traditional picture of our emotional nature on its head, Sartre has cast romantic love as a choice. Just as you must choose to love, you must also choose to be loved. Naturally, your partner must do the same. We are not, as Romeo declared, 'Fortune's fool'. Instead, we play a conscious role in deciding exactly how our lives will go. Lovers create their relationship, for better or for worse. Where most people say they *fell* in love, Sartre would say they *jumped*.

From Stranger to Lover

Standing only five-foot-one, and notoriously negligent with regard to personal hygiene, Sartre managed to overcome his physical shortcomings with hyper-self-confidence. Sartre confides that he was once very melancholy because of his ugliness. But he came to see this attitude as a weakness and successfully rid himself of it.

Sartre not only won over many lovers, but also made many friends. He came to regard friendship as a crucial middle stage in the progression from stranger to lover. For Sartre, the friends we keep are rarely a matter of circumstance. It's not simply that our friends are our roommates and neighbors and co-workers. We have plenty of roommates and neighbors and co-workers more or less by accident. Our friends, in contrast, are *chosen*. And we choose our friends on the basis of, among other things, our conception of ourselves.

This is not to say that friendship is essentially narcissistic. We do not necessarily choose friends that are *like* ourselves. On the contrary, we may choose friends who are radically different from ourselves. If I'm not very witty, and concerned about my lack of wit, I might make friends with the wittiest of my peers so that their wit may rub off on to me. I do this in an attempt to improve myself.

How I choose to improve myself depends on my self-image. If I consider myself intelligent, I may make friends who are intelligent so that I can enjoy their company. Or I may make friends who are not intelligent so that I may prove how smart I am. Ultimately, the purpose of the friendship is mutual reassurance; I will approve of you on your terms, if you will approve of me on my terms. The result is a partnership that benefits both individuals.

We identify ourselves through our friends. But because we have so many friends, that identity becomes diluted—less potent. We don't depend on any one friend to determine how we view ourselves; however, when a friendship turns into a romance this changes. The exclusive nature of a romantic relationship amplifies our self-conception. And with this amplification comes an element of control. Sartre sees romance as a strategy designed to win over the other so that they may see you as you see yourself.

To get a better picture of this, imagine your first date. Beyond the anxiety and stress, you dress a certain way, you talk a certain way. All of this is designed to get the other person to think of you a certain way. Your goal is to win them over. More specifically, you want to win them over to your way of thinking. In short, what we find with love, contrary to the ethereal way that we often think of it, is a concrete struggle. We endeavor to seduce the other in order to reinforce our own values.

A similar line of thought can be found in the writings of Russian-American novelist and philosopher Ayn Rand. She writes that friendship and love, in order to be meaningful, must contain an element of the selfish. Whether choosing a friend or a lover, you seek pleasure that the other can provide.

It might be easy to be discouraged by this account. You might argue that it takes all the *love* out of love. However, that couldn't be further from the truth. To love is to express one's values. Conversely, to be loved is the sublime reward for one's own values and characteristics. This is why love cannot be universal and unconditional. No one should indiscriminately love all human characteristics. To do so would be to have no values at all. True love's exclusivity is perfected and symbolized in the lover's ultimate act.

Sex

For the majority of Western history, society has been taught that it is wrong to view someone as a sex object. We're told that to do so would be the moral equivalent of "using a person." In more recent times, feminists have argued bitterly over the sexual objectification of women. However, it would be dishonest not to acknowledge that there is a sense in which sexuality always reduces the other to a sexual object.

Sartre points out that when you make love, the areas of your partner that become most attractive to you are precisely those parts of a person that are least human—the most fleshy, the least mental. This then raises the question, when we love someone for their personality and intelligence, why is it that sex tends to treat them in a way that doesn't leave very much room for those traits? Why does sex seem so animalistic, so biological?

Sartre would insist that these questions are moot. Humans make love in a way that no other animal on Earth does. It is part of what's most human about us. In having sex we are conscious, and we are self-conscious. We are aware of the other person, and we are aware of the other's awareness of us. So sex, like love, is a kind of strategy: it aims at winning over the other to our own self-conceptions.

Contrary to the popular, romantic notion of love-making, Sartre introduces an element of brute reality. He forces us to acknowledge that love and sex are not merely the passive receipt of emotional and physical bliss. Instead, we are proactively responsible for the partners we choose and for our actions in relation to them.

This point is made in the 2004 film, *Closer*. In it, the main character Alice (Natalie Portman) is consumed with sorrow over the infidelity of her boyfriend, Dan (Jude Law). After discovering what he did, Alice declares: "Oh, as if you had no choice? There's a moment, there's always a moment, 'I can do this, I can give in to this, or I can resist it', and I don't know when your moment was, but I bet you there was one."

Here we see Alice expressing Sartre's idea of radical freedom. For Dan, the belief that he "fell in love" was good enough to excuse his behavior (as if he had no role in deciding this fate). On the contrary, as Sartre tells us, and Alice knows, we *always* have a choice. And to that extent, we must be accountable for those choices—freedom demands it of us.

With all this talk of selfishness and choice, it's easy to wonder whether there is any value in a committed exclusive relationship. If you choose to be promiscuous, and you're willing to accept the responsibility, then why not do it? Rand offers a compelling answer:

> Sex is an expression of a man's self-esteem, of his own self-value. But the man who does not value himself tries to reverse this process. He tries to derive his self-esteem from his sexual conquests, which cannot be done. He cannot acquire his own value from the number of women who regard him as valuable. Yet that is the hopeless thing which he attempts. (Ayn Rand, "The Playboy Interview," *Playboy Magazine*, 1964)

For Rand, romantic involvement brings the reward of profound self-esteem. Men and women who have not developed their own values cannot hope to identify the value of another. They will never find true love. On the other hand, to love and to be loved, is to love yourself enough to love another—completely and truly. As Rand once put it, "To say 'I love you' one must know first how to say the 'I'."

In Praise of Selfishness

The contribution Sartre and Rand have made with regard to the nature of love and sex cannot be understated. Their positions may seem a bit harsh, but that does not make them any less valuable. These two great thinkers have managed to reclaim love and sex for the real world. With love removed from its ethereal perch, we're now in a position to appreciate the constructive, proactive role that we play in our romantic relationships. That is, we are to love and be loved *discriminately*. You love someone because he or she is a value—a selfish value—just as you are a value to him or her.

So what, then, can philosophy tell you about your lover? Philosophy reminds us that our lover loves him or herself. In fact our lovers love themselves enough to love us! Moreover, you must regard yourself as worthy of being loved. Love as the result of an unearned exchange is ignoble. Contrariwise, the *real* love you share with your partner is priceless. It is the simultaneous affirmation of your worth, and the worth of your lover.

As a human being, your responsibility to yourself is unmatched. The force of that responsibility demands that you share yourself with only those who are truly worthy—those that are equally as valuable.

IV

Intercourse

14
The Single Life

WEAVER SANTANIELLO

A married philosopher belongs in comedy.

— FRIEDRICH NIETZSCHE

In my early twenties I fell in love with the drummer in a local rock band. For several years, every weekend two girlfriends and I would cheer on the band—and I would typically be the first one on the dance floor jumping around and getting the crowd going.

Exchanging winks and glances, the drummer and I rarely spoke—yet we knew each other, partly because of my love for his music and because I was friends with his younger sister.

The admiration between "Glenn" and me was taboo because he was married. His wife was a beautiful Marilyn-Monroe-type model. Yet his marriage was publicly known as an impending disaster: he didn't want his wife attending shows because she made a fool of herself through excessive use of drugs and alcohol. I figured that, if Glenn wanted to end that relationship, I could be a Good Samaritan and lend him a hand!

Though everyone knew I adored him, most thought it was one sided. I wasn't sure myself until one summer night when Glenn, in front of everyone at the club (except his sister, who didn't attend), approached me during a break and gave me a long, tender kiss. In the bright lights I stood there stunned as he whispered in my ear: "They say it's better the second time around."

At the time, I had no idea what that meant—but as he walked away I was virtually staggering with joy, confusion, and

145

yes, guilt. But not that much guilt! After the show we resumed our newfound relationship in the parking lot and talked for hours in his car—about the marriage, about "us," and so on. He said he had never cheated on his wife; he never had a "reason" to.

I was flying high as I returned home during the wee morning hours; I flew even higher when I heard he and his wife broke up shortly thereafter. Was she pissed because he got home so late in the morning? She always had issues with tomboyish me.

I gushed to myself: "I am going to marry this man."

In deep distress over the impending divorce, Glenn told me over the phone he would never marry again. I wanted to speak with him in person, but sadly, the end of his marriage coincided with the end of the band. It was difficult to figure out how I was going to see him again in a discreet manner, especially since he lived in a neighboring state.

About a month after our phone call, I still hadn't heard from Glenn. A friend convinced me to take action: we would surprise him by bringing breakfast to his home. I didn't feel comfortable with the idea—and I couldn't cook—but she assured me that, once we got in the door, we could always eat cereal!

And so, one morning, after shopping for supplies, we made the long drive to my beloved's house. Scared to death about how he might react to our unannounced visit, I took a deep breath and finally rang the bell.

The unthinkable happened: a woman in a robe opened the door. She was very attractive and clearly had just gotten out of bed!

Totally humiliated, I threw the groceries on the front steps, stammering: "Give these to Glenn!" Then I grabbed my friend's arm and stormed off.

I still blush when thinking about this incident because it remains one of the most embarrassing moments of my life. As it turned out, the woman answering the door was actually just renting the house with her husband because Glenn was broke and needed the money.

Oops!

The incident, which happened almost thirty years ago, changed my life forever: I hated the (unfounded) jealousy that consumed me; I hated the passion I felt for a man whom—I had to admit—I barely knew; I hated my impulsive action, which must have made Glenn's life even more miserable. And, tragically, I severed my friendship with his sister.

That fateful morning made me want to live life in a more independent way. It made me realize that romantic love is most often the pursuit of an unattainable ideal. I didn't want to be a victim of the Cinderella complex, counting on a prince to adore me and whisk me away from the realities of adult life. Even if there ever was such a thing as a fairy tale ending, I would rather write a story of my own. Reading some philosophers on the subject of love reinforced my resolve to do without a lover forever.

Cynical Schopenhauer

Nineteenth-century German philosopher Arthur Schopenhauer expresses amazement that, even though love plays such a vital role in the history of humanity, only a few philosophers have discussed it. Plato, he says, only talks about it in terms of jokes, myths, and fables; Kant's analysis is superficial; and Spinoza's account is positively amusing in its naiveté. Thus, Schopenhauer concludes that he is on his own in the effort to advance philosophical understanding of romantic passion.

Schopenhauer proceeds to make the argument—scientifically ahead of its day—that all forms of love are a trick of nature. The romantic passion we feel is a delusion designed to support the instinct to perpetuate our species. The supposed attraction between opposite sexes is really the desire to create a new and improved copy of oneself. Only the strongest emotional experience could provoke one to sacrifice oneself in service to humankind this way. Like ants laboring endlessly to preserve the colony, lovers deny their autonomy to secure the next generation. Thus, everyone who is in love eventually finds themselves duped.

If only the delusion stayed as pleasant as it seems at the outset! Schopenhauer explains why lovers so quickly become so miserable.

We are biologically driven to seek out unsuitable partners because we want to cancel out our own imperfections. Bent on producing healthy offspring, we look for a partner who has traits we do not possess. For example, short women seek tall men, and vice versa; but tall men rarely seek tall women because they unconsciously fear that they will create giants.

Although Schopenhauer's example is farfetched, he has put his finger on an important principle of the theory of evolution (which Charles Darwin had not yet published). Female peacocks are drawn to male peacocks with impressive feathers without knowing that this is because the feathers are an outward sign of mating potential. For human beings, though the signs are more complicated, they function in the same way and serve the same purpose.

The result, for Schopenhauer is that happiness and marriage cannot go together. The will to reproduce thrusts us into relationships we don't really want. "Love" would be completely abhorrent if it weren't for the prospect of sex. The will of the species is so much more powerful than that of the individual that we are blind to what would otherwise be repulsive.

If one must marry, says Schopenhauer, an arranged marriage based on practical considerations is to be preferred. Yet these too are problematic because money often becomes the most important issue, once again ignoring the day-to-day compatibility of the couple. Regardless of how a marriage comes about, it's bound to be unhappy in so far as its principle aim lies in a projected future rather than in the present.

Ultimately, Schopenhauer finds the sexual instinct to be ignoble because it is directed to all without individuality and strives to preserve humanity through quantity rather than quality. Romantic passion is an insult to human dignity because even the most rational understanding of it cannot overcome its irrational demand. If the fulfillment of desire remains denied, it can lead one to the madhouse or suicide.

While Schopenhauer must be credited for attempting to apply scientific principles to a topic that was traditionally regarded as a spiritual mystery, he concludes more than he is entitled to. Granted, human beings experience evolutionary instincts just like other animals; granted, this explains certain tendencies among our species. This does not prove, however, that we are biologically determined.

There are many scientists today who believe in determinism—the view that all human action is entirely caused by the physical conditions of our existence. Yet there are also many scientists who believe that human beings, despite being influenced by physical conditions, still have free will. Philosophers expend a great deal of time and energy examining the free will versus determinism debate. There are good arguments on both sides, and in my view the issue just is not settled.

For example, Schopenhauer's claim that love is nothing but a function of the instinct to reproduce does not explain the romantic passion that exists among same-sex couples or among couples who are past childbearing age. Nor does it explain why a heterosexual couple might deliberately choose not to have children. Though determinists have proposed various possible explanations for these phenomena, none have been conclusive or entirely convincing.

And yet, there is one sense in which Schopenhauer's theory rings clear as a bell to me—namely, it explains some otherwise puzzling cultural attitudes.

Consider adultery, for example. Schopenhauer contends that men are by nature inclined to inconstancy in love, women to constancy. A man's love decreases when it has achieved satisfaction, a woman's love increases. This is because men can beget a hundred children a year, whereas women can only give birth every nine months. While the man pursues other women to perpetuate the species, the woman clings to him for the security of future offspring. Thus, fidelity for the man is "artificial," and for the woman "natural."

This provides a clue to why adultery has traditionally been considered much less pardonable for a woman than for a man. A woman's infidelity violates her nature—a man's infidelity is only natural. Even today, especially within radical monotheistic religions, women adulterers are unmercifully belittled—and even stoned.

In like manner, Schopenhauer's theory illuminates why childless couples are often disdained. DINK couples (Double Income No Kids) are widely viewed as selfish for not having or even *wanting* children. I know this from personal experience.

Over drinks one evening, my cousin (a scientist) conveyed to me his bafflement that his brother and his wife not only don't want kids, they don't *like* kids! Regarding his own children my cousin exclaimed: "*That* is what life is all about." As a self-proclaimed "OINK" (One Income No Kids), I smiled: "That is what *your* life is all about." I was tempted to discuss with him

Schopenhauer's suggestion that we would not assent to reproduce unless we first had lost our minds—but I didn't want to ruin the evening.

There seems to be a cultural expectation that everyone should want to be in a permanent heterosexual relationship, and that every such couple should reproduce. Still today, the Catholic Church maintains that the primary reason for marriage is reproduction. And unfortunately, that argument is used by conservative religious groups to deny the legalization of gay marriage.

So, while Schopenhauer has not proven biological determinism, he has at least identified strong biological tendencies. Many people, aware of these tendencies within themselves, make the unwarranted inference that they and everyone else should choose to live in accordance with them. The result is bigotry and intolerance of contrary choices.

While I would never choose to be single just to prove Schopenhauer or my cousin wrong, I suspect that the counter-cultural nature of my choice is a big part of its appeal for me. Philosophers have been standing up to tyrannical societal expectations since the day Socrates—the founder of Western philosophy—was executed. It is the philosopher in me that refuses to go along with the fairytale of romantic passion.

Elitist Nietzsche

My other main source of inspiration on this issue is Friedrich Nietzsche, another nineteenth-century German philosopher. Though strongly influenced by Schopenhauer, he nonetheless rejected Schopenhauer's notion of the will of the species as the primary life force, substituting his own notion of the will to power.

The will to power is striving to achieve greatness that transcends mortal existence. All human beings, in virtue of being human, experience this urge to some degree. The human will *needs* a goal: it would rather will nothingness than not will.

Yet most people waste their will on trivial pursuits. Family life is, for Nietzsche, the prime example of a trivial pursuit. Of course, family life consumes the vast majority of time for the vast majority of people—whether one is actually taking care of family members or working outside the home to support them. Family life turns the majority of humanity into slaves.

Whereas Schopenhauer argued that the servitude of family life makes people unhappy, Nietzsche's concern is that it makes people mediocre. One cannot achieve greatness when tied down in a committed relationship. Truly ambitious individuals must therefore practice the ideal of asceticism.

Asceticism is a sublimation of biological urges for the purpose of focusing energy on creativity. According to Nietzsche, those who have traditionally practiced asceticism throughout history have often done so hypocritically. The composer Richard Wagner, for example, practiced chastity in order to elicit the intense emotion that would lend drama to his music. Asceticism became for him an artificial device to accomplish a contrived result. Likewise, priests deny themselves out of reverence for God and thereby alienate themselves from the mass of humanity, whom they are supposed to be shepherding.

For the philosopher, on the other hand, asceticism is not hypocritical but necessary in order to promote contemplation. True philosophers abhor marriage as a hindrance to their craft. Heraclitus, Plato, Descartes, Spinoza, Leibniz, Kant, and Schopenhauer were all unmarried. Thus, Nietzsche jests: "A married philosopher belongs in comedy." The exception is Socrates—but Socrates married ironically just to prove that the free spirit cannot abide domesticity.

Nietzsche insists that Socrates never let Xanthippe get the better of him. By making his house inhospitable, she drove him more and more into his strange profession—hanging out in the marketplace so that he could discuss philosophy with everyone whom he met. In spite of herself, Xanthippe helped turn Socrates into "Athens's greatest backstreet dialectician." Devoting his life to the cause of encouraging philosophical thought among his fellow citizens, Socrates compared himself to a pesky horsefly on the sluggish beast of tradition.

Socrates was seventy years old when he was sentenced to death for corrupting the youth. Nietzsche contends that Socrates, in part, drank the hemlock *because* of his views on women, or rather, because of his rejection of conventional, domestic life. This is evident from various accounts of Socrates's trial and execution, which portray the women of Athens blaming Socrates for abandoning a wife and two children. They cried and lamented and disturbed the thinker's twilight peace to the point that he was happy to drink the poison.

It is significant that his last words were: "Have someone take these women away!"

Nietzsche recommends that philosophers avoid three things: fame, princes, and women. But philosophical asceticism should be neither hateful nor pathetic. It consists of an independent, cheerful will that is natural for supreme spirituality. Philosophers do not deny existence, they affirm it—but only their own: "Let the world perish, but let there be philosophy, the philosopher, me!"

Opposing Schopenhauer on the free-will versus determinism debate, Nietzsche insists that the will to power can rise above any biological tendency. Unlike Schopenhauer, who thought both men and women seek love in order to reproduce, Nietzsche attributes this motive only to the woman. For her, the man is just a means to the end, which is always a child. The vast majority of women are largely determined by their reproductive function because they are the weaker sex and have far less capacity for the will to power than men.

Nietzsche basically views love between a man and a woman in terms of domination. Originally, women idealized the concept of love to make themselves more desirable in the eyes of men and thereby vicariously increase their power. But over time, women ran into their own "net" because they forgot the reason behind the original ideal of love. As a consequence, they are now more deceived than men and suffer more from the disappointment that the ideal of romance often brings.

Doomed to a life of servitude, women strive to secure male support by making themselves seem more submissive and subservient than they really are. For example, they can use childcare as an excuse to avoid work as much as possible and they can make a fuss about housekeeping so that men overestimate their activity tenfold. Hence, among the ordinary mass of humanity domestic life is domestic strife.

While it's hard to take Nietzsche's bald disdain for ordinary, work-a-day people, his effort to encourage his reader to rise above ordinary, work-a-day thinking is valuable. Being ordinary is a choice. If you can summon the courage, you can break out of the mold and realize your true potential. Nietzsche's emphasis on asceticism also calls attention to our society's obsession with sex—from advertisements, to books and movies, to news programs—which surely is an unfortunate distraction from more admirable pursuits.

Is there any way to salvage Nietzsche's attitude toward women?

Displaying his often complex state of mind, Nietzsche grants that there have been noble women capable of realizing the will to power. Their existence makes it possible to conceive a higher interpretation of marriage as a spiritual friendship. A free-spirited woman could join with a free-spirited man to form a productive union. However, such a union would require the aid of a concubine. Nietzsche explains: a good wife who is a friend, helpmate, child-bearer, mother, head of the family, manager—who perhaps has to run her own business—can't also be expected to put out. It would be asking too much of her.

Here Nietzsche comes close to appreciating the value of motherhood and housekeeping. In 2007, a report assigned a salary of $138,095 to a stay-at-home mother, based on the ten most common jobs she does in a normal week: housekeeper, day care center teacher, cook, computer operator, laundry machine operator, janitor, facilities manager, van driver, CEO, and psychologist. Moms who have jobs outside the house would earn another $85,939 for their mothering work, beyond what they bring home in existing salary. I heard last year on CNN that stay-at-home moms are now worth approximately $145,000.

In a way, Nietzsche gives credit where credit is due. The domestic life is a choice and it is a choice that comes at a price. We can't blame anyone but ourselves if we become ensnared in its web. For many people, this web is all they ever wanted or needed. For others, it is nothing but a tyranny. Though Nietzsche is too strongly biased in favor of his own choice, his insistence on human free will is worth bearing in mind through every juncture of life. Fancying myself a free-spirit (but not a creative genius), I find the independent and self-sufficient path worthy of aspiration.

The Single Life

So, we have seen how two nineteenth-century German philosophers blew a hole in the fantasy of true love. I am not enough of a cynic or elitist to follow either of them faithfully. And I must confess that I haven't entirely lived up to my resolve to go it alone. Yet no lover has lured me for long from the single life.

Once in a blue moon I wonder if something's "wrong" with me for wanting to be single. Knowing that philosophers have often rejected and criticized marriage eases my mind to some extent. And I find the theories of Schopenhauer and Nietzsche especially provocative in directly challenging the assumption, ubiquitous in our culture, that everyone must find their true love. Even so, I know my ultimate motive for dropping out of the dating game is not philosophical.

In the song, "I Never Cry" my childhood hero, Alice Cooper, wrote: "I may be lonely but I'm never alone." To that I would counter: "I may be alone but I'm never lonely." I have two beloved dogs (Turbo and Plato) and a very small circle of loyal friends. My aging parents live three miles away. I love doing work around the house, teaching, writing, playing racquetball, spending time with friends and family, and watching the Red Sox. I can honestly say that my hands are full. I really don't have the time or inclination for much else!

This year Glenn, the renowned drummer, received a prestigious music award. Since I had not spoken to him in almost thirty years, it took all the guts I could muster to send him an email of sincere congratulations. Did my heart skip a beat when I saw his return email arrive in my inbox? Yep, it did. His note was brief, kind, and provided some sense of closure—at least for me. He also mentioned he might be playing in my area in the near future. I told him, if that were the case, I'd be there. Hopefully, this time around, the wisdom of sages will go with me!

15

Who Do You Love, Simone de Beauvoir?

Margaret Betz

Bo Diddley probably wasn't thinking about the philosophical significance of the question, "Who do you love?" when he penned the song by that name in 1956. It's about a slick and dangerous badass looking to entice a woman named Arlene by telling her, among other things, he's got a chimney made out of human skulls. By the end of the song, Arlene is taking him by the hand—evidently willing to follow him off into the sunset.

Diddley's song came before second-wave feminism challenged the ideal of the compliant female. In the 1950s, a woman couldn't get a credit card in her own name and husbands maintained control of their wives' property. Heterosexual courtship was relatively straightforward precisely because it was limited. Women had so little choice, power, or control that they didn't need to think much about whom they ended up with.

All of this began to change in 1963 when Betty Friedan published *The Feminine Mystique*. Friedan's message was that a whole generation of post–World War II women was unfulfilled by the traditional roles of marriage and motherhood. *The Feminine Mystique* presented the subversive suggestion that women have been duped into believing these things should be enough.

Friedan raised the question: Is there something more? And freedom began with that question mark.

Though second-wave feminism brought freedom, it also brought complication. As Jean-Paul Sartre points out, the onslaught of choices that come with freedom can be so overwhelming that many people would rather not be free. But

Sartre condemns this rejection of freedom as "bad faith." Living authentically means recognizing and embracing radical possibility, despite the anxiety and confusion it can bring.

As feminism grew and women began forging new lives for themselves, the question of heterosexual love became more opaque. Women like me, born in the midst of second-wave feminism, faced a new relationship frontier. Henry Kissinger once joked, "Nobody will ever win the battle of the sexes. There's too much fraternizing with the enemy." Exactly.

What does romantic love look like in a feminist era? Are heterosexual women doomed to choosing only the Sensitive Pony Tail Man skewered in the 1990s movie *Singles*? Ironically, Bo Diddley's question, "Who do you love?" has become a provocative feminist question, one I have had a hell of a time answering on my own.

Beauvoir's Philosophy

Who better to turn to for feminist advice about heterosexual love than the twentieth-century French philosopher Simone De Beauvoir? In trying to navigate through the relationship minefield, I found her writings insightful in a surprising way.

Beauvoir's classic work, *The Second Sex* (1949) is an early feminist examination of the question "What is a woman?" In it, Beauvoir turns the concept of woman over and over, unfolding its historical, biological, sociological and philosophical meanings. In doing so, she develops her groundbreaking notion that "woman" is the classic "Other," an oddity ultimately incomprehensible to men. Since men control the official point of view in our society, women are officially incomprehensible. They can be defined only in terms of their non-maleness.

The "Other" status has been bestowed on many different groups throughout history—Jews constituting a prime example. Being oppressed has usually allowed such groups to turn to each other and form a self-identified "We." Women, however, are unable to do this because they lack concrete means for organizing themselves into a unit. They live dispersed among the males—attached to them as their daughters, wives, and mothers. Many of them enjoy economic security precisely because of this unique relationship with the oppressor. It is understandable, therefore, that it's very difficult for women to emancipate themselves. Every "Real Housewives" reality show is an extreme testament to that.

Though emancipation is difficult, it is not impossible. Beauvoir juxtaposes the "feminine" woman against the "emancipated" one, arguing the former makes herself prey to men. The feminine woman lures a man in by arousing desire in him, submissively making herself a "thing." The emancipated woman, on the other hand, is active—a "taker"—and refuses the passivity man tries to impose on her.

Beauvoir believes men and women will only see each other as peers when stereotypical femininity finally disappears. The vicious cycle of women and men enjoying benefits from the perpetuation of femininity continues unabated because each camp is giving aid and comfort to the enemy. Nonetheless, both men and women need to move beyond the traditional gendered mindset that diminishes women's status, overcoming women's "Other-ness" in favor of more authentic relationships.

More than anything, Beauvoir advises women to gain economic independence, which has the power to transform their lives. She recognizes, however, that the mindset of individual men and women, as well as the collective cultural psyche, likewise needs to change. We need to abolish the feminine-masculine dynamic and learn to see men and women as equal in every way.

While this androgynous world might seem frightfully dull to many, Beauvoir argues such a perspective lacks imagination. True, some of the relics of past gendered roles would disappear just as relics of the antebellum South disappeared with the abrupt end of slavery, but Beauvoir asks that we courageously move forward to envision new forms of love and happiness. She predicts that with a little creativity, new relations of both "flesh and sentiment" can arise between the sexes. Human heterosexual tension and desire are not tied to gendered existences. Creativity and courage. Just imagine the possibilities!

Beauvoir's Life

In her writing, Beauvoir comes across as a confident, liberated woman, yet the facts of her life complicate this image.

The crux of the problem was her relationship with fellow philosopher Jean-Paul Sartre, which has become the stuff of legend. They met in Paris in 1929 as students studying for the *agrégation*, the competitive exam for a career in the French school system. She was twenty-one and he was twenty-four. It was Sartre's second time taking the exam and, although the examiners found Beauvoir to be a more gifted philosopher, Sartre was awarded first place and she second.

Oddly, Beauvoir didn't seem resentful at all; in fact, she appears to have been irresistibly drawn to the troll-ish yet charismatic Sartre. She later declared that her relationship with him was her "greatest achievement in life." It was a relationship that would last fifty-one years.

With the advent of World War II greatly shaping their thought, Sartre and Beauvoir developed similar existentialist views, built on the premise of radical freedom. Determined to live their philosophy, Beauvoir and Sartre committed themselves to the idea that their relationship avoid the bourgeois conventionality of the rigid roles found in the institution of marriage.

Sartre was the first to introduce the possibility of other lovers in their lives. He called theirs an "essential love" but suggested to Beauvoir that it would be good for them to experience contingent love affairs. They wished to be true equals, sharing their love, their work, and even their outside sexual experiences. We can imagine Beauvoir applying her idea of courageously and creatively envisioning post-sexist relationships to Sartre's proposal.

Even as far as "contingent love affairs" go, however, theirs were unconventional. As a high school teacher, Beauvoir had access to many pretty young girls, and more than one became the lover of both Beauvoir and Sartre. In the spirit of sharing everything, they made a pact of "brutal honesty" regarding these outside dalliances, sometimes relishing details in letters to each other.

Beauvoir arguably displayed more "freedom" than Sartre by taking both female and male lovers, one of whom was American novelist Nelson Algren. Sartre typically chose to seduce very young, pretty (often troubled) women, women he once characterized as "drowning." Beauvoir was often the one to arrange these affairs.

Despite her ardent philosophical commitment to a liberated outlook on sexual pursuits, Beauvoir was constantly jealous.

This is clear enough from her letters, which make petty comments about the other women, some of whom were quickly dropped when Sartre and Beauvoir grew tired of them.

Sartre challenged Beauvoir by insisting that jealousy, like any passion, is an "enemy of freedom." He accused her of allowing jealousy to control her, when she should have been controlling it.

Beauvoir apparently agreed with Sartre's harsh assessment. It is as though she stayed committed to her avant-garde lifestyle for theoretical reasons even though it was deeply troubling to her in practice.

Many experts have posed the delicate question of why the twentieth century's best-known feminist thinker would have endured such an oftentimes humiliating arrangement. Beauvoir's description of woman's secondary status seems eerily represented in aspects of the life she constructed with Sartre.

Reading about Beauvoir's life, I had to ask myself, where is the self-assured voice of *The Second Sex*? It began to seem that Beauvoir may not be the model of feminist heterosexual love I was looking for. I hoped my friends would stage an intervention if I ever settled for a Sartre.

Visionary Feminist or Compliant Partner?

Some maintain that, on many levels, Beauvoir's lifestyle *was* progressively feminist, especially for the time. After all, while maintaining her lifelong "soul marriage" to Sartre, she avoided the legal and social indignities of early twentieth-century marriage. She also avoided the traditional role of motherhood, leaving her free to write and build her career.

Some suggest it was Beauvoir and not Sartre who orchestrated their arrangement—*she* who rejected marriage. Although Beauvoir certainly didn't enjoy her sexual freedom to the extent Sartre did, theirs was an innovative commitment to love between equals at a time when women enjoyed little sexual freedom and power, even within marriage.

But this rosy picture of shared lovers and perpetually fresh sexual passion is hard to uphold given the less savory aspects of their situation: the jealousy, the exploitive choice of women, and (the creepiest detail of all) both conducting brief affairs with young women they would eventually adopt.

Sartre financially supported many of his lovers (some of whom didn't know the others existed) and referred to his daily visits to the collective lot as his "medical rounds." Despite their pact of "brutal honesty," they *did* hide details from each other. Sartre once proposed to a French woman he met in America but somehow failed to mention it to Beauvoir. Their elaborate system of lovers ultimately seemed heavy on the "brutal" side and light on the "honest" side.

Beauvoir's revolutionary ideas on gender intertwined with the more troublesome aspects of her life left me without any answers about choosing a lover. Her feminist philosophy seems to directly imply that one should not choose the likes of Jean-Paul Sartre. And yet she did choose him. She built her life around him.

Perhaps I was missing something.

Turning back to Beauvoir's own writing for some clues, I gained, I think, a deeper and more generous understanding of her. In the section "Woman's Life Today" in *The Second Sex,* Beauvoir includes a chapter entitled, "The Woman in Love," in which she considers the typical difference between men and women involved in romantic relationships.

Beauvoir argues that, for men, love is about taking possession of the woman while remaining "sovereign subject." For women, in contrast, being in love means relinquishing everything for the benefit of the master. Beauvoir quickly adds that this difference has nothing to do with the respective natures of men and women and everything to do with "their situation." (In other words, it could be otherwise.)

Insisting that every woman in love is a masochist, Beauvoir contends woman is raised from childhood to see the male as something she cannot equal: the best she can hope for is to merge with him. The only way out is for her to "lose herself." Her body and soul become his, and he becomes the only absolute. Women desire this enslavement. Every moment of their lives, all that they are, must be dedicated to their man.

Is it a stretch to imagine Beauvoir had herself in mind as yet another "woman in love today"? Beauvoir, after all, described her relationship with Sartre as "the greatest achievement" of her life, despite her considerable intellectual achievements (and the fact that many of his most famous philosophical ideas may have actually been hers). Perhaps by way of explaining her own situation, Beauvoir writes that the "transforming" power of love is so intoxicating that men can arouse passionate attachments even if they are physically lacking. It's worth mentioning that Sartre was once physically described with the explanation: "his skin and teeth suggested an indifference to hygiene."

If a woman in love is unable to make her lover happy and keep him interested, her narcissism will become self-hatred, pushing her towards self-flagellation. This can turn into a lifetime of being a "voluntary victim." A woman in love takes on her man's perspective and makes it her own; she becomes him. He dictates her reality while she creates "a hell" for herself.

All this reveals the most important truth about a woman's love. Although it comes in the form of a gift, it is really a tyranny. The tyranny stems from the jealousy that ensues when the man looks at others and ceases to be present to her. It is the jealously of a "jailer." A truly "authentic love," on the other hand, would consider the other's faults and limitations without pretending to be a mode of salvation. But is this authentic love possible?

Not in the present circumstances—that is, in an oppressed society. Although a woman tries to be everything to her man, she cannot be. This reality forces her either to suffer or lie to herself. Most women lie to themselves, Beauvoir claims. While the more fervent will end up in an insane asylum, the "normal woman," will eventually accept reality. A "wise" woman in love becomes "resigned." While she may not be "necessary," she may still be "useful." She can choose to accept her servitude without demanding the same in return.

Although she labels jealousy a negative emotion, Beauvoir insists this is pretty much the perpetual status for a woman in love because she can never feel perfectly loved. She writes that the "bitter taste" of her dependence is "a maddening torture" for the woman. Authentic love is based in a reciprocal recognition of freedom, which allows the lovers to make a true gift of themselves to each other. Add to that economic independence, and "love in equality" is possible.

Caught Between Two Worlds

In the end, what I found in the puzzling case of Simone de Beauvoir is that feminist love is a hard business. As she says, it demands creativity and courage. Beauvoir's dedication to a life-long love affair with Sartre proves to be a window into the complex relation between a philosopher and her own philosophy.

She herself was caught between the two worlds of antiquated gender limitations and a vision of the future. Her philosophy informed the unique lifestyle she constructed with her lover. We can see how her relationship with Sartre was a blend of her feminist vision and her resigned acceptance of what it means to be a woman in love with a man "today"—while sexism is still the norm.

It's not that Beauvoir was one or the other—visionary feminist or compliant partner—in reality, she was both. Beauvoir likely believed she had creatively transcended much of the sniveling negativity of the inessential woman's existence. But factually we know she did not transcend it all. Perhaps she was proud of overcoming jealousy enough to actively invite other lovers into her relationship with Sartre but she suffered through intense emotion as he voraciously pursued younger women in a way that could rival Hugh Hefner.

Beauvoir knew she did not "identify her whole being" with Sartre. After all, being a philosopher does not mean escaping the foibles of everyday human existence. It is undeniably impressive that she forged her unconventional life long before women in France even had the right to vote. Yet she was still caught up in her time. Beauvoir the philosopher and Beauvoir the woman were evidently capable of very different things.

She ends the chapter "The Woman in Love," by proclaiming,

> On the day when it will be possible for a woman to love not in her weakness but in her strength, not to escape herself but to find herself, not to abase herself but to assert herself—on that day love will become for her, as for man, a source of life and not of mortal danger. (*The Second Sex*, Vintage, 1989, p. 669)

Ultimately, in revealing so much about herself as a lover, Beauvoir does tell us something about heterosexual love in a feminist era. The emancipated woman must insist on economic independence from her lover. She must refuse the dehumanizing role of "wife." She must invent her own identity. And, unlike what is still typically true for most women today, she must allow no one person to own her sexuality.

That's a pretty good model for the rest of us to start with. Beauvoir's answer to Bo Diddley's question, "Who do you love?" was: "Someone who will accept the bare minimum of loving me as an independent, intelligent person."

So, we can be grateful to Beauvoir the philosopher for envisioning and putting on paper a theory that might give even greater inspiration and courage to women of the twenty-first century.

16
The I Who Says "We"

STACEY E. AKE

It is always an I who says "we."

> — JACQUES DERRIDA

One of the most difficult things to navigate in this era of "fuck buddies" and "friends with benefits" is the terrain between the two (or more) people involved. In what regard does each party in the relationship hold the other(s)? Is one partner merely affectionate whereas another is deeply in erotic love with that partner? Can friendship really be maintained when sex has entered the relationship? Are we a couple or are we simply two ships that are passing in the night?

These are the questions that haunt the post-modern lover and beloved. But I think all these questions and doubts can be narrowed down to one single question: Are we a "we"? In other words, do I have the right to say "we"? The answer to this question lies in a careful examination of four different kinds of love.

Affection Creates Loyalty

Affection is probably the most silent of loves. It sneaks up on us unawares and sometimes even against our will. It's also the least talkative of loves. It exists in a nice, warm, and comfortable space between two (and perhaps more) persons.

Affection is the quiet love of things as they are. Perhaps one of the best examples of affection is seen in the film "Good Will Hunting" where the psychotherapist, played by Robin Williams, speaks of missing his late wife and one thing in particular—the fact that she passed gas during the night while she slept. No doubt flatulence is a strange thing to become nostalgic about, but isn't it also the case that this flatulence was an example of who his wife was, part and parcel of her existence? As such, it was one aspect of his wife that, over time, he got accustomed to.

To accommodate silently and without question the idiosyncrasies of another is the work of affection. One need not be intimate with someone to have affection for them. The janitor who stops to chat as he goes about his rounds of an evening, the way a co-worker always brings in donuts on the last day of classes, or the office mate whose nose blowing sounds like the trilling of a bird all can arouse affection in us. We would (and will) miss these things when they're gone.

Yet the janitor who stops to chat will also be the one who lets you into the building one night after you've locked your keys in your office, and the co-worker who brings the donuts might just make a special effort to include the particular kind you like. You might even get the office mate a box of tissues covered with tropical birds in honor of his nasal trilling. All of these things are done with a kind of trust that is best called familiarity. It can also be called loyalty—the loyalty of constant contact.

Contempt rings the death knell for affection. Consider the following saying; it has two interpretations: "Familiarity breeds content" and "Familiarity breeds contempt". We say of someone as we begin to hold them in contempt that "they rub us the wrong way." Such a tactile metaphor is apt. Just as an itchy piece of clothing or a small rock in your shoe can be ignored consciously for several hours, there comes a point, subconsciously, where such constant irritation cannot be tolerated any longer. And often one's expression of such long-term suffering comes out not at the rock in your shoe but at some poor, harried clerk at Wal-Mart.

But when affection or the loss thereof is oriented toward others we know more intimately, such as a lover or even a friend, the explosion of irritation is directed at them. If the explosion of irritation is kept under wraps, if the irritated person feels themselves above such shows of temper, then irritation is guarded by a stoic silence that little by little gives way to contempt. Often the person hiding their irritation feels themselves to be in a superior position vis-à-vis their irritating friend or lover because they are being so long-suffering about their partner's failings as well as not showing their anger at said failings. This is contempt, and it carries with it that peculiar pleasure of suffering and superiority. This is how someone becomes a thoroughly modern martyr—but a martyr to their own pride.

Thus affection, that most silent of loves, when it is irritated and still maintaining its silence festers into contempt. We see also that affection is not reciprocal and need not be reciprocated. I can feel an affection for my office mate that he does not feel for me; nor need he feel it. Whether he feels it or not, I still have affection for him. This is not a love where an I says "we"; this is a love where all an I can say is "I."

Camaraderie Assumes Equality

People who work together, people who play on a sports team together, or people who are serving on the PTA together all share common pleasures and common pains. They all are putting up with the micromanaging boss, the onslaught of the opposing team, or the lack of parent participation in school events. This shared experience leads to camaraderie among the participants.

Probably the most notable attempt to deliberately develop camaraderie is seen in the Soviet use of "comrade"—one who shared the views and the goals of the Russian Revolution. Perhaps also it meant one who ought to share those goals and views. But comrades do not have themselves in common; they have something they share in common.

This sharing leads members of a group to have a certain appreciation and, occasionally, respect for one another. Perhaps one appreciates another's ability to handle crisis situations, or to flag a fly ball, or to organize a bake sale. More importantly, this is the first I that can say "we", but only inasmuch as the "we" refers to the factor that all have in common. We—the people who put up with our stupid boss, or we—the people who have gone undefeated all season, or we—the people who organized this year's school picnic. It is a very narrow and particular commonality that this "we" refers to.

To speak of a "we" in something more than that commonality is presumption. This distinction first rears its ugly head when some topic beyond the one at hand is broached: say politics or religion. Then you discover that unlike yourself the person sitting beside you on the committee is a staunch Catholic or an avid Republican.And here the sense of "we-ness" evaporates. You don't have as much in common as you supposed. The shared commonality, the camaraderie, ends at the office or the playing field or the all-purpose room.

But the "we-ness" of camaraderie introduces a new element into the idea of we. It brings to the fore the difference between the inclusive 'we' and the exclusive 'we'. When, by 'we', I mean all of us standing here over against *you*, then I am using the exclusive 'we'. This we represents the us in "us versus them." Quite literally, our we does not include you, the other. An inclusive 'we' includes both the speaker and the other. With the advent of camaraderie, we see the limitations for an I who says 'we'. It is a narrow 'we'; it can be in error, presuming things in common that the group does not share, and it is the first use of the exclusive 'we', since the 'we' being spoken about is a 'we' that exists only in virtue of shared experience. Here, the I that says 'we' must be very careful that it has acknowledged the correct commonality and the correct participants in that commonality.

Because all the people sharing the commonality are free agents, one of the most dangerous things that can develop is a feeling of dependence in one person for another. No matter how much pleasure or pain is shared, each person is only putting part of themselves (and maybe not an authentic part) into the shared experience. Moreover, inasmuch as the shared experience is concerned each person is considered an equal participant in the situation. All are equally office workers, teammates, or concerned parents. What they may be at home, in their sex life, or in their religious beliefs are irrelevant to the matter at hand. For this reason, the camaraderie ends once work is over, people have left the locker room, or the floor is swept up after the holiday pageant.

Yet, for some people, camaraderie may be the closest they have come to the beginnings of friendship or the vestiges of care. It can be very difficult for such people not to read too much into the camaraderie they have been feeling, if only because they do not have enough experience to distinguish one love (friendship) from another (camaraderie). But within this I that can speak either an inclusive or an exclusive we resides the fact that, at the end of the day, each I at the office, on the sports team, or serving on the PTA always says I. Camaraderie makes for a very temporary we.

Friendship Implies Authenticity

As mentioned above, it is sometimes the case that camaraderie is confused with friendship. And it must be noted that friendship can and does arise from camaraderie. Two office-mates might become fast and thick friends when they discover a common love of music. Two sports aficionados might find a friendship has been sparked when they discover they belong to similar synagogues. And two members of the PTA might become lifelong friends over the discovery that they are both avid amateur quilters. In each case, these two people found that there was something they each had in common with the other beyond the office, the sports team, the committee. This appreciation is the stuff upon which friendships are made.

Friendship has gone the way of all flesh in US culture. I think this has to do with the conceptual sexualization of all interpersonal relationships. I first ran across this, or rather smack dab into it, when I noticed how many younger people (thirty-five and under) assumed from the *Lord of the Rings* movies that Frodo and Sam had a homosexual relationship. The idea that Frodo and Sam might be stalwart friends could not even cross their minds. Their relationship was "gay"—and perhaps in both senses of that word.

It must be remembered that J.R.R. Tolkien is writing based on his experiences in World War I. For a subordinate to become an intimate friend of the officer he was assigned to was apparently a common occurrence. The same relationship between a servant and an officer can be seen in Dorothy Sayers's Lord Peter Wimsey mysteries where there is such a relationship between Lord Peter and his very able servant Bunter. What is remarkable about such relationships is that they crossed class boundaries, something that was very difficult to do in the Britain of that time. A similar conundrum confronts us with the contemporary, and very post-modern, BBC series, *Sherlock*. As with the relationship between Frodo and Sam, the relationship between Holmes and Watson has often been under scrutiny for its homosexual elements—despite Watson's evident relish and pursuit of "the fair sex".

It is open for argument whether Holmes is homosexual or asexual. In the contemporary series *Sherlock* I think the implication is that Holmes is gay but asexual by choice, considering himself married to his work. But something the contemporary show brings out, by building up the character of Watson, is that Holmes and Watson trust each other in virtue of their individualities. Each appreciates the oddness of the other; they both have in common the need for violent excitement—not a trait common to many in the world. This shared need, this peculiar desire, is the thing that cements their friendship.

I think what sexualizes the relationships between Frodo and Sam, Holmes and Watson, is the fact that friendship by its very nature creates an exclusive 'we'. There is no doubt that when Frodo or Sam says something like "We are going to Mordor alone" that the "we" meant here is Frodo and Sam and no one else. The distinction between friendship and mere camaraderie can be seen when Gollum joins their group; he is at best a comrade but never a friend, for friendship reflects (it does not create) a kind of intimacy.

But this intimacy can only exist among those—whether two or three or four—who are truly being themselves. One can try to fake friendship but never successfully and never for long. Friendship is too easy-going, too spontaneous, to give someone feigning it enough time to plan and implement their next move. To be a friend, one must be truly, authentically, interested in the thing the friendship is about—getting a magic ring to Mount Doom or solving puzzling criminal cases. Friendship requires the commitment of and to authenticity.

Authenticity, however, is a difficult thing to acquire. Yet you cannot have real intimacy without authenticity. To be authentic to someone else one must first start by being authentic to yourself. To admit who and what you truly are starts a person on the road to authenticity. This also means you need to admit what and who you are not. The Sherlock Holmes of *Sherlock* has not mastered all (or most) of the social graces. Then, again, Watson is not as intelligent as Holmes. What kind of friendship could they possibly have if they did not admit these things to themselves? Could one imagine what their friendship would be like if Watson was constantly competing with Holmes in order to prove he was just as smart as Holmes? Authenticity requires an acceptance and perhaps even a celebration of our limitations as well as our gifts.

But to attempt authenticity requires courage. You need courage to look yourself in the eye and say, "I am this, yes, but I am not that." You need courage to give up the simulacrum you have of your self and exchange it for the reality of your self. Yet you can never be a true friend until you are a true self.

I remember an undergraduate student of mine who came out his junior year of college. He was surprised and disheartened by the friends he lost as a consequence of this. But, as hard as it was to accept, those "friends" had never been friends with him; they had been "friends" with a simulacrum, their projection, of who he was. The fact that he was gay undid their image of him in their heads. The student that they had been friends with was not this student. He made a move toward authenticity and found himself rejected.

But if I am your friend, it does not matter what your sexual orientation, religion, or ethnicity are since we are friends about or according to something. It doesn't matter what Holmes's sexual orientation is; Watson and Holmes are friends about solving crimes. This creates an intimacy between them not shared by those who aren't interested in solving crimes. They cannot help this intimacy, the exclusivity, from existing, because they are authentically interested in crime solving, and this separates them from others—whether they like it or not. And to find yourself separated from others requires great courage as well. Real friendship is probably the opposite of popularity.

Eros Requires Humility

Now we come to the love that is the most difficult to talk about, because everyone already assumes they know what it means. Eros, erotic love, is the love that people "are in" when they say they are in love. Eros is the love that is based upon desire, most often sexual desire. It is not exclusively sexual love, and not all sexual love is eros, as we'll see.

When we talk about friends with benefits, what precisely do we mean? Are these people friends or comrades? Perhaps all they have in common is the urge to have sex. And this is an understandable urge, but it is an urge nonetheless. It may appear to be desire, but as is made very clear in this day and age, this is a biological urge akin to hunger or thirst. Unlike hunger, which we are supposed to be able to manage given all the weight loss programs and lose weight gimmicks, not much is said today about tempering one's sexual urges. Just do it. Don't hold yourself back. Lose your inhibitions, and so on. Strangely, all these admonitions could be just as easily coupled to an advertisement for expensive chocolate. And sometimes they are.

I am not interested in talking about this kind of sex or sexual relationship, the shared genital massage between two consenting adults. I am interested in that kind of love that is the product of abundance and need, between plenty and want, between wealth and poverty: eros.

Oddly, the first kind of eros I want to talk about is not sexual at all—despite the above-mentioned tendency to sexualize all human relationships, for this erotic love is hero worship. To the young person (gender irrelevant) who idolizes a sports figure or a rock star or some other celebrated person (again, gender irrelevant), they are finding in their hero something they themselves lack and would like to have. They don't want to have this person sexually, although they may lack the vocabulary and thus speak in sexualized terms; rather, they want *to be* that person. Whether it's Madonna or Gandhi, the hero worshipper sees something in that person they desire to emulate, that they desire to be. This is erotic love; it is a lover seeking a glorious and wonderful beloved. It is also an excellent example of the major requirement of erotic love: an admission of poverty. It is an admission that the beloved is something (not someone, not yet) greater than I. It is the admission of humility. To worship a hero is to see yourself as not a hero. This is humility, and humility is an erotic necessity.

To fall in love—a turn of phrase that sounds as if falling in love were a fortuitous accident like falling over a cliff—to be in love is to encounter an other who, at first at least, seems amazing, wonderful; it's a miracle that they exist! But as experienced lovers know, this stage of love—of being head over heels in love—does not last long. It definitely does not last forever. Then, again, I'm not sure that this is the kind of love fairy tales are promoting when they say "and they lived happily ever after." To live happily ever after means to get on with the project of living—something that is often overlooked in the more passionate and mind-numbing states of being in love.

One of the weaknesses of being in love is viewing the beloved as perfect . . . for me. It's easy to see the beloved as the perfect accessory to your life. It's very difficult to see the beloved as himself or herself. They are so perfect . . . according to our specifications. When this way of viewing things exists between two people who say they are in love with each other, and who are actually in love with how perfectly the other fits into their lives, disaster is imminent. Because someday one will disappoint the other or, perhaps, one only disappoints oneself. But the dream is gone. The belief that through this person I will be saved, that everything will be all right, has been undone.

Erotic love runs the danger of being a we that says "we," but without defining each individual 'I' that makes up that 'we'. Any outsider—and everyone is an outsider to a couple in love—can hear that 'we' and wince or sneer accordingly. This is the we that says "We have everything in common," and "We both love cherry ice cream," or "We're going to be so happy together." It is this we that is the dream of love.

Can such a love withstand waking up? I think it can—if we remove the magical thinking from it. There is in US culture this strange belief that love is a mysterious, uncontrollable event. There seems to be little, if any, emphasis on loving as a process, as something we learns to do and choose to do. It's as if we want all responsibility for love taken off our shoulders. "I couldn't help myself"—in either falling in or out of love—sounds inane when said by an adult. I can understand one not being able to help themselves where sneezing is concerned. We really cannot help ourselves there, but in loving? With humility we find that loving is an attitude toward the world.

The same ecstasy that we feels upon falling in love we can also feel when discovering beautiful music or a sacred space or an amazing movie for the first time. We stand in awe of it; we're humbled before it. Sometimes this loving awe grows as we come to appreciate our beloved music or movie more and more. Sometimes it goes away, and we say maybe weeks or years later "There wasn't anything in it after all." We have outgrown our love. And we can feel that we've outgrown a love, a beloved, whether it's our love for music, movies, or another human being.

This feeling that we are somehow better than what we once loved, the fact that we no longer stand in awe of our beloved, has a single source: pride. And because we can no longer find within ourselves the humility we once had, we may even go on to disparage our once having had it. "Well, I was just a kid then. Now I know better." Really? I suspect one of the reasons children find the world so wonderful is that they have no choice but to be humble before it. Everything is at once a surprise and a mystery. It is easy in the attempt to seem sophisticated and "grown up" to lose that humility and thus the concomitant wonder. "Been there; done that; bought the T-shirt," beautifully encapsulates lost humility and lost wonder. There's a reason this is the generation of 'whatever'. When you feel you've seen it all—or believe that you should act as if you have—there isn't much left in life to surprise you. Is it any wonder then that, if life has been emptied of all its wonder and spontaneity, it should take that long for another person—once our beloved and our possible salvation—to be as readily emptied of meaning?

Because falling in love can be as unreflective as affection, it falls prey to a similar vice. Contempt is not all that different from pride, except pride is generally more articulate than contempt. So, is it possible to stay in erotic love forever? Yes, and no. No, you cannot remain in the state of 'being in love' for long much less forever. But you can stand humbly and respectfully before the other person, the beloved, for as long as you like. We often forget that every individual is a world unto themselves, a kind of Cantorian infinity. To humbly bow before such an infinity, to realize that we stand in poverty before such richness, even if it is merely the poverty of one's knowledge, is to keep the spark of erotic love alive.

Charity Honors Otherness

The final love I wish to speak about is charity. It is a shame that the modern use of the word has reduced charity to a kind of benevolent alms giving, a smiling and polite philanthropy. Historically, charity has been associated with bounty and sumptuousness. It's the love that keeps on giving. Moreover, charity is a virtue, a strength. It is the strength of the deity when it is written that God is love. Charity signifies a virile and unending benevolence.

As such it would seem that perfect charity can only be performed by God; some would say that for humans perfect charity can only be done through God. I would not argue with that statement. But my interest lies elsewhere; I am interested in imperfect charity. I am interested in charity as it is practiced by flawed and failing human beings, for this is charity in action.

Charity requires a species of graciousness few of us have and even fewer are interested in developing. It's the act of loving the unlovable and forgiving the unforgiveable without losing ourselves in the process. There's a sense in the contemporary world that to forgive the unforgiveable or to love the unlovable is tantamount to surrendering or betraying oneself. Such charity smacks of weakness, of giving in to someone or something more powerful. But is this the case?

Consider Nelson Mandela's work to bring healing and peace to South Africa. This has not been done by overlooking justice—the Truth and Reconciliation Commission sees to that, but it has been done in order to avoid the bloodshed that might have come with a very understandable retaliation on the part of black and colored South Africans. Mandela treated his enemies—and I will not deny that we all have real enemies—with charity. This charity was his strength and perhaps created his strength as well.

But how do we as individuals practice charity, when our hearts are broken and our hopes destroyed? Not easily; it requires a great deal of strength and courage to overcome our basic urges to retaliate or seek vengeance. But it can be done. The first step is to step away from ourselves and look at the other as an other. Sayings such as "Do not judge a man until you have walked a mile in his shoes" intimate what is the necessary element: empathy.

Empathy should be distinguished from sympathy. Imagine a friend of yours finds themselves stuck in traffic on the way to a job interview resulting in their arriving late to their destination. When they later tell you this story, one possible response is to say: "I understand how you feel. I remember when I was held up in traffic trying to get to my niece's wedding. . . ." This is sympathy. You have had the same feelings (or believe you have had) as your friend. Empathy responds differently. Empathy says: "That must have been very distressing for you.

I know how important it is to you to be punctual. . . ." Empathy sees the other as an other, separate from yourself and wholly as real as yourself. It is with empathy that charity begins.

One of the first persons toward whom we should have empathy and thus charity is ourselves. When we are ignorant of our own motivations and desires, we are dangerous creatures. We act according to whims and willfulness. But if we're aware that we are often in the dark about our motivations and desires, we can extend empathy toward another who may be just as ignorant as ourselves. If we can admit that we have our own dark moments, we can more readily recognize and more easily accept that someone else has their own dark moments as well. Strangely, only when we see ourselves as ourselves are we able to see the other as an other.

But when we see ourselves in a shining light—as the innocent victim or as the wholly beleaguered spouse or as the persecuted co-worker—we are being presumptuous. We are presuming that we are of a different category than the person who has harmed us. To presume that we are perfect in light of another's imperfections makes the practice of charity impossible. No matter what our feelings are, we are all stumbling around in the dark, and it should be no surprise that we occasionally run into each other. The important thing is to remember we are all equally in the dark.

As I said above, charity is not easy, and it tends to go against our most immediate and seemingly natural inclinations.

But there is something else that is required of charity. This is the capacity to see the other as an entity in their own right. Charity, then, is the I that says 'you'. It is the I that has enough strength to let the other say 'we', if it is going to be said at all; charity does not need to say 'we' for itself. Charity allows freedom and autonomy to the other; it is not dependent upon the other for its identity and strength. Furthermore, only a person willing to accept another's charity—who does not feel their identity swallowed up in such magnanimousness—can say 'we' and mean it. Only an I who is known as a you can look at another, see them as a you, and with meaning and forthrightness say 'we'. A true we can only exist between people who see each other as you and are thus aware of the agency and complexity of the other half of their we. Only the I that says 'you' can ever become an I that says 'we'.

The "I" Who Says "You"

One of the most striking things about the I who says "you" is that it is not a special love in and of itself. It can be used to extricate any of the other four loves from trouble. It can rescue affection from contempt and camaraderie from dependence. Charity requires a return to authenticity on the part of a friend and reminds the erotic lover of her or his humility before the other. This is the love that rescues all other loves.

As such, it must be there, lingering in the background, as we go about our daily loves—affection, camaraderie, friendship, and eros. But perhaps the most tragic thing about charity is that one only discovers one does not have it at the very moment when it is most necessary: when affection dies, camaraderie fails, friendship frays, and eros falters.

Perhaps, however, you can practice charity before it becomes necessary by working as hard as possible to see others, any other, as a you—as a person as real as yourself. Consider all the people we pass by everyday and whom we treat as "human furniture"—the bank teller, the janitor, the checkout clerk at Wal-Mart. All these people are you's in their own right. Do you know the janitor's name? Have you ever inquired? What about the bank teller's children? A photo of them sits on his or her desk. Have you ever asked? Have you ever noticed how tired a checkout clerk often looks? Have you ever said anything to cheer him or her up?

Start doing these things today and you will begin to practice charity. Be an I who says 'you' so that you may become an I that can say an authentic 'we'.

17
Friendly Lovers

RONDA LEE ROBERTS

Have you ever wondered why we treat our friends better than our lovers? Anyone who has gone through a nasty (and I mean low-down, no holds barred, and quite bitter) breakup has asked themselves this question. Is it because love is closer to hate than it is to indifference? Still, it seems contrary to intuition that two people who were so in love could bring out such intensely negative emotions in one another.

This puzzle shows that romantic relationships have a thing or two to learn from friendship. In fact, successful romantic relationships are built on a foundation of friendship and when two individuals seek different things in a romantic relationship it is doomed to fail. Through examining some of the things that philosophers have said about friendship, we can gain some insight into romantic relationships.

Aristotle and the Types of Friendship

Think about your best friends. Do they make you happy? Do they make your life more worth living? Aristotle famously asserted that friendship is necessary for the good life. He sorted friendships into three categories: the friendship of utility, the friendship of pleasure, and the ideal friendship based upon mutual pursuit of the good. As it turns out, the same categories apply to lovers.

Friendships of utility arise because we *need* something from someone. Some examples are the friend who provides us with a ride to and from work, the classmate who lends us his or her notes, or the teenager who babysits for us. In John Steinbeck's novel, *Tortilla Flat*, the friends of the main character, Danny, are friends with him because of what he is able to provide them—a place to live.

Likewise, romantic relationships of utility arise when one person depends upon another for something. For instance, one partner marries the other for stability or health insurance. We tend to describe these relationships as ones where one person is *using* the other person.

Friendships of pleasure are those in which we pursue pleasurable aims with another. For example, one might enjoy going to the movies or playing tennis with someone. A tennis partner may not also go to the movies and a movie friend may not also play tennis. Hence friendships of pleasure are very activity-oriented. While they are quite enjoyable for both individuals, they are still a long way from what Aristotle means when he talks about the best type of friendship.

Romantic Relationships of pleasure are often fleeting. Sometimes the couple will meet while engaging in a mutually enjoyable activity, but after a period of dating will find they have little else in common. When one partner decides that they no longer have interest in the shared activity, the relationship falters.

Friendships where both individuals mutually seek the good are the ones that Aristotle holds in the highest regard. In this type of friendship each individual strives for happiness—or as Aristotle called it, *Eudaimonia*. This requires that the friends encourage one another to be virtuous. This sort of friendship, Aristotle believes, can only exist between two individuals who are committed to living the virtuous life.

According to Aristotle, virtue is cultivated by habit. Rather than give us a prescriptive definition of virtue, Aristotle simply recommends following the golden mean. One should aim to do the right thing, in the right way, in the right time, with the right tool, to the right degree. This is something we can only learn through practice.

One does not learn to refrain from drinking too much if one has not yet had anything to drink. Abstinence from alcohol comes with its own problems, but so too does over-indulgence in alcohol. Someone who drinks too much quickly becomes sick. Thus, those who intend to imbibe alcohol in a "virtuous" manner, learn how to temper their intake.

The same goes for the other virtues. For example, courage is a balance between cowardice and rashness. We do not say that the untrained citizen who runs into a burning building is courageous—instead, often he is scolded as being rash. On the other hand, the individual who freezes when faced with danger is said to be cowardly. The person who balances fear and fearlessness displays courage—a mean between the two extremes.

A friend who is aiming at leading a virtuous life can be a great compatriot when it comes to leading your own life of virtue. That friend who encourages you to go out at night may also be the one who encourages you to stop drinking when you've had too many—and stages an intervention if that is necessary.

Friendship, for Aristotle, is also a relationship that exists between equals. A good person cannot be friends with a bad person. Instead, the good are friends with the good, and the bad are friends with the bad. This is because there must be some commonality between friends, and ultimately, lovers. The friends must get the same things from one another. In other words, it would not make sense for one person to derive utility while the other derives pleasure. This would not be a friendship in the Aristotelian sense.

The friendship of virtue, for Aristotle, is an exclusive relationship. He argues that just as one may not be in love with many people at the same time, one may not have a perfect friendship with many people at once. This friendship takes time, and must be painstakingly built.

When you think about how most people form bonds, it is evident that they tend to have something in common. They work at the same company, they have a class together, or they frequent the same gym. No matter what the commonality is, it is a vital part of formulating the relationship. They might begin to partake in pleasurable activities together. Eventually, they might go on to share in the virtuous aims and goals of one another. For Aristotle these commonalities are crucial.

However, not every philosopher believes that commonality is a necessary condition for friendship (and ultimately love) between two people. A twentieth-century philosopher, Jean-Paul Sartre, asserted that in order for true friendship, and ultimately a beneficial and healthy love-relationship, to exist between two individuals, there must be conflict and support. This conflict and support will ultimately lead to a friendship of virtue, where each friend encourages the other to lead the good life.

Sartre on Friendship and Love

You may know Sartre as the guy who said that as human beings, we are condemned to be free, yet in our freedom we also have absolute responsibility toward others. This doesn't make immediate sense—responsibility implies necessity while freedom implies no necessity.

Sartre avoids this apparent contradiction by arguing that freedom requires acting with intent. To illustrate this, Sartre contrasts the careless smoker with an employee of a construction company. Imagine the difference between the smoker who recklessly tosses her cigarette into a pile of explosives and thus causes an explosion and the worker who rigs the dynamite to cause an explosion. In the first example, the person has acted without intent. In the second example, the person acted with intent.

Sartre also argues that our intentional choices fill the emptiness that exists between the current state and the future state. As I type, each letter I choose fills the gap between the present and the future end of this chapter.

This outlook on freedom, then, requires us to release our idea of causality. Sartre argues that we cannot see actions as having a definite cause nor can we see them as having a definite end. At any point, we could always choose differently, and nothing is ever finished. There is always something else to achieve.

For this reason, true friendship comes with elements of both support and conflict. It may seem obvious to say that friendships have an element of support—*of course* they do! After all, as we saw with Aristotle, there has to be something in common—the striving toward the good, a mutual need, or a mutual pleasure—that drives the friendship. However, when Sartre uses the concept of support, he means something much more.

He asks us to imagine standing on a moving trolley and watching someone running after it. Many people are simply bystanders: they watch—some may laugh, some may avert their eyes. However, for whatever reason, you decide you're going to help that person onto the bus. You extend your hand so that she may grasp it. In order to do that, you have to brace your body so that you are prepared to support her weight. There is a common goal shared by both of you: to get her from the street onto the bus. Rather than seeing her as a body running after a vehicle—as those who do not jump in to help see her—you see her as a human individual with a need. In order to help her, you must see her as a person with her own goals, projects, and most importantly, *freedom*. You take on her goal to determine the manner in which you can best help her.

So it is with friendships. To be an authentic friend, not merely a friend of utility or pleasure, I must take on my friend's goals. If my friend's goal is to pass logic class, then I must take on as my goal his ability to pass logic. If I happen to be a logic goddess, then I do this through helping him to understand derivations in logic to help move forward the project of passing. So long as I do this with respect for his goals, projects, and freedom, I have been a good friend.

However, I have to be careful when I'm sharing in a friend's goals. I cannot impose my own agenda or concepts of how that person should be. Thus, conflict enters into the friendship.

There are two ways we can view those whom we love. We can love the person who stands in front of us, as he or she exists. This first form of loving accommodates unexpected and unforeseeable outcomes that come with that presence. Alternatively, we can love the idealized image we substitute for that person when they are absent from us. This second form of loving is static and unchanging.

Conflict comes in when reality confronts our image of the person. On the positive side, this allows us to adjust to the reality of that person. To be a good friend—a true friend—I have to love that person even during the spontaneity of action that occurs when the friend is present to me. Because of this, consistent effort is needed in that relationship. Friends who see one another often tend to become close while people who lose touch cannot maintain a friendship.

If I am concerned about my *perception* of someone's goals, rather than their actual goals, then I'm unlikely to be able to be a good friend. My perception is static and unresponsive to the person's changing needs. Being open to change, on the other hand, and to the friend's changing goals, will allow me to be a better friend to her. To be a good friend, I have to share in my friend's goals and projects, but most of all I must respect her freedom. If she's to be truly free, then she also must have the ability to change her mind at will.

Turning from friendship to romance, consider for a moment your most recent (or current) romantic relationship. Most fights occur in relationships when the actual person clashes against the idealized person. When first dating a potential lover, there's a gap between the person we are getting to know and the person that we will come to know. We fill this gap with many expectations based upon past relationships, our hopes for future relationships, and assumptions we make about the individual based upon what we've seen *so far.* At some point, that potential lover will do or say something that is in contrast to this idealized notion we've formulated. Enter conflict.

Conflict is valuable to a friendship's growth. For Sartre, conflict is both inevitable and beneficial. Likewise for Aristotle. If your lover or friend steers off the course of virtue, in order to get him or her back on course, you'll need to have some conflict. Returning to the alcohol example, if your friend has been drinking too much, you'll need to intervene (at least if you're to have a virtuous friendship). Your friend will likely be unhappy with you. He or she may even try to fight with you, but you're concerned, so you step in anyway. This helps to keep your friend on the path to virtue.

Not all conflict is helpful—or virtuous. While Sartre does not say this, it would seem as though conflict that does not aim toward the good is unhelpful and that it does not benefit the friendship. In fact, it might tear the friendship apart. Imagine a couple who have been married for a few years. The wife wishes to return to work after their children have all begun school. The husband vehemently opposes this because he's afraid that it will take her attention from him, and he is afraid she may stray. He begins to argue with her to trying to dissuade her from pursuing a career for his own selfish reasons. This may drive a wedge in the relationship and may even show that it's an unhealthy relationship. Would we treat our friends this way? No, not our good friends, anyway.

Looking at the Lover as a Best Friend

Many people say that their lovers are their best friends, but do they really mean this? After the discussion of Aristotle and

Sartre, it can be said that a "best friend" ought to be someone with whom you pursue the good life, someone with whom you share goals, and someone with whom you move through the conflict of real verses ideal.

A best friend will be there for you—supporting you in your goals, helping you to do the right thing, and seeing you as you are while remaining open to your changes as you grow as an individual. A healthy, happy, and long-lasting romantic relationship also has to do this. The relationship where you are obtaining some benefit—either financial or sexual—from your partner is unlikely to survive. Even relationships where the "use" involved is merely an ego-boost are doomed to fail. Once the "need' for that quality is extinguished so too is the relationship. Sometimes these relationships continue because "We need to be together for the sake of the children" or "I couldn't possibly afford to leave him or her." However, even when they do last, it's hard to say they are "good."

Relationships based on pleasure also seldom last long. This is because these relationships are again built on that static, idealized notion of the other. Whether the pleasure involved is sexual or based upon a mutual enjoyed activity—tennis, video gaming, cooking, movies—once one person in the relationship either tires of the activity or decides it's time to pick up a new hobby and the once mutually enjoyed activity loses priority in his or her life, the relationship begins to fizzle out. Sometimes the individual cheats on the other individual with a new individual sharing the new interest. The person left behind often becomes resentful, longs for the changing individual to be "the person I fell in love with," and cannot let go of the static idealization.

Even lovers who aim for the good can encounter problems if they do not recognize the aspect of conflict inherent in long-lasting relationships. It is unlikely that the person you fall in love with will be the same forever. We often hold our romantic partners to higher standards than we would hold our closest friends. Even close friendships can end if they are not maintained and if they are based on idealizations.

It's not enough for both individuals to be "good Christians" or "pious Jewish people" or "moral individuals." It's not enough to aim at the "good." For a friendship that seeks out virtue, one must combine Aristotle with Sartre. Each individual in the relationship must participate in the other's goals, projects, and most importantly freedom. For example, suppose at the outset you and your lover viewed church as optional, but one of you decides five years in to attend church weekly and become more religious. It's crucial to allow for that change.

To be a good friend, and just as importantly, to be a good lover, we have to embrace the spontaneity that comes with dealing with real people. We cannot have relationships with our idealized versions of others. When we hold onto the idealization while that person is present, confronting us with the reality of his or her own goals, projects, and freedom, then we face conflict. This is the time when people say "I love you, but I don't like the things you do." People who make this statement do not really love the other person but only their idealization of the other person. They must reflect and determine whether they can continue to share the goals of the other. Unhealthy, abusive, and controlling relationships often arise out of an inability to share in the goals of the other.

Thus being a good lover is much like being a good friend. In fact, we treat our friends better than we treat our lovers precisely because we are more prone to idealizing our lovers. By analyzing our relationships in terms of Sartre and Aristotle, we can begin to recognize areas for improvement. Sometimes, such an analysis tells us we need to leave that lover behind, and find someone new—especially when their idealization of us will not allow us the freedom to change our goals and life projects.

Romance, domestic partnership, and marriage are not static but dynamic relationships. We must change with our lovers in order to help them reach their goals. This, of course, is not an easy thing to do. In order to build a virtuous love life, we must take the time to build a virtuous friendship. This requires a mutual commitment to seek the good and a shared understanding of freedom.

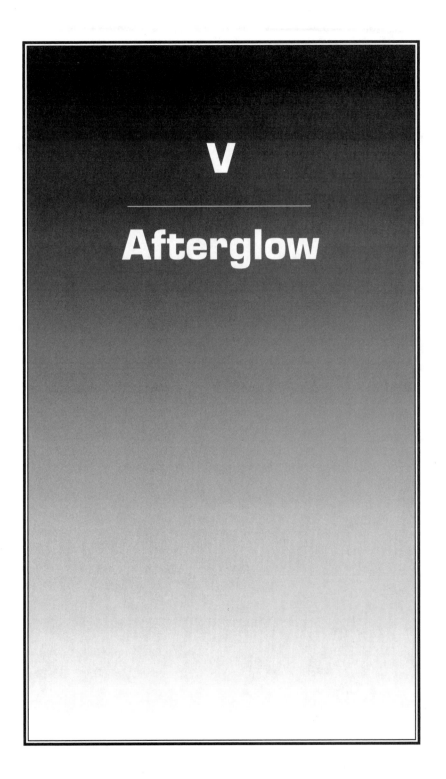

V

Afterglow

18
Up All Night with Socrates

BENJAMIN STEVENS

We all know about 'love at first sight.' At least we've heard of it, even if we haven't experienced it. But we've also heard—or, unfortunately, discovered first-hand!—that 'appearances can be deceiving'.

Being deceived isn't necessarily bad, if we want to be taken in. Something like a movie, for example, requires that we suspend our disbelief. We do this easily, even seemingly naturally: although we *know* that the movie isn't real, we're able to *pretend* that it is. When it comes to something like a movie, then, we happily let our *knowledge of fact* give way to our *desire for fiction*.

But a movie or other work of art is one thing. 'Love at first sight' would seem—at least at first glance!—to be quite another. If appearances can deceive, when we seem to fall straight into love, are we only deceiving ourselves? "How do we know when it's love?"

This is a philosophical question famously posed by the Eighties rock band Van Halen. And we needn't stop there. How do we know that there is such a thing as 'love' at all? The problem is that, as in our movie example, we may not be positioned rightly to see whether 'love' is a *fact* open to knowing or 'only' a desirable *fiction*. If 'love at first sight' is possibly only *fictional*, even a falsehood, is there such a thing as 'true love'? May the fictional, by definition not factual, nonetheless be 'true'? What, if anything, may wanting, desiring, or loving help us to learn—ultimately, most importantly—about 'truth'?

Questions like these have kept philosophers up all night for thousands of years. The ancient Greek philosopher Plato argued that we need to look for truth beyond the physical world because everything in the physical world is known through the senses, which are notoriously deceptive. Supposed truths of the physical world are attractive but fleeting and false. Plato therefore recommends ignoring the physical world, including physical bodies.

But many of us are interested in bodies! And not merely attracted to them, but more deeply and meaningfully desirous of them, wanting them in ways that involve our whole human being. *We love our lovers' bodies!* Can it be right, then, that 'loving wisdom' means *not* loving bodies? Is there really no bodily—loverly, sense-perceptual, sensual, even sexual—path to 'truth'?

Getting to Know You

Plato developed an elaborate metaphysics, a speculative model of the universe, centering on a theory of 'forms.' Forms are the originals of everything, open only to the intellect; while 'everything'—every object in the sense-perceptible world—is only an imitation of one or another form.

For example, Plato distinguishes a bed (!) from the thought of a bed and from the form of 'bed.' His point is that bodies in general, being things in the world, aren't forms. More pointedly, bodies change—as we know from personal experience! And anything that changes cannot be fully real. Since bodies are not fully real they cannot lead us to the truth.

Ancient Greek culture was highly erotic—from pornographic pottery to nude bath houses. Plato was not insensitive to such pleasures. He argues, however, that contemplation of the desirable human body should be only a first step on an ascent towards 'truth' that is ultimately not sense-perceptual but intellectual.

The irony is that Plato develops his anti-physical metaphysics in a series of dialogues—staged conversations between characters. Both the characters and the conversations were modeled on real life. Plato also founded a school for philosophy. The word "philosophy" comes from the Greek words for "love of wisdom." Lovers of wisdom would gather at Plato's school and seek the truth face-to-face with each other. So, it seems that, for Plato, truth requires at least a minimal interaction among bodies after all!

Even if bodies aren't 'really' real to Plato, they still seem somehow meaningful to him. And if they're important to Plato, then they are all the more important to Western philosophy more generally. It's been said, with little exaggeration, that the European philosophical tradition consists of a series of footnotes to Plato. It is possible, then, that a mainline of Western philosophy, in seeking so vehemently to deny any value to the body, has protested too much!

Trying to see how this foundational philosopher finds meaning in the human body, especially as the body is object of desire, will therefore take us a long way towards answering the crucial question of whether there is a bodily—loverly, sense-perceptual, sensual, even sexual—path to 'truth': whether, in other words, we who love our lovers' bodies are *therefore*, in a deeply meaningful way, *also* lovers of wisdom, 'philosophers'. For this, we don't need to propose an alternative metaphysics. It's enough to wonder whether there is something philosophically meaningful in the feeling that a lover can become 'our whole world'!

Is our feeling of living in that world, of loving a lover's body, 'real enough' to reveal any 'truth'?

A Flirtual Reality

In one dialogue, the *Phaedrus*, Plato sets his characters, Socrates and Phaedrus, along a riverbank under a tree whose spreading branches provide deep, cool shade from the hot Mediterranean sun. Could a more relaxed, more sensual setting be imagined? And *this* is where philosophy, in the form of an active and intimate unfolding of conversation, takes place: in the dappling shade, amidst the sound of the breeze and running water, two bodies reclining together on the warm and fragrant earth. . . .

For Plato, philosophy proceeds in response to, and in the context of, earthly beauty, which he imagines as imitating heavenly forms. And this gives us a clue to what matters most of all in philosophy, namely, ethics, or the question of how best to live. For Plato, this was the urgent human question, a matter of reason above all, overpowering our desires even if ostensibly in balance with them. Ethics is a question of the interaction between our human and animal natures. The former overtakes the latter, such that desire for bodies leads to intellectual or even spiritual experience of bodiless truth.

First of all, then, bodies are animal—and yet they are necessary for the intellectual or rational to take place. So the question arises—must it be that 'truth' comes when an erotic, desirous, or loverly feeling is *subordinated* to an intellectual one? It seems to me that there is evidence to the contrary in our own experience. It's tempting to suppose that Plato actually knew this and was not ultimately denying the body, but putting it off in some kind of tantric philosophical foreplay.

Philosophy or Phoreplay?

Phaedrus and Socrates aren't obviously lovers. They may not even seem particularly intimate, meeting as they do by chance and making no physical contact. Yet we may imagine that more intimate interaction is wished for by one or the other or both. Their conversation centers around the topic of rhetoric but touches on erotic love . . .

. . . and Plato is just getting going. Though the loverly aspects of his philosophy are a slow burn, he shows how philosophy can include intimacy aplenty: spiritual, emotional, and—be it sublimated or delicately symbolized—physical. So as we move on from *Phaedrus*, we move from flirtation to more proper foreplay!

Towards the end of the dialogue *Phaedo*, Socrates, who has been condemned to death for corrupting the youth with philosophy, is required according to ritual to cleanse himself before his execution. And so he takes a bath 'off-stage'. This may seem far from a loverly interest in the body, and indeed the ostensible philosophical point of the *Phaedo* is rather that the body, being mortal, is much less important than the soul, which may be immortal.

A longer look, however, reveals that bodies abound in this dialogue and that intimate attention to them runs deep. This is true not only of Socrates's body—what distinguishes a living body from a corpse? It is also true of the bodies of the people who talk with Socrates—what is different about being present for the philosophical inquiry, as opposed to hearing about it by proxy? As in the *Phaedrus*, so in the *Phaedo* the scene is carefully staged, with friends and a range of lovers or sexual partners all around, including Socrates's own wife and children.

Plato dismisses Socrates's family on the grounds that they would respond to his death with excessive emotion, which would be not only unseemly but also philosophically useless. It is as if Socrates, expecting eternal life with the divine, must guard against the interference of those who are not capable of the mystical assent of the mind.

Here, too, then, we may wonder whether philosophy is protesting too much or rather, in Plato's ironical mode, engaging in an oblique kind of foreplay. For the attention paid to bodies is of a particular sort. Despite the compelling intellectual power of Socrates's argument that the soul is immortal, the people he talks with are all moved by what they feel is the untimely end of his being in his body. They seem less interested in the content of Socrates's teaching than they are in continued contact with their teacher. Socrates's physical presence is clearly what has brought them all together.

In the same way, Socrates's resolve about his coming absence is precisely what is tearing them up inside: his sanguinity about his body's demise is more than they can stand. Plato repeatedly employs the metaphor of liquid measure. For example, the bath itself is either a bath as we would understand it, with water and soap, or a cleansing of the body with olive oil, effectuated by a smooth bronze scraper. This sensuous liquid image makes it seem as if everyone's invited to share the same drink, as if everyone foretastes the bitter poison hemlock Socrates is sentenced to drink.

But not everyone gets to take part. Socrates goes 'off-stage' for the bath, leaving the sight of the narrator as well as most of the other interlocutors. But he doesn't go alone: he takes a certain young man, Crito, with him. Thus, against the dialogue's argument that the mortal body matters infinitely less than the immortal soul, the bath—enticingly hidden from view—indicates a deep attention to the body and, no less, a deep and shared intimacy between the two men. There is something that Socrates and Crito are able to share in private that, at least so far as Plato is concerned, cannot be expressed in the public language of the dialogue. We are not told what they shared, but we may imagine. Whatever it was, being shared between the men at this most charged of moments, it was intimate. Having to do directly with Socrates's body, it was by definition sense-perceptual, by extension sensual. It was also emotional—mournful and deeply meaningful.

Was it sexual? Socrates seems to be famous for his abstinence, but mostly this reputation derives from his refusal to sleep with the beautiful and otherwise beguiling Alcibiades. Was his avoidance of sexual or physical contact more general, even total? Could he—would he—have acted differently at such a moment, at this last *bodily pleasurable* moment of his life? At that time, would any such physical intimacy really have stood in the way of philosophical 'truth'?

We may wonder. The clear separation of Socrates and Crito from all the others may mean that here, at this last moment, bodily contact became, as it is expressly in the description of other dialogues, a step towards the truth: a touch, a gentle cleansing, a kiss, or sex as such, whatever its mode.

A Loverly Intimacy?

As in *Phaedo*, so in *Phaedrus* it is at least not clear whether what we see traced in conversation was, in fact, something more: whether the two main interlocutors were also, or wished to be, lovers. If not the remarkably abstemious Socrates, then Crito may have been open to a more physical intimacy. He may even have sought it out. Already in the *Phaedo,* Crito's special feeling for the master is marked by intimate gestures: he is implicitly first to cry when Socrates drinks the poison hemlock, and is explicitly the one who, after the death, closes Socrates's mouth and eyes.

Such small, meaningful gestures are also found in the dialogue named after him. Taking place in the earliest morning and set before the *Phaedo*, the *Crito* opens with Crito watching the condemned Socrates sleep peacefully. The dialogue begins with Socrates's first words upon waking. He asks Crito about the time of day, how long he's been sitting there, indeed what he's doing there. It is just before dawn. Crito expresses amazement at Socrates's apparent peace. He himself is too disturbed with grief to sleep, and we may imagine him having sat awake to watch Socrates for quite a while. Clearly it wasn't nearly long enough.

We are therefore given to infer that there has been an extended period of silence, marked perhaps by the sounds of the waking city as well as by the light of the rising sun. By definition, then, there can have been no conversation, but Crito's fraught explanation makes clear that the time spent thus, in silence, was nonetheless very much worth his while as a kind of contemplative act that seems to be *both* loverly *and* philosophical. Crito sought to come closer to understanding Socrates's equanimity in the face of extraordinary adversity.

Crito has not completely succeeded in coming to such an understanding. In addition to wishing, simply, to see Socrates a while longer, he pleads with Socrates to let Crito break him out of jail and into a longer life in exile away from Athens. Socrates refuses: his body being less important to him than his soul, he must subject it even to an unjust law, since the laws in aggregate have made his life possible.

This argument doesn't offer Crito much, if any, consolation. In the end, he will still feel bereft of his most-beloved companion. But we may nonetheless learn something from it. In Socrates's view, Athens hasn't truly mastered him and can't, for that matter, truly take him from Crito. Socrates knows himself, and so knows that what Crito loves is more than, and other than, his body. No matter that I must die, Socrates argues, for my death is surpassed by what we have shared in life.

An Anti-Climactic Climax?

For Plato to have focused so much attention on the body in its final moments is perhaps understandable. In the *Phaedo*, he portrays Socrates claiming that philosophy itself is a preparation for death. It must therefore be able to deal with death meaningfully, as the moment when the soul may ascend towards 'truth'. But is the body, even Socrates's body, really only a means to that end?

Plato gives his most direct answers to this question in a dialogue called the *Symposium*. The word 'symposium' comes from the Greek words for 'drinking together'. Plato is writing about a drinking party with a twist: the participants, all but one of whom are badly hung over, agree to moderate their drinking so as to maintain a higher level of conversation. The topic is competing definitions of 'love', or more precisely competing ways of praising Love as a divinity.

The conversation is enhanced by the setting: the intimately close and sensually suggestive confines of a dining room. It is a boisterous celebration (one of the participants has taken first place in a playwriting competition). There is drinking, of course, as well as eating. But there's also the question of who is to lie next to whom (it was customary to eat and drink while lying on large couches), and the closely-related question of who is—or could be—whose lover.

The men arrange themselves in pairs, most in sexual partnerships. Classical Athenian culture approved male-male homoerotic relationships. These relationships typically took place between an older lover and a younger initiate. The latter was supposed to inspire the former to transform his feeling of sexual desire (*eros*) into longer-lasting friendship (*philia*) and deepened commitment to the society. Amidst flickering torchlight—a variation on the *Phaedrus*'s setting of dappled shade—all is sensual *and therefore* philosophical: the ultimate question being what if any 'truth' may be known through, not despite, such physical and sense-perceptual relations.

In this charged setting, Socrates and his body are central. There is some friendly bickering over who gets to recline next to him. Everyone knows that this man never gets drunk, no matter how much he drinks. Nor does he ever get sexually overheated. And at the very end of the dialogue, after all has been said and very little done, a surprisingly spry, dry, and chaste Socrates leaves his fellow symposiasts behind . . . *to go to the gymnasium*! In Greek, '*gymn*asium' means the 'place of *naked* exercise'—a disciplined idealization of the body, including wrestling while glistening with olive oil.

At such a moment—a very different kind of 'morning after' than that which opens the *Crito*—we may be forgiven for thinking that Plato is promoting physical, even sensual pleasures as a means to intellectual pursuits. Such a cheeky philosophy, I think, *wants* us to wonder whether our lovers' bodies may be, not merely sense-perceptual means to a philosophical end, but fully philosophical ends in themselves!

If only Socrates weren't so maddeningly, enticingly unusual! First, he is revealed to have refused the advances of Alcibiades, the most attractive young man in Athens. Although they once lay next to each other all night, and although Alcibiades—as he reports it—mustered his flustering best, Socrates nonetheless remained staunchly resistant. We may sympathize with Alcibiades's surprise. Socrates simply *didn't*, while Alcibiades desired and desires still that maddening *and physically unattractive* man!

Second, then, Socrates is revealed to be stunningly attractive *within*. Pug-nosed and pudgy, a little rumpled, Socrates nonetheless captivates. Just look inside, says Alcibiades (who, by now, is feverishly drunk), and you'll see a "golden Silenus." That description is complicated, but may be boiled down to meaning that Socrates could teach even the god Dionysus, the god of wine, a thing or two about intoxication. Despite his seemingly unattractive body, Socrates is intoxicating!

The image of Socrates must confirm the well known truth that 'appearances can be deceiving.' There's more to a lover than what the eyes may desire, what we may at first sight mistake for love. The heart wants what the heart wants or—this being Alcibiades—the part wants what the part wants? But the best lovers let us feel our desire for their bodies as desire for *them* and, in extension, for deeper meanings: just possibly for 'truth'.

Up All Night with Socrates?

Alcibiades was able to describe Socrates's unusual status, but did he really learn anything from it? History suggests he did not. (Because of him, Athens suffered grievously in its war against Sparta.) So we may wonder, *Might* he have learned more—anything at all—from Socrates had the older man accepted his advances and taken him on as a lover? Or is there ever true love in a world of falsehood?

These questions don't have easy answers. Nor should they, for they are questions we should all be allowed to pursue. Plato's suggestion is that we best do this not alone but, as even the abstemious Socrates did, in close contact with others, and with our minds open to the possibility that the body may indeed lead us to 'truth'.

19

Socrates the Seducer

CHELSEA C. HARRY

An old man watches a young lad from afar. The boy plays happily in a sandbox. The old man is attracted to the boy, but something stops him from saying anything. A strong desire is met with caution, and a flame has to be set on a back burner. In the future, perhaps, the two will meet again.

*   *   *   *   *

The name "Socrates" elicits a sense of reverence. Socrates was executed by a democratic state because he advanced "dangerous" ideas. He was famous for pushing people to question their beliefs beyond the comfort zone. While he didn't write any treatises himself, he is featured as a key participant in most of Plato's dialogues. Plato, who was Socrates's most famous follower, portrayed Socrates as a strong-minded critical thinker, revered among other philosophers for having as much moral conviction as intellectual prowess.

We don't picture Socrates as a Don Juan. In a dialogue called the *Phaedo*, Plato shows Socrates shooing his wife away for being overly emotional, and choosing instead to spend his last couple of hours before execution discussing philosophy with friends. Plato's Socrates is the epitome of steadfast rationality. He advocates a life of moderation and encourages friends to search for truth among its many semblances in life.

On the other hand, there is a dialogue called the *Alcibiades I* that presents a very different picture. It is not traditionally included in Plato's collected works because the stuffy old scholars who put such collections together are reluctant to admit that he really wrote it. Regardless of whether or not Plato really wrote it, we still glean important lessons from it, just as we do from Shakespeare's unauthenticated plays. The *Alcibiades I* combines the usual Platonic argument structure with something not found in Plato's other works. Namely, Socrates is not just trying to get his opponent, Alcibiades, to take up philosophy, he is trying also to get him into bed.

Is it any wonder that the *Alcibiades I* has been at certain times in history the most popular of the dialogues? The conversation between Socrates and Alcibiades is highly erotic; it is a game of cat and mouse, and we all want to know if Socrates will get the guy in the end. Not only this, but we read, riveted, as Socrates shows off his skills for seduction. Just how good are these skills?

Seduction Tip #1: Make It about Your Beloved, Not about You

Alcibiades was not only a man of great potential; he was a stud. Blessed with both beauty and strength, he was truly the Athenian "golden boy." Since Socrates, in contrast, was a bit of a troll, not to mention that he was much older than Alcibiades, the challenge ahead of him was significant.

The *Alcibiades I* purportedly records the first ever conversation between Socrates and Alcibiades. In it, Socrates admits to having loved Alcibiades for a long time. This is Socrates's first and maybe only chance to win Alcibiades's heart. Being at a disadvantage, Socrates has to be crafty. He begins by showering Alcibiades with compliments and praise. Once he has Alcibiades's attention, he offers to help his Adonis-like friend to achieve his political ambitions. Socrates goes so far as to insist that sticking with him is necessary for any future success. Socrates plays to Alcibiades's desire for power, telling him that he alone can help him achieve his aspirations for greatness.

While Socrates's approach is over the top, it is at the same time indirect. He makes one goal obvious while another goal rests just under the surface. Socrates doesn't come right out and declare his own desire for Alcibiades. Instead, he offers his services and commits to proving that he can deliver. In telling Alcibiades that he has something that Alcibiades wants, he de-emphasizes what he himself wants, portraying himself as an asset to Alcibiades's career.

This effectually reverses the dynamic. In portraying himself as committed to the seducee's goals, the seducer transforms himself into an object of desire. As long as the beloved "bites," the seducer has something to work with. With his foot in the door, the seducer no longer needs to appear physically desirable to his beloved. The beloved is willing to talk to the seducer a bit longer. This makes what might have been an uphill, if not impossible, battle into something more manageable.

So, for the seducer, the first objective is engagement. Everyone has their advantages and disadvantages. As a seducer, you must identify your strongest advantage and use it to distract from your disadvantages. Once you have established a relationship based on this advantage, you will have a chance to state your true intentions and/or to make a move.

Seduction Tip #2: Find a Hook to Draw Your Beloved into a Conversation

Socrates was famous for having a personal daemon. In ancient Greece, the *daemon* was believed to be a spirit who "spoke" to a person, preventing him from making mistakes. At times, the word is even interchanged with the Greek word, "*theos,*" meaning God. Socrates invokes his *daemon* a number of times when talking to Alcibiades, first explaining how the *daemon* prevented Socrates from interacting with Alcibiades when Alcibiades was a wee one and then claiming that the *daemon* now permits their conversation.

Talking about the *daemon* serves two functions for Socrates, as seducer. On the one hand, it takes responsibility off of Socrates for any failed attempts at seduction from the past. On the other hand, it lends support to Socrates's current project. If the spirit has encouraged their present meeting, then perhaps Alcibiades should give Socrates a chance. In any case, it is safe to say that Socrates's "name dropping" of the *daemon* early on in his meeting with Alcibiades serves as a sort of hook, which prompts Alcibiades to give Socrates a chance.

Socrates admits to being somewhat of a voyeur, to watching Alcibiades when he was a young boy, for example, while he played in a sandbox. As it turns out, Alcibiades was aware all along that Socrates used to follow him around. Such a situation may have been creepy and altogether off-putting were it not for the *daemon*. In admiring Alcibiades from afar, Socrates was merely following the dictate of the *daemon*. The admiration is a sign of Alcibiades's future greatness, not an old man's infatuation. It is further proof that Socrates is crucial to Alcibiades's illustrious future.

In our society, Socrates's actions might land on an episode of *To Catch a Predator,* daemon or no daemon! In ancient Greek society, however, pederasty was an accepted and even celebrated practice. Older, wiser, usually married, men would court and often engage in sexual relationships with younger, up-and-coming men. Socrates goes so far as to cite his predatory habits as one of his *merits*: he is the oldest and most dedicated of Alcibiades's lovers. And this strategy works, allowing Alcibiades to conclude that he had underestimated Socrates.

Modern day seducers, therefore, take note. While staying away from anyone underage, do try to tap into the child in your beloved. Children love gimmicks and there is no stronger gimmick than a supernatural one. If you can show your beloved that your union was somehow written in the stars or divinely ordained, then you are well on your way.

Seduction Tip #3: Convince Your Beloved that He Has a Lack that Only You Can Fill

Alcibiades is used to getting a great deal of positive attention, and he has had success in gaining popularity among Athenians. In fact, when Socrates speaks to him in this dialogue, Alcibiades is just days away from being elected to the Assembly. Thus, it seems that Alcibiades has things figured out. With good looks, money, smarts, and rising popularity, why would he need Socrates?

Socrates tells Alcibiades that he is not going to give a long speech, asserting reasons why Alcibiades needs him. As a politician, this would be the type of instruction Alcibiades would have been used to. Socrates, on the other hand, just wants to ask Alcibiades some questions. Since this seems harmless enough to Alcibiades, he agrees.

And so, Socrates puts his famous "Socratic Method" to work. Socrates asks Alcibiades whether he really knows anything.

After a bit of back and forth, Alcibiades eventually admits that one only knows what he has been taught or what he has discovered. On this reasoning, then, Socrates is able to show that Alcibiades really doesn't know very much. After all, Alcibiades has been schooled in a limited number of subjects at his young age—he is barely twenty—and up until this point has learned nothing more than writing, harping, and wrestling. Socrates concludes that Alcibiades lacks knowledge of the most important thing of all, namely, what justice is. And where will Alcibiades go to gain such important knowledge if not to an experienced philosopher such as Socrates himself?

At this point in the dialogue, Socrates's soft touch turns firm. Alcibiades has a serious lack of knowledge, something that must be remedied if he is to be a good statesman. Shame on you, Alcibiades, for basing your ambitions on stupidity and ignorance! It seems like this would be a hard blow for Alcibiades to take, but Socrates at the same time excuses Alcibiades by acknowledging that everyone else in his profession has the same deficiency. Taking up with Socrates will put Alcibiades at an advantage over his rivals.

There is a point at which the modern-day seducer has to speak honestly about the lack he is going to help fill. When dealing with self-confident and successful people, it's almost impossible to hint at the ways they might better themselves. Instead, you have to come right out and state what others see as obvious. Nobody is perfect, so there has to be something about your beloved that needs fine-tuning. Figure out what that is and expose it!

Seduction Tip #4: Do Not Completely Crush Your Beloved's Confidence

Alcibiades is used to thinking he's special, and so too, hearing from others how gifted he is and how much potential he has. As seducer, however, Socrates has had to show Alcibiades that there is something he still lacks. If Alcibiades lacks nothing, then he certainly has no need for Socrates. Presumably, then, successful seduction hinges on the seducer's abilities both to expose this lack and to tempt the beloved with the prospect of overcoming whatever deficiency exists.

Showing anyone, let alone a self-confident and successful individual, what he isn't good at is a challenge. No one likes to be told that he is "not good enough," and there is always the threat of offending the person or turning him off. In order to prevent this from happening, the seducer has to string along the beloved with some well-placed compliments, acknowledging that the beloved is talented and, indeed, beloved. This prevents the beloved from coming to feel worthless, or from coming to think that the seducer is a total jerk.

Socrates shines when it comes to this technique. Without coming out and saying anything directly, he shows Alcibiades that his talents are not going unnoticed. Thus, he keeps Alcibiades interested in the conversation. An example of this comes at a strategic point. While exposing the gaps in Alcibiades's knowledge, he manages to slip in the caveat that it is in line with Alcibiades's *kalos*, or beauty, to work things through with Socrates.

Just when it seems that Alcibiades may not have the wherewithal to withstand Socrates's questioning—he begins answering "I don't understand" instead of making confident retorts. Socrates implies that it is in accord with Alcibiades's good nature to be able not only to question what he knows but to come out the stronger for learning to know more and to argue better. So, Socrates is able to advance the idea that there is a way—with his help—that Alcibiades can obtain the knowledge he lacks, and thus can surpass his political competition.

As a seducer, you must take Socrates's cue here, occasionally slipping in words or phrases to flatter your beloved. This technique can come off naturally, coyly affirming your beloved's good looks, intelligence, style, or personality without focusing too much or for too much time on the compliment.

Seduction Tip #5: Accentuate the Positive!

The result of all this is that Alcibiades ends up trusting Socrates. He realizes the ways it could benefit him professionally to keep Socrates around as friend and counsel, but there has not yet been any real talk of personal relations. Socrates must now make his move to secure his intended prize.

It is no use dwelling further on Socrates's garish features. Socrates surely doesn't. Instead, as his conversation with

Alcibiades winds down, he accentuates his best asset in an effort to win Alcibiades's affection. What is Socrates's best asset, you wonder? Why, his soul, of course! This is the point at which Socrates argues that a person's true identity has nothing to do with his body. The body is only a person's tool to get things done. Who and what a person really *is*, depends entirely on his soul.

In an effort to convince Alcibiades of this, Socrates barrages him with a number of analogies. Just as the harpist is different from the harp, the cutter is different from the cutting tool, and so too, the man must be different from the body parts he uses to complete different tasks: he must be different from his body. If he is not his body, nor can he be a combination of his body and soul. Therefore, reasons Socrates, man must be his soul. Alcibiades readily concurs.

Masterfully, then, Socrates turns the conversation to Alcibiades's body. Clearly, he argues, those who love Alcibiades's body do not love Alcibiades; they love his tool. The person who loves bodies instead of souls, cannot be a longtime lover. Bodily beauty fades and when this happens, the lover's love of the body will likewise disappear. On the other hand, those who love souls are longtime lovers. Not only does the beauty of souls not fade, there is a good chance that it amplifies over time. Thus, the lover who loves souls has a love that will not expire.

I'm sure you know where this is going. Socrates's final step is obvious. He tells Alcibiades that the reason he has stuck around all of these years (let's not forget the sandbox incident) is because he is the only one who truly loves Alcibiades. He promises to stick around for the long haul, not forsaking Alcibiades when good looks have worn away.

Socrates surely hopes that Alcibiades will find it within himself to love Socrates's soul in return. But, this is never directly stated. Instead, Socrates begins to discuss the importance of cultivating Alcibiades's resistance to the pressures he will face in the Assembly as he gains popularity among the Athenian people. In particular, Socrates fears that Alcibiades will be promptly seduced by *their* love of him, appreciating the way the many fawn over his good looks and charm, and will forget what he has agreed to with regard to soul-loving.

In order to prevent this, Alcibiades must follow the mandate of the Delphic Oracle to "Know Thyself." This Oracle was believed since pre-historic times to receive inspiration from the God, Apollo. Thus, she was considered to have God-like wisdom and was consulted before all major events and for personal advice. As one might suppose, for Socrates, knowing oneself means knowing one's soul—practicing temperance, courage, and wisdom instead of allowing oneself to be swindled by physical beauty or rhetoric.

Everyone has something about them that is special, something to accentuate. Likewise, most of us have something about us that we wish we could change. If the modern-day seducer is perfect, he probably doesn't have to do much seducing. After all, anything that needs selling is something that the potential buyer does not yet know he wants. Take heed, modern-day seducer, and put forth your best asset! It may just be the one thing your beloved never knew he wanted, or needed.

As the dialogue closes, Alcibiades is putty in Socrates's hand. He vows to be Socrates's personal attendant. In response, Socrates declares victory, comparing his love for Alcibiades to a stork—it established itself within Alcibiades and has now "flown back" to Socrates. This is to say, it has been returned.

*   *   *   *   *

It can't be denied that the *Alcibiades I* is a pretty steamy dialogue. Socrates uses his well-known skills in persuasion to seduce his beloved, Alcibiades, into reciprocating desire. It combines the virtuous "love of wisdom" with something we can all relate to—loving someone else and wanting that love to be returned. Certainly, we won't take home all of Socrates's techniques (predation is not cool, kids!), but as we have seen, there are at least a few that deserve a place in any good seducer's playbook!

20
The Gift

Katarina Majerhold

Where love is, no room is too small.

—The Talmud

Who makes the best lover? Socrates once held a raucous drinking party at which he posed this question. Various Athenian notables were present and they all offered different answers, reflecting every color of the rainbow. The intrepid reporter Plato recorded it all for posterity in a work called the *Symposium*.

Throughout history, many readers have found their answer to our question in one or another of the *Symposium*'s theories, but we have to ask whether even three of its best might be missing something.

Un-break My Heart

According to the playwright Aristophanes, human beings were originally created with two faces and four arms and legs. We lived very happily as these double creatures until our creator, Zeus, cut us in half due to our arrogance and disobedience. Since then, we have roamed the earth, lonely and forlorn without our missing halves. Only Eros, the God of love, can help us find them.

Aristophanes also contends that the original double-humans had three genders: male (with two male halves), female (with two female halves), and androgynous (with one male and one female half). Males descended from the sun, females from the earth, and those who were androgynous

207

descended from the moon. Eros must unite two men in order to restore the male gender, two women in order to restore the female gender, and a man with a woman to restore the androgynous gender.

However, making us complete again is not easy. When Zeus first started cutting the original human beings in half, he cut them in such a way that all they could do when they reunited was kiss and hug. These poor creatures soon died from despair. So, in a rare display of mercy, Zeus began giving each half-human a set of sexual organs. They enable us to merge with our other halves, at least for a little while, releasing us from the unbearable tension of desire. This is why sex is such a powerful governing influence for human beings and rules our lives with absolute sovereignty.

Although it paints a very beautiful picture, Aristophanes's account of true love suffers from two significant problems.

First, regardless of how lovers physically enter into each other, they remain two persons—the full merger is impossible. This suggests that not even true love can bring true happiness, which is wrong, we hope!

Second, how do we explain such a high divorce rate, especially when divorce so often occurs after the couple has raised a family together? It seems that in such situations, erotic desire disappears because the initial movement to create a union was completed. The same goes for couples who split up after reaching other milestones, such as building a house, establishing a business, or creating a work of art. People do not stay in one place with one passion. The very notion of there being a single right other half for each of us is therefore too simple. It reduces the lover to a pure functionality, reproductivity, while disregarding other dimensions.

Don't Stand So Close to Me

Opposing Aristophanes's account, Socrates himself offers an interesting alternative. In his view, true love is ultimately the relationship between a philosopher (someone seeking wisdom) and the wisdom he seeks. The object of erotic desire is not actually another person at all but something immaterial that gives us an anchor within ourselves. In this way, our passion and happiness does not depend on our lover but on our ability to gain wisdom and thus become self-sufficient.

For Socrates, this implies that couples always consist of a teacher, who is older and wiser, and a student, who is younger and ignorant. Neither of the lovers desires the other; they both desire to achieve the greatest knowledge—with one another's help. Their relationship is based on strict roles: the older instructs while the younger inspires the instruction.

The greatest knowledge, which all human beings long for, concerns three things we do not possess: beauty, goodness, and truth. Eros itself is neither beautiful nor ugly, neither good nor bad, neither wise nor foolish, neither god nor mortal. Eros is something neutral in the middle. He is a great "daemon," or intermediate power, who conveys to the gods the prayers of men, and to men the commands of the gods. As something in between, love is always a process, always unfolding—perpetual movement towards fulfilment.

The lover is a philosopher because his attainment of truth, beauty, and goodness constitutes his supreme happiness. Ultimately, true love is the desire for this happiness. And when something makes us happy we do not want to lose it, we want to keep it forever. In fact, it would be difficult to be happy while knowing our happiness was about to disappear. So, in our yearning for possession of the greatest knowledge, we desire immortality.

We witness our desire for immortality most obviously in our urge to reproduce. But we also see it in other urges, such as in the quest for fame and in artistic creativity.

Socrates advises that he who would seek wisdom should begin by loving one fair form, and then many, and then proceed by learning the connection between them. From beautiful bodies he should advance to beautiful minds, and the beauty of laws and institutions, until he perceives that all beauty is of one kindred. From institutions he should move on to the sciences, until at last he beholds the vision of a single science of universal beauty. Then he will behold the everlasting nature which is the cause of all, and will be near his goal. In his contemplation of that supreme being of love he will behold beauty, goodness, and truth, not with his bodily eye, but with the "eye of the mind." The vision will inspire virtue and wisdom.

At this stage, the lover is dependent neither on the beloved nor on the outside world. No one will ever be able to exploit, betray, surprise, or dump him. His love is now freed from pain, moodiness, and instability because his beloved (immortal beauty, goodness, and truth) is always available, always stable and always with(in) him. He has become divine.

Socrates kept his promise to provide a theory in which lovers are not dependent on one other, thereby avoiding Aristophanes's mistakes. The relationship he delivers, however, begins to look disturbingly unequal. While the "teacher" achieves the all-important vision, the "student" cannot do so unless he grows into the role of teacher himself. If and when that happens, however, we lose the delicate balance of instruction-inspiration, developing a potential conflict between two instructors instead.

In practice, this arrangement can also make for an exploitative situation. One can't help but think of the older, wealthy man choosing a woman twenty years younger than him. She depends on his knowledge, connections, and fortune to help her achieve what she desires. He, in exchange, enjoys her youthful beauty and naivety. He may enjoy wielding power over her to such an extent that he hinders her progress toward independence. Treating someone as a means to an end, even if that end is itself noble, represents a selfish attitude that cannot be suitable for lovers.

Only You

The politician Alcibiades, disagreeing with Socrates, presents yet another intriguing account of love in the *Symposium*. Alcibiades was a stunningly beautiful and desirable man. An acclaimed war hero, he had won many prestigious awards, and was universally admired in Athens. He could have just about any lover he chose. Astonishingly, he chose Socrates.

He announces to the revellers at the dinner party that he fell in love with Socrates because Socrates is an enchanting speaker who ravishes the soul and changes the hearts of men. Alcibiades was surprised to find that beneath Socrates's old and unattractive appearance lay the greatest treasure of all. This made him compare Socrates to Marsyas the great flute-player. For Socrates produced the same effect with his voice as Marsyas produced with his flute. He used the commonest words as the outward mask of the most divine truths.

Alcibiades also compares Socrates to the busts of the great sculptor Silenus. They portray people with pipes and flutes in their mouths but they are made to open in the middle, and have images of gods inside them. To Alcibiades, the words of Socrates are divine.

Alcibiades was irresistibly drawn to something very unique he saw only in Socrates. In so doing, he demonstrates a theory of love that explains why we fall in love with one person instead of another. The twentieth-century French philosopher and psychiatrist Jacques Lacan calls this uniqueness "agalma."

According to Lacan, romantic desire points towards a peculiar feature which makes a certain person stand out of the crowd, seeming to exceed all others. This is why, of all the lovers Alcibiades ever pursued, Socrates is the only one he considered to be worthy. Lacan adds, however, that the agalma is actually a subjective projection not reflecting something real in the person. And this explains Socrates's mysterious reply to Alcibiades invitation to become his lover—he said, "Look again, and see if you are deceived in me."

So we see that Alcibides fell in love because he saw something unique in Socrates—treasures hidden from the eyes that can be found only if you go deeper into the person—treasures of words and thoughts that help you to get to know yourself. Alcibiades says that upon first meeting Socrates, he felt as though he had been bitten by something in the most sensitive spot where it hurts the most. Socrates awakened in him the uncomfortable awareness that he ought not to live as he was, neglecting the improvement of his own soul. Discovering your true self gives you the greatest self-satisfaction and happiness. At the same time, it shows you how to become a better person and help others.

Of course, Socrates devoted his life to this mission. He called it "midwifery"—helping others bring to light the wisdom that was all along within themselves. It doesn't matter how you look, how successful you are, how popular, or how important. What matters is striving to be a good person who is happy and free, knowing yourself and helping others.

The problem with Alcibiades's account of love—as Socrates, who never fell for Alcibiades, points out—is that it is more imagined than real. The man who has everything hears of a new computer or jet airplane unlike any other that has existed before, and he decides that he must have it. He infuses it with the ability to solve all of his problems. And yet, somehow, when he finally has it, it becomes just another conquest.

No doubt a great part of Alcibiades's obsession with Socrates actually hinged on the fact that Socrates was the one person in Athens who had the nerve to say 'no' to him. Alcibiades could have anyone—anyone except Socrates. Socrates was therefore the final conquest, so completely enticing precisely because he lay just beyond reach.

The Gift

While I find each of the three accounts of love deeply insightful, I think that they are all missing something. They all presuppose that a romantic relationship should bring a person something they have been looking for. In so doing, they conceive of the lover as a shopper going to the market.

When we go shopping, we have a list of the things that we want and need. We browse through the available products, and we buy the ones that we believe will meet our requirements. We make a predictable transaction, an exchange designed to be mutually satisfactory to the buyer and the seller.

I propose that such a pragmatic approach will always undermine the true nature of love. A lover cannot be regarded as some kind of acquisition. Although the three accounts of love we surveyed were very different, they each suffered from this misconception. For Aristophanes, we must acquire our missing half, for Socrates, we must acquire a student to inspire our intellectual assent, and for Alcibiades, we must acquire the one thing no one else has. In all of these perspectives, the lover becomes a kind of burden to be evaluated, rather than spontaneously experienced. While such a deliberate approach may result in a relationship of some kind, it will not result in true love. True love must be experience on its own, without any preconceived expectations.

A lover need not be beautiful, knowledgeable, of a certain race, social status, or level of success to be worthy of love. As a child you are loved no matter who you are—how you look, how you walk, how you talk, with deformities or without. It is enough that you just are and the other just is. This is the primal model for all true love, including romantic passion.

So the necessary mindset of the lover is to be oneself and to let the other be him- or herself. Love flows everywhere and between everyone. Only a state of mind that is kind, all-embracing, accepting, understanding, and humble can be called love. Another person can only be truly valued and cherished when imperfections are disregarded. We are all imperfect. Imperfect beings are needy, dependent, fragile, vulnerable, and mortal. We all need love to feel complete and worthy of existing. In the end, love is as essential as breathing.

As adults, we have many obligations, responsibilities, and tasks to perform. As a result, it is difficult not to see everything in pragmatic terms. But true love can exist only for its own sake. It does not exclude, bargain, exploit, or possess. If you can achieve this kind of state, then you can love anybody and can be loved by anybody. But, of course, no one can fully achieve it. The thrill of romantic passion is being able to achieve it to some degree. The "magic" or "mystery" occurs exactly at that moment when our preoccupation with ourselves and our own agenda shifts and we dare to embark on a completely new adventure.

And this is the moment that enables us to truly see, hear, smell the other for the first time—to truly meet. The lovers stretch out their hands and they reach for each other, holding hands for the first time. Giving your lover what he needs and wishes means that you see him as the most beautiful and precious gift, regardless of how he is. This liberates him from his old ways and the two can now proceed to discovering new ways of being together. Love gives them wings to fly.

What makes the *Symposium* accounts so valuable is that they give us diverse images of what love can be. It can be finding your other half; it can be finding an inspiration for intellectual ascent; it can be finding the one thing no one else has. It can be any of these things and more. But it cannot be sought out as any one of those things. Rather, it must be received and appreciated for whatever it turns out to be.

By presenting various partial accounts of what love can be, the *Symposium* tells us that love is a gift. When you receive a precious gift you treat it with respect. It makes you feel grateful, and with gratitude comes happiness. Thus, our lovers are a source of happiness. To cherish them as they are and we must be ready to embrace them in their entirety. They will not be what we thought we were looking for!

21
Winnie the Pooh in Love

ADAM BARKMAN

> Piglet sidled up to Pooh from behind.
> "Pooh!" he whispered.
> "Yes, Piglet?"
> "Nothing," said Piglet, taking Pooh's paw.
> "I just wanted to be sure of you."
>
> A.A. MILNE, *Winnie-the-Pooh*

In *Winnie the Pooh* stories there are no lovers, yet there are plenty of persons who love. Or better, there is no discussion of what the Greeks call *eros* ("sexual love"), but plenty of discussion about *storgé* ("affection"), *philia* ("friendship"), and *agapé* ("sacrificial love").

If our subject is "lovers," it might seem odd for *Winnie the Pooh* stories to come up; however, this is strange only if we think of lovers as persons of *eros* and nothing more. Yet this assumption is mistaken since perfect lovers—and here I'm taking inspiration from *Pooh*—must have not only *eros* but also *storgé, philia,* and *agapé* as well. Moreover, the basis of these loves is, according to *Winnie the Pooh*, individuality.

In *A Very Merry Pooh Year*, Rabbit becomes so infuriated with Tigger, Piglet, Pooh, and Eeyore that he expresses his distaste for the characteristics that make them unique: Tigger's love for bouncing, Piglet's timidity, Pooh's love for honey, and Eeyore's pessimism. Out of love for Rabbit, the four try to change these defining features about themselves; however, when Rabbit finds himself in a bind and only the original characteristics of his friends can help him, he realizes that he doesn't want them to change. We learn that such defining features form the basis, and perhaps even one of the goals, of love in general. As Pooh wisely reflects, "If you weren't you, then we'd all be a little less we."

Storgé

Storgé or affection is the most basic of loves and can be enjoyed by virtually anyone. A young boy like Christopher Robin may share it with his inanimate teddy bear; two students in the same class may share it simply by being in the same class; and a man may feel this way toward his favourite sweater or brand of scotch. This kind of love can also be seen in the relationship between a woman and her pet and even between two pets, such as a dog and a cat raised together. Patriotism is a form of *storgé* since the criteria for this love is very simple: the object of this love must simply be familiar.

Storgé is the least discriminating and broadest of the loves. It's homely, comfortable, humble, and familial. We witness it when Kanga baths Roo, Pooh (mis)spells the word "hunny," Piglet puts an ornament on the Christmas tree, Tigger bounces through Rabbit's garden, and, tellingly, when Rabbit scolds Tigger for doing so. Even Gopher, who seems to have no particular interest in anyone but himself, is, in the Hundred Acre Wood, "good old Gopher." *Storgé* says with Pooh, "As long as we are apart together, we shall certainly be fine."

Lovers enjoy *storgé* when they watch their favourite shows together, when they take comfort in just knowing the other person is in the house, when they give each other pet names such as Sweetheart or Dear. The twentieth-century novelist C.S. Lewis, who wrote a book about the four loves, once said he felt that the fatness of Falstaff (the beloved buffoon in three of Shakespeare's plays) was more an essential quality than an accidental one. Though the metaphysics of this statement is questionable, the sentiment is indisputable. Likewise, Eeyore *ought to* be slouchy; Pooh *must* wear red T-shirts; Owl *has to* speak some Latin. In fact, women and wives, who I may safely say are less aesthetically demanding than men and husbands, may be quite satisfied with their man's bald head and hairy back just because of *storgé*. Aspects such as these, which we may find objectively distasteful, we may love—or better, *come to love* (since *storgé* takes time)—simply because they are ours.

But lovers must also be careful of perverse *storgé*. While affection is certainly natural and good in its proper place, a lover can't always be expected to feel it to the degree or at the exact time that the other lover would like. How many husbands complain that their wives aren't home to cook them a meal even when their wives may very properly deserve an outing with their friends? How many girlfriends complain about their boyfriends not wanting to talk on the phone 24/7? And how many lovers ridicule each other's interests simply because they don't include the other? *Storgé* is quite proper when it enjoys the individuality of a familiar presence, but it's distorted when it wants to subsume the other into one's self.

There is no selfishness, egotism or inordinate love of self in wanting to feel affection from those around one's self; but there is much selfishness in wanting to be loved by the familiar at all costs, even at the cost of robbing the other person of their freedom, identity and proper enjoyment of other things. Jealousy, then, isn't unique to *eros*, and the feeling of suffocation brought on by the other's sense of abandonment is a common feeling one has when *storgé* sours.

But suffocation isn't the only perversion of *storgé*. A couple may feel bored with each other because they have only *storgé* and none of the other types of loves. They may feel things are dull or uninteresting when *storgé*, the humble servant, is inordinately elevated to the king of the loves. Or again, rudeness is often a corrupt form of *storgé* because people, including lovers, often confuse being *comfortable* with being *uncouth*, being *casual* with being *free from manners*. This, of course, is another instance of *storgé* being elevated above its correct station.

The home may be a place where a man can take off his tie and a woman can remove her makeup, but the home is still under the sovereignty of goodness. Morality should never be disregarded—not only because it is good in and of itself, but also because proper comfort and relaxation *require* the higher love. We feel *storgé* when Tigger bounces Rabbit, not because jumping on people against their will is good, but because this familiar situation is tempered by Tigger's genuine good intent toward "Old Long Ears."

Philia

Philia or friendship is probably the least understood of the loves. "Friending" on Facebook is more an effect than the cause of a predominate confusion between *storgé* and *philia*. *Storgé* will be felt in some measure between all who spend enough time together. Colleagues at work ususaly share *storgé*, yet they need not share *philia*. Time spent together is not sufficient for friendship. Common loves and interests—not just common situations and circumstances—are what's needed.

And here's the test: If you think a person is your friend, try spending some years apart; then, meet up again and see how things go. If, after the initial excitement brought on by reminiscence, things become a bit uncomfortable and you find there is little for you to say to each other, then almost certainly you were simply acquaintances, colleagues, or comrades (even though you may have thought of the other person as one of your dearest friends). However, if you find that reflecting on "the good old days" to be fun but almost beside the point—if you feel a hunger to get on to talk about the things that the two of you have in common, in particular, ideas (be it of war, art, Dickens novels, video games, cooking, or whatever)—then there's a very good chance that you are, in fact, friends, for *philia* typically stands two people side-by-side, looking at a third object in common, while *storgé* has no interest in such third objects.

Because *eros* accompanies procreation and *storgé* is the glue of the family unit, these two loves are widely found among both animals and human beings. *Philia,* on the other hand, is rare among humans, and impossible for animals (except the fictional kind that can talk). The shared love of ideas that is central to *philia* requires rationality.

Especially important to philosophers is the fact that the shared love of ideas in no way implies that all ideas must be shared: *philia* may very properly develop between two people who disagree on nearly everything so long as they both share the same love of discussing the ideas in common. In fact, what makes the conversation better is precisely the differences of each in the group. Individuality is vital: one friend asserts what he thinks and the other does likewise and through the meeting of two different persons, a single beautiful friendship emerges. As Pooh tell us, "It's much more friendly with two."

. . . And perhaps three or four as well since *philia*, often unlike *storgé* and *eros*, is not jealous when another friend or two enters the mix. Thus, in *A Very Merry Pooh Year*, although Tigger, Rabbit, and Piglet enjoy discussing with each other their shared loves of Santa, theatre, and how to hunt heffalumps, they still feel impoverished when Pooh, the fourth member of their group, is missing. Each of the four is different, and yet all are united in a common love of the topic before them and have become richer—far richer than real animals—because of friendship. This is why the great ancient Greek philosopher Aristotle elevated *philia* to a position of honor in life's feast.

Lovers, then, ought to make friendship one of their aims. The old saying about finding a girlfriend who is a friend first is a good saying, yet the order may not be as important as the desire to see *eros* and *philia* meet. Although most couples begin their relationship with *eros* and end it with *storgé*, a couple that doesn't share some of the same interests, in particular, interests requiring discussion, remains all too animal. Since human beings aren't merely animals, this is often a sad state of affairs.

The lurking danger in *philia*.is when a friendship forms around an immoral interest. Convicted murderers Paul Bernardo and Karla Homolka may share many of the same interests, and thus can be seen as friends in one sense. However, in another, more profound sense, the ancient Roman writer Cicero is right when he declares, "There can be no friendship between evil men." Why? If the two do not love goodness and justice *first*—that is, if they don't desire to treat all people as they ought to be treated—then there's nothing to stop them mistreating each other. "A little consideration, a little thought for others," Pooh tells us, "makes all the difference"— in friendship, as in all the loves.

Eros

We can't conceive of perfect lovers without *eros* or sexual love. The phrase most associated with *eros* is "being in love," which may be thought of either in a very high minded fashion or in a very base, animalistic fashion. Both understandings of *eros* are correct, yet are ideally joined. A middle-aged couple that has become disenchanted with romance is impoverished since *eros* as romance ennobles the object of its desire. Songs are written, wars are fought, lives are given in the name of romance.

And so, couples need to keep romance alive—wives must not carelessly let their looks go, and husbands must keep things interesting. The adventure of seeking out the mystery in the other is something good in and of itself. How wonderful it is that a young man in love would *truly* rather kiss his beloved than have sex with her. Nevertheless, young people or people who remain wildly romantic can also commit the error of making *eros* a god, when, in fact, he is also part animal. Perfect sex requires the mind and imagination, to be sure, but it also requires other, more physical parts.

While *storgé* simply wants the other around, and *philia* stands friends side-by-side to discuss a common object, *eros* stands lovers face-to-face. And here is where we need some insight from *Pooh* again. In its perfect form, *eros* is tempered by justice such that it sees and wants the other to be his or her true self. Individuality is the key to proper *eros* since the lover wants to go on admiring the splendor of the other, especially in his or her physical form. True *eros* avows, "I would have you above any other." Of course, this ought to mean "I would have you above any other *person*" since *eros* can only love truly when it loves justice first. We may admire Romeo and Juliet's passion for each other, yet it is unjust to commit suicide out of despair.

Though a man and the woman must remain themselves in order for their *eros* to be true, they must also become one. This is a great mystery that must not be perverted. Perverse *eros* sees oneness as the dissolution of the other's individuality into the self. It desires only the pleasures the other can provide—a feeling of sexual excitement and release. This is why a husband may cheat on his wife with a woman (or the computer image of a woman) who is less attractive than her.

The union of the two individuals in *eros* is proper when each, loving justice above all, elevates the other as persons equal to, or above, themselves. Moreover, because each respects the individuality of the other, this relationship is freely entered into and the cage, so to speak, remains open. Of course, perfect lovers never fly out or, rather, they never fly out alone, since they want to be together. They want *each other* and they want each other *forever*. They see their monogamy as divine.

While this relationship ought to be freely entered into and the individuality of the other must be respected at all times, there is no sense, in *eros*, that the lovers must in *everything* be thought of as equals. They are equals as rational souls and persons, but not as gendered beings. Chivalric knights very properly lay down their lives for their ladies, and their ladies, very properly, receive this. Women want a champion— not just a man—who will shelter them when the storms of life are too much. None of this, of course, is to say that a woman can't rescue a man or that a man can't find comfort in a woman's arms; but such moments are the exception, not the rule.

Women rightly like a man who can talk about his feelings, but none desire a man who cries at the slightest hardship. This is part of the truth in the old saying "girls love bad boys."c If the individuality of persons matter, then the gender differences of each matter as well. Only a mistaken understanding of gender as a social construction rather than a given, and justice as equality, rather than as treating each as they ought to be treated, would say otherwise. Even in *Pooh*, the hierarchical differences, not of gender, but of intelligence, physical strength and so on matter very much to the relationships between the individuals: Owl is *wiser* than Pooh; Tigger can bounce *higher* than Piglet; and Gopher digs *better* than Rabbit. They properly delight in this, as do we.

Agapé

Even more than *philia*, *agapé*, or sacrificial love, requires rationality. A doe may sacrifice herself for her fawn but she does so out of instinct and *storgé*. Bull elephants may fight to the death for a mate, but they do so out of bare *eros*. *Agapé* completes each of these loves and *philia* as well. None of the loves can be perfect without *agapé*, and so perfect lovers simply cannot *be* without understanding and implementing this love. Good lovers are, first and foremost, good people.

In its purest form, *agapé* is a love that values the other more than is required. It goes so far as to *risk* itself for another. Making itself vulnerable in this way, it can easily be hurt. That is what Pooh means when he says, "Some people care too much; I think it's called love."

Because of the costly nature of *agapé*, some philosophers have failed to see its value. For example, the ancient Greek philosopher Epicurus thought it foolishness to risk being hurt, and the Buddha taught that enlightenment requires extinguishing all desires that cause suffering. Nevertheless, most great thinkers throughout history have sided with Pooh on the importance of *agapé*—even Mahayana Buddhists quickly found the Buddha's dethronement of this love too rash.

If justice loves each thing as it ought to be loved, then *agapé* perfects this: it loves each thing *more* than it ought to be loved. Christianity illustrates the point. Justice demanded that Adam love Eve more than the animals and the rest of nature, but less than God (lovers take note). Adam could have acted unjustly by either loving an animal equal to, or more than, his wife (a greater thing), or by loving her equal to, or more than, God (the greatest person). Now, when I say that *agapé* loves each thing "*more* than it ought to," I do not mean that *agapé* contradicts justice in this sense. Rather, as the perfection of justice, *agapé* should be seen as going beyond the call of duty—of helping those who have no claim to be helped, showing mercy to those who have no claim to be shown mercy, forgiving those who have no claim to be let off the hook.

Justice itself allows that individuals have the freedom to pay the price for someone else's injustice or to suffer something that they don't deserve to suffer on behalf of another. This supremely free, giving love is *agapé*. Justice demanded that God love his creation, including Adam and Eve, to some degree, but not to the extent of giving his life, which is greater than all of creation, for them. Likewise, when Tigger ruins Rabbit's garden, Rabbit is wronged and Tigger is morally to blame. Rabbit could ask Tigger to compensate him for the injustice he suffers and justice would demand Tigger comply; however, Rabbit usually takes the injustice upon himself and, through *agapé*, forgives Tigger, freeing him from blame. Good lovers ought to imitate actions such as these in all things.

"Huggable"

Inspired by *Winnie the Pooh*, I have argued that perfect lovers need four types of love: *storgé* or affection, *philia* or friendship, *eros* or sexual love, and *agapé* or sacrificial love. While all of these loves are unique, *agapé*, the perfection of justice and the defender of individuality, is the king of loves. All of the other loves need it in order to be complete. If there were a book called *Winnie the Pooh in Love*, it would tell us that romance is not enough. We need to be affectionate, friendly, and sacrificial—in a word, "huggable"—whether stuffed with fluff or not.

22

A Single Soul in Two Bodies

SHAI BIDERMAN AND WILLIAM J. DEVLIN

Have you ever fallen in love? We're sure that anyone reading this will say "yes." But have you ever *truly* fallen in love? If so, do you remember what it's like falling head over heels?

Bill vividly recalls meeting his true love for the very first time. Once introduced, he couldn't stop looking at her. Finding her blue eyes to be the most beautiful eyes he ever looked into, he couldn't forget his first meeting with her. Even afterward, before he began courting her, Bill couldn't stop thinking about her. Unable to capture exactly what he felt, he continuously turned to the Beatles' song, "I've Just Seen a Face" to help encapsulate how he felt. He found that he couldn't forget when and where he met her. Realizing that she wasn't like other girls, he knew that she was just the right girl for him. He wanted everyone in the world to know that they met. It was clear to him that he was falling deeper and deeper in love with her by the day.

Shai has also found true love; however, he had to wait nine months until it happened. After learning that his wife was pregnant, Shai spent many hours staring at the bean-shaped smudge on the ultrasound printout. Even with the strongest dose of imagination, Shai couldn't see the smiling baby girl soon to emerge from this Rorschach-like image. Their first encounter in the maternity ward was love at first sight. One-sided, for the time being, but nevertheless the feeling of true love was complete and pure. A year later, and his love for his adorable cutest munchkin is still growing. What amazes him even more than the magnitude of his love for his daughter is the natural manner by which he seems to have "slipped into" it. Although she is his first-born child, and he never experienced parenthood before, he didn't expect the loving feelings to be so immediate and so overwhelming.

The experience of finding true love is unforgettable. Likewise, the feeling accompanying true love is so exciting, so pure, and so unique, that it, too, is unforgettable. There are some who maintain that the love we've discussed is essentially problematic: it's a delusion that tricks us into making mistakes; it's inherently selfish and egotistical; or, even if it is something of real value, it is doomed to end in failure.

However these pessimistic opinions about love are mistaken insofar as they misunderstand the notion of *true love*, or authentic love that exists between two individuals.

Love as a Single Person Divided

Think about the last time you told your husband, your wife, your girlfriend, your boyfriend, your child, your parents, or your friends that you love them. What do you mean when you say "I love you?" What is "love?" And *why* do you love the ones you love? These are tough questions.

We can begin by thinking of love as a feeling, or a sentiment, or a state of mind. But what specific feeling or sentiment or state of mind is it? This is where certainty begins to unravel. When Bill thinks of his true love, he finds that it's the feeling he has where he can't live without her. When Shai thinks of the true love for his daughter, he finds that he wants to take care of her and guide her through her life. When we both think of our loves, we think of *The Princess Bride*, where Westley would always tell his true love, Buttercup, "As you wish."

But the problem is that our brief descriptions don't exhaust the real feeling, or sentiment, or state of mind that we have. Furthermore, as our mention of *The Princess Bride* suggests, it is so difficult to capture what we mean by love, we often turn elsewhere to find other references to help us express it.

We may remind ourselves of the scene in *Jerry Maguire* where Jerry tells Dorothy "You complete me. And I just . . ." to which she interrupts by saying "Shut up, . . . you had me at 'hello'." Or, we may think of Elizabeth Barrett Browning's poem, "How Do I Love Thee? Let Me Count the Ways." Or, perhaps we prefer the poet Robert Burns, who wrote that his love is like a red, red rose. Or, maybe we'll turn to music and find the right love song (as Bill does with "I've Just Seen a Face"). We turn to movies, poetry, songs, or stories to represent the love that we feel for another.

There are many different kinds of love and falling in love need not be with a lover, as our opening remarks indicate. The songs and poems mentioned above could apply to the relationship between parent and child, other family members, or best friends. Nevertheless, because the case of lovers is particularly vivid, it provides a kind of model for the rest.

The playwright Aristophanes presents a famous story about lovers in a dialogue called the *Symposium*, by the ancient Greek philosopher Plato. Aristophanes describes what love is through a myth.

> Once upon a time, each person was double what a person is today—they had two heads, four arms, and four legs. Being twice what they are today, these people were very powerful and their power threatened the gods. To limit the humans' strength, Zeus cut each person in two, covering the gash by tightening the skin and fastening it at the navel. So each person today is half of the person he or she was. But we each long to be re-united with our other half. Love, then, is the desire and feeling each individual has to become whole once again. It is our desire to return to our original nature. The feeling of love serves as our guide in life to find the one true other—the one person that completes us.

When we find our other, matching-half, Aristophanes explains, something wonderful happens. The two people who are re-united as one feel that sense of love, affection and belonging with one another. Filled with their desire for one another, they cannot separate themselves from one another and do not want to be apart for even a single moment. Instead, they will long to spend the rest of their lives together.

Even when such people are re-united, and spend the rest of their lives together, they may find it difficult to say exactly what it is they want from one another. It's certainly not just sex, or the intimacy that sex can provide, since the joy of being together is far too deep for just a physical action. The souls of two lovers long for something more than just sex. The love they have for one another is so strong, that they want as much of a union and bond to each other as possible. It is so strong that, should Hephaestus, the craftsman god, offer to weld them together, they would both eagerly say yes. Bound by their heart's desire for each other, they would choose to be re-united in such a way so that they could lead a single life together, die a single death together, and be together, as one, in the afterlife.

So, what is love for Aristophanes, as reported by Plato? It's the desire and feeling of being reunited with our other half. Why do we love the one we love? Because it is that person, and *only that person*, who completes us. The myth provides an explanation of what love is, and why, say, Bill loves his partner. Here, Bill's other half is his true love. And so, the feeling he has of being with her is the feeling of being reunited with his other half. As Plato's student Aristotle says, "Love is composed of a single soul inhabiting two bodies." Bill and his true love are one soul within two bodies: they have now finally reunited.

Love as a Delusion

While some may find that Aristophanes's myth is beautiful and romantic, others will say that it's bullshit. Love doesn't exist and so this myth is just that: a myth! It's fake, maybe hokey, and perhaps meaningless. Whether it's Aristophanes's myth, *Jerry Maguire*, Browning's "How Do I Love Thee?" or any of the countless cheesy romance novels that plague our bookstores, what they all talk about is an illusion.

Or perhaps, as John Milton remarks in *Devil's Advocate*, love is "overrated, . . . biochemically no different than eating large quantities of chocolate." Or worse, maybe love is a trap, because it deludes us into believing in a mythical thing, and so entices us to make stupid decisions in our lives.

The nineteenth-century German philosopher Arthur Schopenhauer encapsulates this tirade in his account of love. Schopenhauer argues that love is a clever psychological ruse that is part of our human design. Unconsciously, we seek intimate and sexual relationships with others for the sole purpose of the propagation of the human species.

Even the object of our desire is no mystery to Schopenhauer. For him, we unconsciously select an individual that makes up for our imperfections and so is someone we think will be the proper co-parent for the offspring we're driven to produce. The feeling of being in love with another is just a method of tricking ourselves, making us believe that there is something noble, or romantic, about a relationship when, in fact, the sole reason for the relationship is the sexual impulse the human being has to reproduce.

Schopenhauer's account of love is very egotistical, since it is driven by the person's selfish desire to maintain his individuality, as well as his species, through procreation. Love is a self-delusion that leads to obsessions, attachments, suffering and misery because creating a child, in the long run, generates endless work, hassles, and responsibilities.

Going on this account, the only thing valuable about the love delusion, should it be successful, is the offspring brought about by reproduction. But, for Schopenhauer, even the love for one's children should not be seen as anything but biological and egotistical. The love a parent has towards his child is a paternal instinct, one that is also rooted in the drive to live. The parent is securing his individuality in the child and in maintaining the life of the species as a whole.

So, Schopenhauer would argue that Shai's love for his daughter is simply a paternal instinct that is part of his biological make-up. Shai loves his daughter, not in a genuine or pure sense, but because she possesses his genes, and so she continues his identity. He cares for her out of a selfish desire to continue his own line of descendents.

What is love for Schopenhauer? If anything, it's a trick. And it's a trick that we naturally play on ourselves, to hide the egotistical drive to continue our existence and secure our identity through procreation. Why do we love the ones we love? Because they serve our own ego by compensating for our imperfections and extending our own selfish desire to live.

If you're like us, you'll find Schopenhauer's biting criticism of love to be bitter and cynical. You may also feel insulted by such an outrageous denial of love. You may think, "He just doesn't get how I feel when I'm in love!" But if Schopenhauer's wrong, why do we have such a hard time expressing what love really is? And when we do try to explain it, why do we turn to the metaphors, allegories, and images expressed in films, songs, poetry, fairy tales, and fables? If anything, Schopenhauer does give us a more concrete, empirical, and objective account of what love is, as it is rooted in a physical human drive. It seems as though, if we want to say Schopenhauer is wrong, and that love is something real, something tangible, something that transcends the physical drive for sexual reproduction and individual identity, then the burden of proof is on us. So how can we give a concrete definition of what love is?

Love as Personal

Our response and defense of love begins by admitting that Schopenhauer does have a point. There are people who connect with one another because of selfish needs. There are people who hook up, have one-night stands, and use each other solely for their own personal gain. There are even people who trick themselves, or are tricked by others, into thinking that they love someone else when in fact they do not. These people fit Schopenhauer's general account: any idea of love that's tossed around in such relationships would be a self-delusion for some underlying egotistical drive.

But we need not say that these people are "in love," per se. Rather, such people are best understood to have feelings of lust or infatuation. In these cases, those who lust are infected with a foolish obsession that can lead to stupid decisions in their lives. Here, we can find ourselves unreasonably attached and dependent upon the object of our lust, tortured by our own obsession. Ultimately, we are likely to wind up suffering and in misery when we lose the one we sought, or realize that the one we lust after cannot satisfy our egotistical desires in the first place.

But this is not love. Lust and infatuation are not true love; they are not real, authentic, love. True love is the kind of love that cannot possibly be grasped entirely with the mind; rather, love is expressed and understood through the heart. And, as the seventeenth-century French philosopher Blaise Pascal writes, "The heart has its reasons of which reason knows nothing." In other words, love is found in our passions, and so we cannot rationally understand it. But if we cannot formulate a solid account of love through reason, then we cannot accurately express what love is, or why we love someone, in words. Love thus cannot be fully captured by reason and language.

True love is elusive. If we attempt to capture the essence or meaning of true love with a rational or logical approach, we're doomed to instant failure. A better approach may be to remain silent when asked, "What is love?" or "Why do you love the one you love?" The nineteenth-century Danish philosopher, Søren Kierkegaard adopts this approach, focusing specifically on the love of God. Kierkegaard begins by making a distinction between two kinds of truth.

First, there are objective truths, or truths that are universal, factual, and rational. These truths can be understood by others, and so we can communicate them to one another. We can say that "Bill met his partner in 2010" or "Shai's daughter was born in Tel Aviv" are objective truths. So, when we share these truths with you, *you*, as rational readers, can understand them as truths. Likewise, you could prove us wrong if we are wrong. Maybe Bill and his partner met in 2009. Or maybe Shai's daughter was born in Jerusalem. Regardless, these truths can be analyzed, proven, and defended in a logical manner.

Second, there are subjective truths, or truths that are personal and inward, beyond logic and reason. Such truths are lived truths in the sense that they are experienced with great passion. Furthermore, such truths are private—they are understood by the person who holds them, but they cannot possibly be shared with others in the public arena of rational objective language.

Kierkegaard focuses on the love of God as a prime example of subjective truth. One who loves God is a "knight of faith," who finds that such love is a personal and private truth. But this truth cannot be understood rationally. It is beyond an objective, analytic, factual truth for all to see and understand. Instead, it is a truth that is felt inwardly; it is a truth of the heart and not the mind. Recognizing that reason falls short, the knight makes a "leap of faith" in God. Since such truths cannot be communicated to others objectively, the knight remains silent about his love and faith in God.

After All, It's Your Love

We can use Kierkegaard's distinction between two kinds of truths, to address the pessimistic account of love. Schopenhauer's criticism of love is mistaken because he misplaces love in the category of objective truth. By reducing love to a psychological delusion rooted in our biological drive for reproduction, he treats love as a truth that is universal, factual, and rational. Even if we disagree with Schopenhauer, we can all understand his account of love. And it can be evaluated rationally. But this is exactly why he is wrong.

While lust and infatuation may belong in the category of objective truths, true love is a subjective truth. It is a truth that is lived and felt in the heart of the individual who holds it. This is why we find it so difficult to fully express what love is or why we love the ones we love. True love is a private truth, a truth that we find to be unconditional and unadulterated. Still, we struggle to explain it and even when we describe it, we always find ourselves saying, "I still haven't captured exactly what I mean!"

Love is ineffable, when we think about it in an objective, non-personal sense. But given our passion towards our loved ones, we choose not to keep it completely private, or remain silent about it. Instead, we turn to the poets, to the songwriters, to the fables, the movies, and any other way to speak about love metaphorically.

This explains why we cannot fully define and describe love. Furthermore, it explains why we turn to metaphors, analogies, and other images when challenged to give an analysis of love. This is why Bill turns to the Beatles' song "I've Just Seen a Face," or Aristophanes's myth in the *Symposium*, or Browning's "How Do I Love Thee?" or *Jerry Maguire* when he thinks of his true love, and how he's madly in love with her. This is why he calls her his "soul mate" and thinks of them together as "a single soul inhabiting two bodies."

Likewise, this is why Shai turns to Brown's "Red, Red Rose," or *The Princess Bride* when he dotes on his daughter, his own princess. This is why he calls her his "cutest munchkin" and why, when he first saw her, it was "love at first sight."

And, finally, this is why you all have your own, *personal* poem, or film, or song, or trope or fairy tale that you turn to when you think of your true love. Whether it's the love for your lover, the love for your child, the love for your parents, the love for your friend, or any other kind of true love, it is *your* love.

Only you can truly know what that is and what that feels like. And we think that's just great! All you need is love. And love is all you need.

Under the Boardwalk

♀ **STACEY E. AKE** is an Associate Teaching Professor in Philosophy at Drexel University in Philadelphia. An avid traveler, she is certain that love does make the world go 'round.

♂ **ROBERT ARP** is a philosopher and ontologist. His most recent books include *Critical Thinking: An Introduction to Reasoning Well, Philosophy DeMYSTiFied,* and *What's Good on TV? Understanding Ethics Through Television.* He loves the idea of being loved by lovers who themselves love the idea of being loved by lovers.

♂ **ADAM BARKMAN** is Assistant Professor of Philosophy at Redeemer University College. He is the author of *C. S. Lewis and Philosophy as a Way of Life* and *Through Common Things,* and is the co-editor of *Manga and Philosophy: Fullmetal Metaphysician.* Despite daily rendezvous with his favorite mistresses, wine and books, he still truly professes all four loves for his amazing wife of nine years, Ashley.

♀ **EMILY BARRANCO** is a graduate student of philosophy at the University of California, Davis. She works on methodological problems in the science of happiness. She didn't know whether to be insulted or flattered when her lover told her he liked talking to her even more than having sex.

♀ **MARGARET BETZ** lives in the Philadelphia suburbs where she teaches philosophy at local universities. She is the author of *The Hidden Philosophy of Hannah Arendt* (2002) and several articles on continental philosophy, feminist theory and animal ethics. She is raising two sons in the hope of producing men any feminist would love.

♂ **SHAI BIDERMAN** is a doctoral candidate in philosophy at Boston University, and an Instructor in Tel Aviv University and the College of Management, Israel. His recent publications include articles on the Coen brothers and Steven Soderbergh and a book on David Lynch. Following the Beatles' dictum "All you need is love," he lives the life worth living.

♂ JAMES BONEY is an adjunct professor of philosophy and PhD candidate at Temple University in Philadelphia. By way of experience, his greatest philosophical accomplishment is recognizing that in order to appreciate the ethereal nature of love, one must first delight in its physical aspects.

♂ WILLIAM J. DEVLIN is assistant professor of philosophy at Bridgewater State University and visiting summer lecturer at the University of Wyoming. His fields of interest are Nietzsche, existentialism, philosophy of science, and theories of truth. He is co-editor of the book, *The Philosophy of David Lynch*, and his essays appear in such volumes as *The Philosophy of TV Noir, The Philosophy of Science Fiction Film*, and *Family Guy and Philosophy*. Though his paper in this volume is about true love, William finds that, even if he were killed and needed to be resurrected, his real reason for living is to blave (and we all know that "to blave" means "to bluff").

♀ CHELSEA HARRY is a doctoral student and instructor at Duquesne University in Pittsburgh. She is a longtime lover of (in no particular order) wisdom, her husband, Chris, and their dogs, Jackson and Wolfgang. In addition to her recent chapter in *The Red Sox and Philosophy: Green Monster Meditations* (2010), she has published an article on Plato's *Timaeus*, "A Platonic Response to J.S. Mill" (2011), and is currently dissertating on Aristotle and nineteenth-century German Idealism.

♂ JACOB M. HELD is an assistant professor in the department of philosophy and religion at the University of Central Arkansas. His recent work includes an edited book, *Dr. Seuss and Philosophy: Oh, the Thinks You Can Think!* (2011) and articles on Free Speech, Kant and Retributivism, and Marx and Marxism. He wonders what Dr. Seuss would tell you about your lover, and would his advice include a Zizzer-Zazzer-Zuzz?

♀ SHARON M. KAYE is professor of philosophy at John Carroll University in Cleveland. Her most recent books include *Critical Thinking: A Beginner's Guide, The Onion and Philosophy*, and *The Ultimate Lost and Philosophy*. Her top three erotica are: samba music, Flamin' Hot Cheetos, and automatic car washes.

♀ Ummni Khan is a professor at Carleton University in Ottawa. Her scholarship focuses on the criminalization of consensual sexuality, from sadomasochism to sex work. She is currently preoccupied with tormented she-wolves (Leah from *Twilight*), misunderstood sluts (Lydia from *Pride and Prejudice*) and sexually repressed half-Vulcans (Spock from *Star Trek*).

♂ Paul Loader lives in London. He has never met Richard Dawkins.

♀ Katarina Majerhold is an independent scholar (researcher, writer, and lecturer) of philosophy of love (emotions) and sex. Occasionally she is a screenwriter and editor. Her books are *Love in Philosophy*, *Love Is All*, and *Living*. Some ten years ago she felt she should become a doctor. When she met Dr. Patch Adams (founder of the doctor-clowns) last year in Vienna she started doing interdisciplinary research in philosophy-medicine-art. She now develops the practical philosophy of clowning with red noses and aims at philosophy with heart, joy, and humor.

♂ Scott F. Parker is author of the memoir *Running After Prefontaine* and co-editor of *Coffee—Philosophy for Everyone: Grounds for Debate*. His hobbies include writing love poems for his wife.

♀ Jordan Pascoe teaches philosophy at John Jay College and Hunter College in New York City. She writes about Kant, colonialism, and African philosophy. She has never had a vampire for a lover, though not for lack of trying. She would like one, if only because she thinks Kant would heartily disapprove.

♂ Mike Piero teaches courses in composition and rhetoric at numerous colleges in the Northeast Ohio area. His most recent work has appeared in *Dexter and Philosophy: Mind Over Spatter* (2011) and *The John Carroll Review*. He thinks that conducting "research" for a book on lovers is reward enough in itself.

♀ M. Pontoppidan is a PhD student at the Centre for Neoplatonic Virtue Ethics at the University of Copenhagen, with a project on Ficino, Plotinus, and Eros. She has published a Minnesongbook (on courtly love songs, with a music CD) and a book on the Magnificent Things about Men. She has also published scholarly articles, including one on how to use naughty words most efficiently according to D.H. Lawrence and C.S. Lewis!

♂ Carol V.A. Quinn is assistant professor of philosophy at Metropolitan State College of Denver. She is co-editing a book entitled

Queer Philosophy. Her research interests also include feminist philosophy and philosophy of sex. After three failed marriages and
numerous failed relationships, she has decided to stick with dogs.

♀ RONDA LEE ROBERTS is an independent scholar and editorial con-
sultant. Her recent book, *Success in Life through Personality
Engineering*, co-authored with Murali Chemuturi, gives tips on
achieving excellence in life. She has made contributions for the
upcoming Avatar and Philosophy and Ang Lee and Philosophy. She
has a habit of falling in love with her best friends.

♀ WEAVER SANTANIELLO is Professor of Philosophy at Penn State,
Berks. She's the author of two books on Friedrich Nietzsche, and editor of *Nietzsche and the Gods*, and has written various articles, including chapters in *What Philosophy Can Tell You about Your Dog*, and
The Red Sox and *Philosophy: Green Monster Meditations* (2010).
Potential suitors can woo her with: real flowers, vanilla-chocolate
candy, expensive wine, and front row tickets to Red Sox games.

♀ STEPHANIE ST. MARTIN is a SWF, non-smoking, 5'4", brown hair,
hazel eyes. She enjoys long walks on the beach by herself, being the
creepy alum at BC hockey games, teaching philosophy at Middlesex
Community College and working at Care.com. Her romantic goal is to
have a 1950s-esque date and share a milkshake (with two straws)
with a fine young gentleman. She seeks a mature, intelligent guy with
no criminal record, no plagiarism record, and no record of ever cheer-
ing for the Yankees. Must have a great sense of humor, seek the life of
excellence and root for the Red Sox (maybe you read her chapter in
The Red Sox and Philosophy: Green Monster Meditations). If you are
this man, you should flirt with her on Twitter @StephStMartin. You
do, however, need to get the approval from a certain professor at
Boston College: bring a double-shot of espresso and two Splenda.

♂ BENJAMIN STEVENS teaches literature and linguistics at Bard
College in the Hudson Valley. Recently he has written on Latin poetry,
science fiction, and contemporary a cappella music. He knows how to
say all the liveliest things in all the deadest languages.

♂ CHARLES TALIAFERRO is professor of philosophy at St. Olaf
College. His most recent books include *The Image in Mind*, co-
authored with Jil Evans. He has contributed to *The Ultimate Lost and
Philosophy* and *The Ultimate Harry Potter and Philosophy*. As a huge
fan of the troubadour tradition, Charles once courted the love of his
life as a knight in a full suit of armor with a bright yellow cape under
a full moon, scaring some of the neighbors.

Adler, Mortimer J., 12
adrenalin, 7
Aesop, 136
affection, 9, 23, 111–13, 174, 177, 227. and loyalty, 165–67; object of, 20, 135. *See also* *storgé*
agapé, 38, 215, 221–23
Alcibiades, 112, 194, 196–97, 200–06, 210–12
Algren, Nelson, 158
Allen, Woody, 127, 132
anal sex, 56
animal, 91, 220, 222; and *Eros*, 41–42; and instinct, 125, 139, 148, 192; part of brain, 7; and love, 87–88, 218–19
Aristophanes, 134–35, 207–08, 210, 212, 227–28, 232; and myth on love's origin, 207–08, 227
Aristotle, 44–45, 114; and friendship, 44–45, 180–82; and love, 219, 228; and relationships, 184–86; and virtue, 180–81
arousal, 7, 13, 15
Aquinas, St. Thomas, 8, 10, 38
Augustine, St., 7–8, 10, 88–89. *See also* Christianity, Church

The Beatles, 225, 232
Beauvoir, Simone de, 126, 156–163; feminine-masculine dynamic, 157, 160; and jealousy, 158–161; life of, 157–163; woman as "Other," 156
Beckett, Samuel, 100
Bella (*Twilight*), 14–23. *See also* Edward; Jacob; *Twilight*
Bentham, Jeremy, 8–9, 96. *See also* pleasure
Bible, 8, 133. *See also* Christianity
Blackburn, Simon, 6
Browning, Elizabeth Barrett, 226, 228, 232
body-image, 58, 60
Botton, Alain de, 125–27, 130
Buffy the Vampire Slayer, 25, 34. *See also* vampire

camaraderie, 167–69, 179; as different from friendship, 169
charity, 9, 135, 174–77
Christ, Jesus, 38
Christianity, 7, 40, 129, 222; doctrine of incarnation, 90; and guilt, 8–9; intellectual

tradition of, 10; and love, 38, 133; and philosophy, 126, 133; and women, 9. *See also* Augustine; Bible; Church
Church, 7–9, 41, 150, 186. *See also* Augustine, Christianity
Cicero, 219
Closer, 139
communication, 101, 118, 121–22
Cooper, Alice, 154
Cyrus, Miley, 64

Darwall, Stephen, 108
Dawkins, Richard, 49–52
dehydroepiandrosterone (DHEA), 4
Derrida, Jacques, 165
Denmark, 81
The Devil's Advocate, 226
Dickens, Charles, 106, 218
Diddley, Bo, 155–56, 163
dignity, 28, 31, 33, 97, 106–07, 148
Diogenes the Cynic, 126
Dionysus, 197

Edward (*Twilight*), 14–23, 34. *See also* Bella; Jacob; *Twilight*
empathy, 175–76
emotions, 121–22, 136–37, 161–62; and desire, 41; and distance, 61; and love, 135, 139, 192; and reason, 30; and relationships, 130
Empedocles, 38–39, 83, 88
endorphins, 4
eros, 9, 11–12, 177, 196, 217–223; and Aristophanes, 207–09; history of, 41–42, 215; as type of love, 11–12, 171–72
ethics, 68, 129; "care," 97; deontological, 97; utilitarian, 96–97. *See also* Plato
evolution, 7, 148

Facebook, 75–76, 218
Falstaff, 224
fantasy. *See* sexual fantasy
feminism, 15, 21, 110, 139, 159–162; second-wave, 155–56
Ficino, Marsilio, 83–88, 90
foreplay, 14–18, 23, 192–93. *See also* sexual fantasy
Foucault, Michel, 126–27
Friedan, Betty, 155
frigidity, 9

Garden of Eden, 7
generosity, 113–14
Girls Gone Wild, 5, 63
Good Will Hunting, 165

Hesiod, 41
Hilton, Paris, 63
homosexuality, 41, 169–170
hormones, 6, 9
Huffington Post, 4

immunoglobin A, 4
integrity, 45, 107–08

Jacob (*Twilight*), 14–15, 17, 19–23. *See also* Bella; Edward; *Twilight*
James, William, 136
Jerry Maguire, 135, 226, 228, 232

Kant, Immanuel, 8, 10, 25–40, 97, 106–08, 147, 151; and desire, 27–35; and kinky sex, 32–35; and marriage, 28–29, 31; and *Metaphysics of Morals*, 26, 30; and morality, 26–28; and moral friendship, 30–32, 34; and pleasure,

32–34; and sex as cannibalism, 26–30
Kardashian, Kim, 63
Kierkegaard, Søren, 231
Kissinger, Henry, 156

Lacan, Jacques, 211
language, 127; of appetite, 28; and love, 230–31; and misunderstanding, 101–02; and Platonism, 88, 193
lesbian, 19, 58
Lewis, C.S., 9–10
limbic system, 7
Lord of the Rings, 169–170
lust, 5–14, 129; Christian attack on, 7–8; definition of, 6; desire and, 6; forgiveness of, 8; and infatuation, 230–32; as type of love, 9–11; Platonic idea of, 84–85, 87–88; as private, 6; vilification of, 5

Machiavelli, Niccolò, 70, 72, 74–75
MacKinnon, Catharine, 55
male genitals, 6
Mandela, Nelson, 175
marriage, 82, 100, 105, 146, 148, 158–59, 186; and Bertrand Russell, 128–29; and end of romance, 98; gay, 150; and philosophers, 151, 153–54; and sex, 28–29, 31–33; and *Twilight*, 16, 22
Marx, Karl H., 49
masochism, 16, 18–19, 21–22
masturbation, 4–13, 40, 49, 55, 126; as "auto–eroticism," 10; and teenage female, 13–14; and women, 4–13
Meyer, Stephenie, 14, 17, 22
Mill, John Stuart, 96–97
Moulton, John, 3, 11–12

mythology: Greek, 41; Roman, 5

Nietzsche, Friedrich, 113–14, 145, 151; and love as domination, 152; and marriage, 151; and will, 150, 152–54
Noddings, Nel, 97

orgasm, 3–4, 11; health benefits of, 4; and meaning, 132; of teenage female, 13; and women, 13, 62
Origen of Alexandria, 126
oxytocin, 4

Pascal, Blaise, 230
passion: romantic, 6, 9–10, 125, 130, 134–35, 147–49, 212–13; and sex, 159; and violence, 18–22. *See also* lust
phenetylamine, 4
philia, 9, 42–43, 196, 215, 218–222
Plato, 22, 147, 151, 154, 193, 196–97, 199–200, 207; as character in Aristophanes, 134–35, 227–28; and chariot analogy, 20–21; and Crito, 193–96; and death, 195–96; and ethics, 191–92; and forms, 42–43, 190–92; and love, 23, 42–46, 81–91; and mind-body split, 89–91; *Phaedo*, 192–95, 199; *Phaedrus*, 20, 191–96; and pederasty, 126; and soul, 192–95, 205–06, 210–11; *Symposium*, 86, 134–35, 195, 207, 210, 213, 227, 232
pleasure, 6, 8, 21–23, 32–34, 56, 87, 126, 131, 138, 196, 220; and desire, 27; of friendship, 179–190; and pain, 8, 16,

18–19, 22, 124, 167–68; Plato
and, 43–45, 190; and utilitarianism, 8–9, 96–97. *See also*
Kant; Plato
pornography, 12–15, 55–65;
and advertising, 58–59; and
cheating, 60–61; and Greeks,
190; industry of, 57–59; and
objectification of women,
58–59, 62–63; reasonable
use of, 61. *See also* sexual
harassment
Potter, Harry, 85–86
The Princess Bride, 232
Pythagoreans, 86, 91
Pride and Prejudice, 15
pussy, 37, 39–46

Rand, Ayn, 138, 140
respect, 26–35, 89, 108–09, 167,
183, 213, 220–21
Rome, 5
Romeo, 137, 220
Rumi, 87–88, 91
Russell, Bertrand, 125,
127–131; and shame, 128–29

Sacher-Masoch, Leopold von, 16
Sappho, 19–20, 23
Sartre, Jean-Paul, 126, 133, 157;
and bad faith, 156; and de
Beauvoir, 158–162; and
emotional experience, 136–37;
and friendship, 137, 181–86;
and freedom, 155–56, 183;
and romance, 138–140
Saussure, Ferdinand de, 101
Schopenhauer, Arthur, 147–154,
228–232; and asceticism, 151;
and love for procreation,
147–48, 228–29
Scrooge, Ebenezer, 133
seratonin, 4
Sex and the City, 73

sex education, 5, 128
sex object, 28–35, 59 139
sexual fantasy, 7, 13–18, 21, 56,
60
sexual harassment, 56–58, 63
Shakespeare, William, 200, 216
Shakira, 49
Shaw, George Bernard, 105
Sherlock, 169–170
Singles, 156
Spinoza, Baruch, 147, 151
Socrates, 8, 86, 111–15, 135,
150, 189–212; and bodies,
192–95; and *daemon*, 201; and
true love, 209–210; and
Nietzsche, 151; and seduction,
200–06. *See also* Plato
soul, 8, 45, 83–85, 88–91, 134,
160; and sex, 127; single soul
in two bodies, 225–232. *See
also* Plato
Steinbeck, John, 180
Stoics, 39–40
Strossen, Nadine, 55
storgé, 9–10, 215–22. *See also*
affection

Talmud, 207
Tronto, Joan C, 110, 112
True Blood, 25, 34, 57. *See also*
vampire
trust, 45, 109–110, 166; of
another, 77, 123; as care, 110;
sex and, 25, 27, 34
Twilight, 14–17, 19–25, 34; and
Breaking Dawn, 17, 22; as
tool for arousal, 15. *See also*
Bella; Jacob; Edward

utilitarianism, 96–97

vampire, 14, 17–19, 28; and

desire, 14, 22; and sex 25, 33–35. See also *Buffy the Vampire Slayer*; *True Blood*; *Twilight*
venus, 10, 12
vibrator, 5

Wagner, Richard, 151
Wedding Crashers, 134
West, Kanye, 75
Wilde, Oscar, 96–103
Winfrey, Oprah, 4
Winnie the Pooh, 215–223

Wittgenstein, Ludwig, 98–99
women: and domesticity, 151, 153; and masturbation, 6, 9; and motherhood, 153, 155; and relationships, 71–78, 86, 221; and reproduction, 152; and sex 26, 30–31, 140, 149. *See also* feminism; pornography

Xanthippe, 111–12, 151

Zeus, 5, 134, 207–08, 227